THE
WILDFLOWER GARDENER'S
GUIDE

Northeast, Mid-Atlantic, Great Lakes, and Eastern Canada Edition

THE
WILDFLOWER GARDENER'S
GUIDE

Northeast, Mid-Atlantic, Great Lakes, and Eastern Canada Edition

HENRY W. ART

Botanical illustrations by Hyla M. Skudder
Garden illustrations by Elayne Sears
Photographs by the author

A Garden Way Publishing Book

Storey Communications, Inc.
"America's Garden Publisher"
Pownal, Vermont 05261

Cover photograph of larger blue flag (Iris versicolor) *by Henry W. Art*

Cover and book design by Andrea Gray

Edited by Deborah Burns

Maps rendered by Wanda Harper

Typesetting by Quad Left Graphics, Burlington, Vermont

Printed in the United States by Alpine Press

Second Printing, January 1989

Library of Congress Cataloging-in-Publication Data

Art, Henry Warren.
    The wildflower gardener's guide. Northeast, Mid-Atlantic, Great Lakes, Eastern Canada edition.

    Bibliography: p. 168.
    Includes index.
    1. Wild flower gardening—Northeastern States.
2. Wild flower gardening—Canada, Eastern. 3. Wild flowers—Northeastern States. 4. Wild flowers—Canada, Eastern. I. Title.
SB439.24.N67A78   1987   635.9'676'0974   86-45713
ISBN 0-88266-450-6
ISBN 0-88266-439-5 (pbk.)

This book is dedicated to the memory of
Richard C. Art
A man who took pride in his northeastern wildflowers

Contents

Acknowledgments ix

PART I
An Introduction for Wildflower Gardeners   1

Wildflowers of Northeastern North America 2

Getting a Start 6

Theme Gardens 13

Plant Descriptions 24

Flowering Season 31

Wildflower Culture 36

Wildflower Propagation 49

MAPS
Vegetation of Northeastern North America 57
Annual Precipitation of Northeastern North America 58
Length of Frost-Free Period in Northeastern North America 59
Hardiness Zones of Northeastern North America 60

PART II
A Gallery of Northeastern Wildflowers   61

PART III
Species of Wildflowers   79

WOODLAND SPECIES (Early Spring)   80

Sharp-lobed Hepatica (*Hepatica acutiloba*) 82
Bloodroot (*Sanguinaria canadensis*) 84
Eastern Trout Lily (*Erythronium americanum*) 86
Dutchman's Breeches (*Dicentra cucullaria*) 88

Common Blue Violet *(Viola papilionacea)* 90
Purple Trillium *(Trillium erectum)* 92
Wild Ginger *(Asarum canadensis)* 94
Eastern Columbine *(Aquilegia canadensis)* 96
Foamflower *(Tiarella cordifolia)* 98
Mayapple *(Podophyllum peltatum)* 100

WOODLAND SPECIES (Late Spring to Summer)   102

Wild Lily-of-the-Valley *(Maianthemum canadense)* 104
Solomon's Seal *(Polygonatum biflorum)* 106
False Solomon's Seal *(Smilacina racemosa)* 108
Yellow Clintonia *(Clintonia borealis)* 110
Bunchberry *(Cornus canadensis)* 112
Partridgeberry *(Mitchella repens)* 114
Wild Leek *(Allium tricoccum)* 116
Shinleaf *(Pyrola elliptica)* 118
Wood Lily *(Lilium philadelphicum)* 120
Wintergreen *(Gaultheria procumbens)* 122

WETLAND SPECIES   124

Jack-in-the-Pulpit *(Arisaema triphyllum)* 126
Larger Blue Flag *(Iris versicolor)* 128
Cardinal Flower *(Lobelia cardinalis)* 130
Groundnut *(Apios americana)* 132
Turtlehead *(Chelone glabra)* 134
Closed Gentian *(Gentiana andrewsii)* 136

MEADOW SPECIES   138

Canada Anemone *(Anemone canadensis)* 140
Bluets *(Houstonia caerulea)* 142
Pasture Rose *(Rosa carolina)* 144
Black-eyed Susan *(Rudbeckia hirta)* 146
Wild Bergamot *(Monarda fistulosa)* 148
New England Aster *(Aster novae-angliae)* 150

Appendixes   153

A. Suppliers 154

B. Botanical Gardens and Arboreta 157

C. Native Plant and Horticultural Societies 164

D. References 169

Glossary 171

Index 176

Acknowledgments

The author and illustrator would like to thank the following people:

M. John Storey for his vision of this project.

Deborah Burns for her sensitive editing, Andrea Gray for her imaginative book design, and Pamela Art for her timely production assistance in this project.

Chris Skudder for his continuous support and encouragement.

Céline Arseneault, Botanist-Librarian of Ville de Montréal Jardin et de l'Institut Botaniques, and Ms. Laurie Band of McGill University for their aid in research of French Canadian common names.

Mary Pockman and Mary Painter of the Virginia Wildflower Preservation Society for their assistance and comments on wildflower conservation guidelines and other parts of the manuscript.

Dr. Joan Edwards of the Williams College Biology Department for many helpful suggestions.

The staffs of the Garden in the Woods, the Brooklyn Botanic Garden, the New York Botanical Garden, the Museum of the Hudson Highlands, Clark Museum, and the Chicago Botanic Garden, where many of the photographs were taken.

Pamela Weatherbee, Kristen Anderson, Robert Hatton, and the Appalachian Mountain Club naturalist staff on the Mt. Greylock Reservation for their aid in tracking down wildflowers to photograph.

Hardy Wieting, Jr. of the Nature Conservancy and Mrs. C. Norman Collard of Operation Wildflower for their enthusiasm and information about their respective organizations.

Michael Canoso and Walter Kittredge for assistance in the use of the Harvard University Herbaria (the Collections of the Gray Herbarium and the Arnold Arboretum).

Sarah McFarland, Lee Dalzell, Barbara Prentice, and David Shea of the

Williams College Library staff for their on-line literature searches and attention to interlibrary loan requests.

Tom Viti and Jerry Cirillo of the Westwood, Massachusetts Library, and many folks on the staff of the Morrill Library, University of Massachusetts for their aid in obtaining illustrative material.

Michael Troughton-Smith of Scan Studios Ltd., Dublin, for his helpful suggestions on the color elements of this project.

The many students of field botany at Williams College who always make working with wildflowers a pleasure.

The hundreds of people associated with botanic gardens, nature centers, arboreta, wildflower seed companies, native-plant nurseries, native-plant societies, and botanical organizations, who responded to the requests for the information that is contained in the appendixes.

PART I

An Introduction for Wildflower Gardeners

This book is about growing wildflowers in the northeast corner of North America, a region extending from Labrador to western Ontario in Canada, and from Virginia to the Mississippi River Valley in the United States. The region includes a variety of habitats, ranging from coniferous to deciduous forests and from dry meadows to wetlands. Of the hundreds of wildflowers that grow in these habitats, 32 of the most easily cultivated species have been selected for inclusion in this book. These wildflowers have been chosen to cover the range of flowering season and garden conditions typical of northeastern North America.

Wildflowers of Northeastern North America

It's been said that if you don't like the weather in the Northeast, just wait a few moments and it will change. While the weather may be variable from hour to hour and day to day, a real joy of living in this region is observing the change of seasons. The seasonal cycle is accompanied by a procession of wildflowers, from the hepaticas, sometimes dusted by snow in the early spring, to the New England asters, which may receive similar treatment in the autumn. But the season for northeastern wildflowers doesn't end with the first snows. Even in midwinter, when most wildflowers are dormant in the soil and the dry seedheads of black-eyed Susans are silhouetted against the snow, species such as bunchberry, partridgeberry and wintergreen, with their lustrous evergreen leaves and brilliant red berries, provide a welcome accent.

Unlike most domesticated horticultural plants, wildflowers have the capacity to make it on their own without human assistance. Many northeastern wildflowers, such as shinleaf and purple trillium, can not only survive without cultivation, but can also thrive in the dense shade of the forests and endure the harsh winters that typify this corner of North America. Other species, such as larger blue flag and turtlehead, are also adapted to grow in waterlogged soils that would kill most conventional garden plants.

WILDFLOWER HABITATS

The wildflowers of the Northeast are as beautiful as they are diverse, and indeed are the products of their varied habitats. While present-day northeastern North America is a patchwork of fields and forests, cities and suburbs, and domesticated and wild landscapes, 400 years ago the region was largely forested. These forests receded as European immigrants established farms and cut trees for timber and fuel. By the mid-1800s the wave of settlement had moved west to the more fertile lands of the Midwest and Great Plains. In its wake, many northeastern farms were abandoned and then slowly reclaimed by forests.

The disturbance of the landscape of northeastern North America is recent relative to the time-scale used to measure the evolution of the wildflowers growing there. The wildflowers we enjoy so much today evolved in the primal forest and forest clearings over tens of millions of years. The following is a brief guide to the habitats that for millennia have nurtured the wildflowers of northeastern North America. (See map, page 57.)

Boreal Forest. Parts of the area covered in this book — much of eastern Canada south of Hudson's Bay, the northern border of the United States, and the tops of mountains such as the Adirondacks and the Appalachians — have short growing seasons and very cold winters with deep snows. These areas are largely blanketed with needle-leaved evergreen trees such as red and black spruces, balsam fir, and red, white, and Jack pines. Since these "boreal" (northern) tree species retain their thick needles throughout the year, little light penetrates the forest and reaches the ground below. As a result, boreal wildflowers such as yellow clintonia, bunchberry, and wild lily-of-the-valley are more abundant in small forest clearings, in gaps where trees have fallen and allow the sunlight in, or where deciduous species such as paper birch mingle with the conifers. Conifer needles produce a highly acidic humus as they decompose on the ground, and boreal wildflowers are tolerant of, or sometimes even require, high levels of acid in the soil.

Deciduous Forest. Just south of the boreal forest and at lower elevations, broad-leaved deciduous species dominate the forest. Those wildflowers such as wild leek, trout lily and bloodroot that grow in the deciduous forest not only enjoy milder winters than those of the boreal forest, but can also take advantage of abundant sunlight in the early spring, before buds burst on the trees overhead and dense foliage shades the ground.

The cooler, moister, and more northern regions of the deciduous forest are dominated by species such as sugar maple, American beech, yellow and black birches, black cherry, white ash, and other trees associated with moist soils. Various species of oak and hickory are more abundant in the warmer and drier regions of deciduous forest. The fingers of forest that outline the major rivers in the midwestern prairies are also largely dominated by oaks and hickories. Although some species of wildflowers, like the wild lily-of-the-valley, can be found in many different types of forest, others, like bunchberry, which is associated with high-elevation forests, have much more restricted distributions.

Meadows and Wetlands. Even before European settlement, the broad expanses of virgin boreal and deciduous forest were punctuated by occasional openings of meadows or grasslands, where trees had fallen naturally or where soils were too wet or dry to support them. Native wildflowers like the New England aster and wild bergamot are adapted to growing in full sunlight and coping with periodic stresses of drought or disturbance.

European settlement of northeastern North America made openings in the forest much more extensive. Now, however, native meadow wildflowers faced increased competition from introduced weeds, such as foxtail grass and mullein, and even native weeds, such as broad-leaved plantain. This last species was called "white man's foot" by Native Americans when they observed its phenomenal spread following the disturbance of the landscape by Europeans.

While the extent of upland meadows may have increased over the past several hundred years, the pockets of low-lying wet meadows, swamp forest, and coastal salt marsh have decreased in area. These perennially wet habitats are reservoirs of intense biological activity and support a surprising diversity of stunning wildflowers, such as cardinal flower, larger blue flag, closed gentian, and turtlehead. Not only are wetlands places of great beauty, but they are highly productive as well, providing food for many wildlife species. By absorbing a large quantity of water and then releasing it slowly, wetlands often protect adjacent uplands from the hazards of floods. It is only relatively recently that we have recognized the ecological value of wetlands, and that state and federal legislation has been enacted to slow the destruction of what were once considered to be wastelands.

THE JOYS OF WILDFLOWERS

Regardless of the habitat in which you live, both mind and soul can be refreshed by introducing wildflowers into your garden. This pleasure can come from getting to know even the most common of native species.

The Common Blue Violet. Consider the common blue violet, found in open woods, meadows, dooryards, vacant lots, and railroad embankments throughout the region. Botanists have fought pitched academic battles over this unassuming yet beautiful spring wildflower. Some feel that the enormous variability of leaf shape and flower color seen in populations of the common blue violet indicates that it is merely a group of hybrids of other species of *Viola*, rather than a true biological species itself. Others disagree.

There is no question, however, but that the common blue violet has developed an intriguing way of producing flowers. Two completely different types of flowers appear at different times of the year. In midspring, the familiar flowers with petals ranging from deep purple-blue to light blue-gray are visited by a variety of insects searching for nectar. In the process they pollinate the flowers, and without the insects these flowers cannot produce seeds.

Then, in summer and early autumn, inconspicuous flowers with permanently closed buds emerge on short horizontal stalks, hidden beneath the mound of leaves. Self-pollination occurs inside the closed buds, and seeds are produced without the aid of insect pollinators. Since no pollination has occurred, the seeds give rise to plants that are identical to their parents, much the way a rootstock cutting is genetically the same as the plant that produced it.

Although the early, showy flowers generally produce fewer seeds than these late, petalless ones, they benefit from having genetic contributions from two different parents. Often the plants arising from seeds produced by petaled flowers have better chances of survival in habitats that are different than their parents'.

Other Species. A wildflower garden may have other delights awaiting discovery. The sex of the flowers of the Jack-in-the-pulpit, for example, may change several times throughout its life. The plant doesn't flower at all the first year, but as it matures it produces male flowers first. If the plant becomes robust in later years, it switches to producing female flowers, or in rarer cases, both male and female flowers. The sex may then change from year to year depending upon growing conditions. The vigor of the plant in the previous year is the best indicator of the likely sex of the plant the next season, male flowers appearing after poor years and females after good years.

Other species have intriguing stories as well. The flower of the purple trillium has a faint odor of rancid meat (a bit like a wet dog) to attract the flies that pollinate it. The closed gentian flower appears to lack an entrance for pollinators, but large bumblebees find their way in with ease through a concealed passageway where the petals meet.

The larger blue flag is an elegant native iris whose unusual arrangement of flower parts ensures cross-pollination. Pollination takes place when a bee lands on the flower and inadvertently sheds some of the pollen it is carrying. Dark purple lines direct the insect to the sweet nectar, and en route it picks up a new load of pollen, which it carries to the next flower.

These are but a few of hundreds of wildflowers that are worthy of introduction into gardens in northeastern North America. And although some of us greatly enjoy studying those intricacies of wildflower life cycles that require close observation, others may be content simply appreciating the subtle colors and graceful forms of these elements of our natural heritage.

Getting a Start

This book presents 32 wildflowers native to northeastern North American woodlands and meadows. Some of these species, such as the common blue violet, may be old favorites of yours, and others, such as groundnut, may be new. The selected species are well adapted to the range of conditions likely to be found in gardens of the region and can be propagated without much difficulty. Although any wildflower becomes scarce near the edges of its natural range, none of the species included in this book is considered to be "rare" or "endangered," and all are available from reputable wildflower suppliers who sell nursery-propagated stock.

It is a delight to watch the parade of wildflowers through the garden from one season to the next, and the species chosen for this edition will provide a succession of flowering from the early spring through the autumn. These wildflowers can also be grown in a wide variety of conditions, from conventional gardens to woodlands, from meadows to wetlands. Some can even be grown in containers on your porch or patio. Hopefully, the wildflowers in this book will be only a starting point for your gardening with native plants. There are many other species presented in other regional editions of *The Wildflower Gardener's Guide*, *A Garden of Wildflowers*, and other books on native-plant gardening suitable for northeast North American gardens.

Some wildflowers, not included in this book, are difficult to bring into the garden because of their demanding soil or cultural requirements. Indian pipes and squawroot lack chlorophyll, for example, and therefore must parasitize the roots of other plants in order to survive. The downy false foxglove, which does have green leaves, is nevertheless parasitic on the roots of oak trees, and nearly impossible to cultivate in a garden. The pink lady's slipper orchid has not been included, because it is so difficult to propagate quickly that organizations such as the New England Wildflower Society and the Virginia Wildflower Preservation Society suspect it is commercially available at present only from suppliers who sell plants collected in the wild. Pink lady's slippers are best left growing where they are in the wild and should be moved into your garden only if they are in imminent danger of destruction by development.

WILDFLOWER CONSERVATION

One safeguard of our native wild plants is the Federal Endangered Species Act of 1973, administered by the U.S. Fish and Wildlife Service. This act gives protection to those native species that are recognized as endangered in the United States. This law applies only to federal lands, however, and to the interstate traffic of rare plants. The protection of endangered wildflowers on other public and private lands is left up to the states, as is the protection of species that might become locally rare or endangered through collection by native-plant suppliers and wildflower fanciers. State laws protecting wildflowers are far from uniform, and even where there is protective legislation, the enforcement of these laws is sometimes weak.

Wildflower gardeners should become aware of their state's laws concerning the protection of native plants. If your state lacks such protective legislation, or if the enforcement of the laws is weak, become an advocate for passage of strong and effective measures. The World Wildlife Fund and the Environmental Defense Fund, whose addresses can be found in Appendix C, can provide information concerning model native-plant protection legislation.

The wildflower gardener is faced with moral and ethical considerations that do not confront the gardener of cultivars. Essential to the enjoyment and appreciation of wild, native plants is the respect for living organisms in their native habitats. The wildflower gardener's code of conduct should protect naturally occurring populations of native plants, not only to let others enjoy them, but also to preserve the ecological roles these plants play. Individual actions do make a difference, both positively and negatively. Wildflower gardeners have the chance to counteract the tragedy of habitat destruction and reduction in native plant populations occurring around the world.

PLANTING STOCK

One of the first questions one might ask is where to obtain seeds or plants to start a garden of wildflowers. Where *not* to obtain plants is easier to answer. *Plants growing in their native habitats should never be dug up for the garden.* Apart from the laws that protect wildflowers in many states, it is unethical to uproot native plants. The propagation instructions given for the 32 species of wildflowers in this book are intended for gardeners who desire to make divisions of their own plants only, not of those growing in the wild. The only circumstance in which it is acceptable to dig up wildflowers is when they are imminently threatened by highway development or construction. In those cases, prior approval must be obtained from the proper authorities, and if possible, plants should be dug while dormant.

Nursery-grown material usually yields the best wildflower gardening results. Before ordering plants by mail or from a local retail outlet, determine

WILDFLOWER CONSERVATION GUIDELINES*

1. Let your acts reflect your respect for wild native plants as integral parts of biological communities and natural landscapes. Remember that if you pick or disturb wildflowers, your action affects the natural world, and that the cumulative effects of the actions of many people can be particularly harmful.

2. Do not dig or take cuttings from native plants in the wild except as part of rescue or salvage operations sponsored by responsible organizations.

3. Encourage the use of regional native plants in home and public landscapes, but before obtaining wildflower plants or seeds for your home landscape, learn enough about their cultural requirements to be sure you can provide a suitable habitat.

4. If you collect seeds from the wild, collect a few seeds or fruits from each of many plants and *only from common species that are locally abundant.* Purchase wildflower seeds only from companies that collect responsibly.

5. Purchase live wildflower plants only from suppliers or organizations that propagate their own plants or that purchase their material from those who propagate them. Ask sellers about the origin of the plants you are considering buying. If there is any doubt about a plant's origin, do not purchase it.

6. Be cautious and knowledgeable in the use of exotic wildflowers. While many of these non-native wildflower species can be attractively used in gardens and landscapes, some species are overly aggressive and these weeds may displace native species. Become aware of your state's noxious weed laws by contacting your state Department of Agriculture or Agricultural Extension Service.

*Adapted for broader applicability from the Virginia Wildflower Preservation Society's "Wildflower Conservation Guidelines."

7. When photographing wildflowers, or inspecting them closely, be careful not to trample plants nearby.

8. If you pick wildflowers, dried seed stalks, or greens for home decoration, use only common species that are abundant at the site. Leave enough flowers or seeds to allow the plant population to reseed itself. Avoid picking herbaceous perennials such as wild orchids, jack-in-the-pulpits, or gentians that, like daffodils, need to retain their vegetative parts to store energy for next year's development. Avoid cutting slow-growing plants, such as running cedar, club mosses, or partridgeberry, for Christmas wreaths or other decorations.

9. Become familiar with your state's wildflower protection laws. If your state does not have laws protecting wildflowers, or if the existing laws are weak, support the passage and enforcement of strong and effective legislation for the preservation of native plants. Report unlawful collection of plants to proper authorities and, when necessary, remind others that collecting plants or disturbing a natural area is illegal in parks and other public places.

10. If you learn that an area with wildflowers is scheduled for development, notify a native plant society in your region. Discuss with the developer the possibilities of compatible development alternatives or of conducting a wildflower rescue or salvage operation.

11. It is important to protect information about the locations of rare species. If you discover a new site of a plant species that you know is rare, report it to responsible conservation officials, such as your state's Natural Heritage Program, a native plant society, Nature Conservancy chapter, or the U.S. Fish and Wildlife Service, as soon as possible and before discussing it with others.

whether the plants have been propagated in a nursery. Do not buy plants that have been collected in the wild, since this practice may adversely affect natural populations of plants deserving protection. When ordering wildflowers you may wish to purchase seeds or live plants from a producer who is relatively close by, since there is a greater likelihood that the stock is better adapted to your local environmental conditions.

Seeds. Much can be gained by propagating wildflowers by seed, even apart from their year-round availability, durability in shipping, and relative low cost. Raising wildflowers from seed also gives the gardener a chance to become familiar with the complete life cycle of plants. Some of the species in this book will self-seed once established, and therefore it is useful to know from firsthand experience what the seedlings of the species look like. Often the leaves of seedlings look different from those of mature plants, and without this knowledge they might be accidentally removed as weeds.

You can collect the seeds of most perennials growing in the wild without fear of significantly affecting their populations, if you take only a small proportion of the seeds that are produced. Since annuals reproduce only by seed, you should collect seeds from them only in locations where their populations are abundant. Prior to collecting any seeds permission of the property owner is essential.

Wildflower seeds are usually available throughout the year from mail-order suppliers. Many perennial wildflowers of northeastern North America have enhanced germination when their seeds are chilled or "stratified" for several months. Check with the supplier to determine whether the seeds you purchase have been pre-treated or if they would benefit from additional cold treatment.

Wildflower Seed Mixtures: Caution! You should be very cautious and fully informed before purchasing commercial wildflower seed mixtures, which recently have been gaining popularity. Some suppliers painstakingly formulate mixtures that are representative of native wildflowers of specific regions or habitats. More frequently, however, mixes are formulated for broad geographic regions and may contain species that are not particularly adapted to your local conditions. Furthermore, it is often difficult to know just what species are contained in some of the mixtures and in what proportions. Some of the producers of the wildflower mixtures will vary the composition depending upon the temporary availability of seeds, so there is no guarantee that the product will be uniform from year to year. Often the mixes contain an abundance of annuals, which provide a splash of color the first year, but have difficulty in reseeding themselves. The lack of perennials in these mixes may mean disappointment in subsequent years. As long as you are investing in wildflowers, you might as well pay for only what you want, not just a pretty can or packet of mostly roadside weeds.

A further difficulty with some of the mixes is the inclusion of weedy, non-native wildflower species which, while attractive, may become aggressive. An analysis by the New England Wildflower Society of various "northeastern" wildflower seed mixes in 1985 found them to be comprised of eight to thirty-four different species, of which zero to 100 percent were native to northeastern North America. The following are some non-native species that have been found in various wildflower mixes:

SPECIES	PLACE OF ORIGIN	SPECIES	PLACE OF ORIGIN
Oxeye daisy	Europe	Dame's rocket	France
Corn poppy	Europe	African daisy	South Africa
Sweet alyssum	Europe–W. Asia	Foxglove	Europe
White yarrow	Europe	Candytuft	S.E. Europe–
Baby's breath	S. Europe		W. Asia
Purple loosestrife	N. Europe	Four-o'clock	Peru
St. John's-wort	Europe–Africa	Queen Anne's lace	Europe
Bouncing bet	Europe–Asia	Chicory	Europe
Bachelor's button	Europe	Cornflower	Europe

Live Plants. Since it often takes several years for perennial wildflowers to bloom when started from seed, the fastest way to establish them in the garden is to purchase live plants from reputable suppliers. Planning is essential. Perennial wildflowers are best shipped and planted when they are dormant. Therefore, most mail-order suppliers ship only from late winter to midspring, and again in the autumn. In northeastern North America there are obvious difficulties with shipping live material during the winter, so you should contact suppliers to determine the season of availability and whether there are any other constraints in shipping the specific live wildflowers you wish to plant.

SUPPLIERS The number of reputable commercial producers and distributors of wildflower plants and seeds is steadily increasing. Some commercial sources are listed in Appendix A, although their inclusion is in no way an endorsement by the author or publisher. Most suppliers have catalogs or lists giving prices of seeds, live plants and other items useful in wildflower gardening. Many of these catalogs are extremely useful sources of information about growing native plants. As is noted in Appendix A, some of the suppliers have a small charge for their catalogs and some refund that charge with the first order. It is a good idea to order catalogs several months in advance of your anticipated planting time. Some suppliers have shipping restrictions across international boundaries, and where these are known they are mentioned in Appendix A. Most suppliers prefer payment in the currency of their own country, and some require it.

If you are planning to plant large areas with mature bulbs and rootstocks, some of the suppliers listed in Appendix A sell large quantities of live plants (and seeds) to the public at wholesale prices. Although many suppliers give wholesale discounts to the public, some sell at wholesale rates only to registered retailers, so check with the supplier first.

MORE INFORMATION

This book may be just a beginning for you. Further information is available from many sources, some of which are listed in the appendixes to this book.

Botanical Gardens. Botanical gardens, nature centers, and arboreta are excellent sources of information about gardening with native plants. A state-by-state listing of such institutions is given in Appendix B. This listing includes the admission fee, if any, the season of operation, and the phone numbers. The resources of these gardens and centers usually extend beyond their collections of living native plants. Many offer workshops, symposia, tours, or lecture series on wildflower gardening. Some publish magazines, newsletters, and brochures that include information on native plants, and they often have shops that sell books on wildflowers as well as wildflower seeds and live plants.

Many botanical gardens offer memberships that entitle members to use library facilities, attend special events at reduced prices, go on field trips to various natural areas, consult with the horticultural staff, use a phone "gardening hotline," and other benefits. If you become interested in the institution's activities, they may have a program in which you could become a volunteer.

There are numerous other places not listed in Appendix B to observe wildflowers. Many local, regional, state, and national parks have preserved areas of native vegetation. National Forests and National Wildlife Refuges are also ideal places to see native wildflowers, as are lands owned by various chapters of the Audubon Society and the Nature Conservancy.

Botanical Organizations. Native plant societies and some horticultural organizations are excellent sources of information about native plants, as well as a means of becoming involved with wildflowers. The activities and resources of these societies are quite varied, ranging from projects to conserve rare and endangered plants to field trips, lecture series, and seed exchanges. Many of the native plant societies periodically publish newsletters or bulletins and have smaller local chapters that hold regular meetings. Some of the societies are affiliated with specific botanic gardens or arboreta, while others have a more regional or national focus. Appendix C lists botanical organizations that are concerned with wildflowers.

One organization concerned with native plants across the continent is the National Wildflower Research Center, located in Austin, Texas. The N.W.R.C., founded in 1982, is a clearinghouse for wildflower information, an institution conducting research on the propagation and cultivation of native plants, and an advocate for wildflower conservation and preservation. The public is encouraged both to contact the N.W.R.C. for information about native plants and to join them in their cause. The address of the National Wildflower Research Center is given in Appendix C.

On a state level, most states in the northeastern United States have Natural Heritage Programs, cooperative efforts between the Nature Conservancy and state departments of fish and game or natural resources to take inventory of rare plants, animals, and biologic communities. The first Natural Heritage Program was started in South Carolina in 1974, to provide that state with biological inventory data augmenting the Federal Endangered Species Act. The offices of Natural Heritage Programs listed in Appendix C can provide you with current information on rare and endangered wildflowers and plant communities in your state.

The National Council of State Garden Clubs, Inc. is also active in wildflower preservation, and advocates using native plants for landscaping roadsides and public spaces. The organization sponsors "Operation Wildflower," a cooperative effort among state garden club federations, state highway agencies, and the Federal Highway Administration to beautify the nation's highways with native species, providing a low-cost, low-maintenance alternative to the exotic grasses and weeds that dominate our roadsides. Since its inception in 1972, Operation Wildflower has extended its horizons beyond the roadside to include projects in public parks, gardens, and wildflower preserves.

References. An annotated bibliography of books and published resources on wildflower gardening is contained in Appendix D.

Theme Gardens

Cultivating native wildflowers of northeastern North America opens new horizons in low-maintenance gardening. A sense of satisfaction comes with the reestablishment of plants that were once more widespread in the region. Whether you use native plants to complement existing gardens or establish new plantings of species with different environmental requirements, you don't have to start out on a grand scale. Some of the most successful wildflower gardens are small flower beds at the corner of a house or small patches of land otherwise unused. Even those areas you can't mow anyway between the roots of the trees in the front yard can be enhanced by plantings of wildflowers.

Another idea is to use wildflowers in a natural setting. Forested areas can become woodland gardens through the addition of wildflowers adapted to that habitat. Similarly, wet and damp areas can be enriched and open areas beautified by planting wetland species or native meadow wildflowers.

HORTICULTURAL GARDENS

Beds and Borders. The simplest approach is to use wildflowers in existing gardens to complement your ornamental plants. Conventional flower beds might include species such as eastern columbine, false Solomon's seal, and wood lily. Larger blue flag, black-eyed Susan, and cardinal flower should also be considered, because their long stems and long-lasting flowers make them ideal cut flowers. While the larger blue flag and cardinal flower are natives of wetland habitats, they also thrive in normal garden beds.

Numerous northeastern native plants are ideal for sunny or shady borders. Bloodroot, foam flower, closed gentian, wild ginger, and sharp-lobed hepatica, with their low growth form and interesting foliage, make excellent border plants.

Butterfly and Hummingbird Gardens. If you want to attract butterflies to your garden, plant species with contrasting-colored flowers that produce sweet nectars, such as New England aster, black-eyed Susan, wild bergamot,

Butterfly, hummingbird, and cutflower garden.

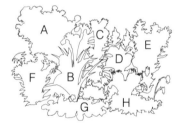

A. New England aster
B. Larger blue flag
C. Wild bergamot
D. Turtlehead
E. Cardinal flower
F. Black-eyed Susan
G. Common blue violet
H. Eastern columbine

NOTE: Wildflowers depicted in this and the following sample gardens may not bloom simultaneously.

bluets, and larger blue flag. All these are used for food by the adult butterflies. Another way to attract butterflies is to plant wildflowers that serve as food for the developing caterpillars. Turtlehead is the primary food plant for the black and orange caterpillars of the Baltimore butterfly, whose adults are mostly black with white and orange spots. The common blue violet is a major food source for fritillary butterflies, but since these caterpillars feed at night and hide during the day, you may not see who has been chewing on the leaves. One of the reasons for refraining from using insecticides in wildflower gardens, obviously, is the harm they cause to butterflies.

Hummingbirds are attracted to red or pink flowers that point outward or hang down. To lure hummingbirds to your garden, try planting cardinal flower, eastern columbine, and wild bergamot. These wildflowers, planted as companions to those that attract butterflies, will provide a prolonged season of winged guests.

Ground Covers. Some of the native species in this book make superb ground covers. If you want a low ground cover for acidic soils, consider partridgeberry, wintergreen, yellow clintonia, and bunchberry. If you desire a ground cover a foot or so high, try bloodroot or the more aggressive

Canada anemone and mayapple. Groundnut, whose vines grow rapidly, is an excellent choice for covering stumps or other unsightly areas, but in the full sun it may become aggressive. Sunny banks and steep areas prone to erosion might be planted with New England aster, black-eyed Susan, pasture rose, and wild bergamot for an attractive, low-maintenance alternative to grass.

Rock Gardens. No rock garden is truly complete without representative native species. By using wildflowers you can create rock gardens for sun or shade, and for acid or alkaline soil conditions. Eastern columbine and the common blue violet grow well in sunny or shady rock gardens as long as the soil is not too acidic; bluets, on the other hand, prefer full sun and relatively acid soils. If your soil is alkaline and you have limestone or marble rocks, try wild ginger, sharp-lobed hepatica, bloodroot, and foam flower, especially in shady locations. If the soils are acidic, however, and you are using granite rocks, then bunchberry, wintergreen, yellow clintonia and shinleaf are more appropriate. It is difficult to grow acid-loving and alkaline-loving plants together in the same garden, and in designing the rock garden you should be careful that water from one type of garden does not drain into the other.

Container Gardening. Growing wildflowers in containers is an easy way to enjoy native plants if you live in a city, if your gardening space is limited, or if your local conditions are quite different from those usually required by a particular species. One advantage to container gardening is you can move the plants seasonally, indoors or out, to match the needs of the species. Wildflowers such as black-eyed Susan and pasture rose planted in large containers provide stunning accents for courtyards, balconies, or patios. Foam flowers also make attractive potted plants when grown in 8–12-inch containers. I have found that one way to enjoy bloodroot, whose flowers are too fragile to pick, is to grow it in shallow pots that can be hung on the porch or even moved into the house.

When growing plants in containers, good drainage is essential to prevent the roots from rotting. The container should have a hole in the bottom to allow excess water to drain out and the bottom of the pot should be lined with a layer of pot shards or gravel. With the plant in place, the pot should be filled to about 1 inch from the top with a sandy or loamy soil mix.

There is a wide variety of containers that can be used: conventional pots, wooden tubs, window boxes, hanging baskets, drainage tile, and chimney flue liners, to mention a few. Containers made of porous ceramic material, like clay pots, tend to dry out faster, so wildflowers planted in them need to be watered more frequently than those planted in impervious glass, glazed ceramic, or plastic containers. If you are rearing a species that prefers wet soils, you may have better success using an impervious container, but be sure it has sufficient bottom drainage.

Most container-grown wildflowers will overwinter best if the soil in the pot does not freeze solid. One way of minimizing winter ice damage is to bury the container in the soil and then cover the top with a layer of insulating leaf or bark mulch. As this technique may not be available to the urban apartment dweller, ice damage can also be reduced by placing the container in a balcony corner next to a wall and covering the pot with straw. Alternatively, you can grow species, like black-eyed Susan, that will flower the first year their seeds are planted, and treat them as annuals.

Container gardening is a way to extend the flowering season for wildflowers, since some pot-grown species can be brought indoors during midwinter and forced into bloom. Wild ginger, Jack-in-the-pulpit, mayapple, bloodroot, purple trillium, Dutchman's breeches, sharp-lobed hepatica, common blue violet and even wild bergamot can be successfully forced, bringing an early spring to your home. Simply bury the pot in the fall so that the level of the soil inside the container is even with the ground surface, and mark the location. The pots can be brought indoors in midwinter, warmed gradually by keeping them for several days or weeks in a cool place, and then set in a sunny window for late winter flowering. It is a good idea not

In terrarium:
A. Partridgeberry
B. Wintergreen

In patio containers:
C. Pasture rose
D. Black-eyed Susan

In pots for forcing:
E. Bloodroot
F. Common blue violet
G. Eastern Columbine
H. Jack-in-the-pulpit

Wildflowers in containers.

to try to force the same individual plants in successive years. Allow them to follow the natural seasonal rhythms the following year.

Terrariums and dish gardens can be planted with small wildflowers to create a miniature indoor garden. Wintergreen, partridgeberry, and shinleaf are good choices. These species prefer acid soils, so use a mix of peat moss, sand, and potting soil to plant them in. As with other containers, terrariums require good soil drainage, even though they lack drainage holes. Place a thick layer of gravel in the bottom of the container, and then adjust your watering regime so that the soil is kept moist but not wet. These plants benefit from cold treatment during the winter. Wintergreen and partridgeberry, noted for their lustrous green leaves and bright red berries, should be chilled at 40°F for about six weeks to ensure continued growth and flowering. If you want to maintain these wildflowers in a terrarium for prolonged periods, put them in a plastic bag once a year with a wad of moist peat moss and give them a six-week rest in the refrigerator. You can even put the entire terrarium in the refrigerator, if you cover the top with plastic wrap to retain its moisture.

NATURAL GARDENS

A highly successful way to use native plants is to plant wildflowers in appropriate natural settings. This also allows you to brighten up areas of your property that are difficult to plant — shady areas, wetlands, dry places. See pages 80–151 for detailed descriptions and illustrations of species suitable for planting in naturalized wildflower gardens.

Woodland Gardens. Woodland gardens are ideally suited to areas with existing trees and shady conditions. For the most effective woodland garden select species for a succession of blooming, from the early spring, when the sharp-lobed hepatica, bloodroot, eastern trout lily, and Dutchman's breeches are in flower, through the summer, when the wild leek, wood lily, and wintergreen bloom. You can expect much greater success in establishing the garden if you use live plants that have been reared in a nursery, rather than attempting to plant seeds directly in a woodland.

In creating a woodland garden, do not just purchase plants and plunk them into the ground. Rather, plan out the season of bloom and try to match the soil, light, and moisture requirements of the plants with the conditions found in the woodland garden site. Much of this information is presented in the charts in this book and in the individual wildflower descriptions in Part III. Pay particular attention to the soil requirements of the plants and adjust the soil conditions according to the suggestions on pages 42–48.

You may need to remove a few of the existing ferns, tree seedlings, and herbaceous plants to give your new woodland wildflowers an opportunity to become established. First, however, learn enough about the species you are disposing of to be sure that they can be sacrificed in your woodland garden.

The best way to clear patches for planting new woodland wildflowers is to use a sharp spade. Dig a hole a foot deep and several times as wide as the maximum extension of the wildflower's roots. This will sever some of the roots of nearby plants which would be competing for moisture with the new arrival.

Pay extra attention to your wildflowers for the first year after transplanting them. If the soil becomes excessively dry, you may need to water the plants until their root systems have become fully established. It is a good idea, periodically, to remove competing weeds that may encroach on the new wildflowers the first season.

Wetland Gardens. If your soils are perennially wet, or if you want to create a garden by a pond, pool, or swampy area, native wetland species can work well. Jack-in-the-pulpit, larger blue flag, cardinal flower, turtlehead, groundnut, and closed gentian are easy to grow and highly adaptable wildflowers of wetland habitats. Although these species naturally grow in continually wet conditions, they can be grown in any soil that is moderately moist. All can be grown in full sun to partial shade, and Jack-in-the-pulpit even tolerates deep forest shade.

All of these wetland species can easily be grown from seed, with the exception of groundnut, which tends not to produce fertile seeds northward from New England. Young plants' survival rate is higher, however, if they are started in flats or seed beds and transplanted to the wet soils after the first year. Larger blue flag, cardinal flower, groundnut, turtlehead, and closed gentian are all easily propagated by root and rootstock divisions. Once established, they will spread by root extension and together form large, showy masses of red, white, blue and pink.

Be careful about the placement of groundnut. In full sun with ample moisture it may become aggressive, and its trailing vines may overrun other wetland species. You can keep it under control by planting its tubers inside large plastic flower pots or rings of lawn edging buried just below the soil surface. And if it starts to become overly aggressive, you can gain the final victory by digging, cooking and eating this subterranean delicacy.

A small wetland garden at the edge of a pool filled with aquatic plants can enhance a landscape by creating a natural transition. If you want to plant a larger area of wetland, or if your garden is situated in an extensive

Rock garden — for alkaline (left) and acidic soils (right).

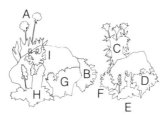

A. Wild leek
B. Wild ginger
C. Wood lily
D. Bunchberry
E. Shinleaf
F. Wintergreen
G. Bloodroot
H. Foam flower
I. Sharp-lobed hepatica

wetland, you should first check with your local conservation commission, planning board, or state environmental conservation agency, to determine whether local or state laws pertain to your planned activities. Many states in the region have wetland protection laws, which regulate the manipulation of wetlands. Some alterations to wetlands require permits from the U.S. Army Corps of Engineers under the Clean Water Act administered by the U.S. Environmental Protection Agency. The addresses of the regional E.P.A. offices are given in Appendix C.

Meadows. Wildflower meadows are becoming increasingly popular alternatives to lawns, and northeastern North American natives such as Canada anemone, New England aster, wild bergamot, pasture rose, and black-eyed Susan can fill open spaces with color from late spring through autumn. If your meadow is damp or has moist soils, several wetland species such as closed gentian, cardinal flower, and turtlehead should be considered. Native wildflower meadows cost less than lawns to maintain, and consume less water, gasoline, fertilizers, and time.

The easiest time to create a wildflower meadow is when the land is bare and you do not have to deal with established, competing grasses, weeds, herbaceous plants and woody seedlings. Meadow seeds can be purchased from many of the suppliers listed in Appendix A. If you are planning to plant a large area, you should inquire about wholesale prices for wildflower and native grass seed. And if you purchase formulated wildflower-grass seed mixtures, be sure they contain only those native species you really want in your meadow.

Natural grasslands and prairies in this region (see page 138) are a combination of wildflowers and grasses. When establishing your wildflower meadow, the grasses you interplant with the wildflowers should be *bunch grasses* — species that grow in clumps. Their shoots will provide support and the ideal amount of competition for the wildflowers to grow straight and tall. Avoid planting ryegrasses or bluegrasses, which will form a sod turf and crowd out the wildflowers.

Native wildflower seeds should be combined with a mixture of native grasses such as little bluestem, June grass, prairie brome, northern dropseed, big bluestem, and switchgrass, with 60 to 90% of the seeds being grasses. The wildflower and grass seed mixture should be sown at a rate of 5 to 20 pounds of live seeds per acre, depending on the species composition. If species with small seeds, such as switchgrass and cardinal flower, make up the bulk of the mixture, the seeding rate should be lower than when species with large, heavy seeds, such as northern dropseed and wild bergamot, are used. The supplier from whom you purchase wildflower and grass seed in bulk can make specific seeding rate recommendations, but typically 6 to 7 pounds of wildflower seeds are mixed with enough grass seeds to sow an acre.

It is best to sow the seeds in midspring or fall on a windless day, broadcasting them by hand or using a whirlwind seeder. Do not plant the meadow in midsummer, when heat and droughty conditions may make it

A. Yellow clintonia
B. Wild ginger
C. Bunchberry
D. Wintergreen
E. Wild lily-of-the-valley
F. Partridgeberry

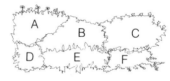

Ground covers, late spring.

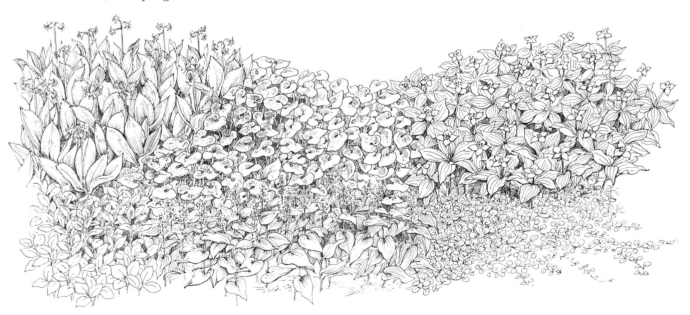

difficult for seeds to germinate and seedlings to become established. Keep the soil moist, but not wet, until the seeds have germinated and seedlings start to become established. A light covering of seed-free straw will help to conserve moisture and reduce erosion until the meadow is established. Do not, however, use baled field hay, which is likely to contain the seeds of exotic grasses, species you want to prevent from invading your meadow. If you cannot plant your meadow until the following spring, plant a cover crop of buckwheat, oats, or annual rye on the area in the fall, and plow it under as a green manure the following spring before sowing the wildflower and grass seeds.

Transforming an Existing Field. More commonly, you are confronted with an existing lawn or field that you want to convert to a wildflower meadow. *Resist any impulses to use herbicides or fumigants to kill the existing vegetation.* Herbicides are likely to create more problems for the wildflower enthusiast than they can solve. Apart from the damage they cause to the environment, they are not likely to save you any time in establishing a wildflower meadow.

The best way to turn an existing field into a wildflower meadow is to start on a small scale by transplanting live plants, rather than scattering seeds among established grasses. The best time to start is in the spring, after planning your strategy and ordering your seeds in the late winter.

In the spring plant the wildflower seeds in beds, flats, or plugs as detailed on pages 49–53 and the section on meadow wildflowers (pages 138–151). Grass seed can also be planted in small pots to make plugs.

As soon as the soil is warm and dry enough to work, dig up patches of the field, turning them over with a sharp spade or a rototiller. The patches should be 3 to 8 feet in diameter and dug in a random pattern, to create a more natural effect than spacing them in straight rows. Remove as many of the existing grass roots as possible, and water the soil to encourage the germination of weed seeds that you have inadvertently stirred up in the process. Then cover the patch with heavy-gauge black plastic sheet "mulch," pieces of discarded carpet, or even thick sections of newspaper. If you do not care for the sight of such coverings, you can spread a layer of bark mulch or even soil on top of them. The covering will eventually shade out and kill off the remaining pieces of grass and the newly germinated weed seedlings. Rain will soak through the carpet or the joints between the newspapers and mulch and should keep the ground below moist. Leave the coverings on the patches through the summer as the wildflower seedlings and grass plugs are maturing in the nursery.

In the early autumn, remove the coverings. If black plastic mulch or carpet sections have been used, it may be possible to use them again. Just place them where you intend to create the next year's patches.

Now plant the grass plugs in the patch, spacing them 12 to 15 inches apart, and transplant the wildflowers in between the clumps of grasses. Alternatively, wildflower plugs or sods can be transplanted into the patches in the fall or spring, and the grass seed sown around the live plants. In either method, the meadow benefits from an initial watering and a light mulch of seed-free straw.

If your meadow already has bunch grasses, and you do not care to introduce new grass species, wildflower plugs and sods can be planted directly into the field. Clear a small patch about a foot in diameter with a cultivator and pick out the grass roots. Set the live plants so the bases of their shoots are at the ground level. Press them down firmly so the roots are in good contact with the soil beneath, and water well.

Wildflower Meadow Maintenance. Repeat the steps each year until you are satisfied with your wildflower and native grass meadow. It may be a slow process, but even in nature a beautiful wildflower meadow, resplendent with a high diversity of desirable plants, is rarely produced in a single year.

Once the wildflower meadow is established it is relatively easy to maintain. The natural process of succession in northeastern North America will eventually turn your field into a forest, unless you take steps to prevent it. Mow the meadow once a year with a rotary mower, in the late fall after seeds have set. Woody plants will be clipped off and eventually eliminated, while the grasses and wildflowers will be relatively unaffected. Be careful of pasture roses if you have planted them in your meadow; they too are woody and do not respond well to being decapitated when the field is mown. To make the mowing easier, plant pasture roses next to the fences at the edge of the meadow.

Meadows, grasslands, and prairies can also be maintained by periodic burning, which kills invading shrub and tree seedlings. Do not burn a meadow until after the second season, but then you can burn it every two to three years. Meadows are best burned in the early spring, on windless days, when the grass is dry but the soil is still wet. If the meadow grass is too thin to support the fire, dry straw can be scattered about and ignited. Be careful to observe local, state, and federal regulations concerning outdoor burning, in addition to the usual safety practices. Check with your local fire department about obtaining an outdoor burning permit.

In some suburbs there are ordinances dictating aesthetic standards for landscaping. If you live in such a community you might want to check with city hall before converting your front yard into a prairie. If there are prohibitions, you can always try to get the law changed to encourage the landscaping use of native plants. Native plants are rarely the "weeds" that these ordinances are trying to prohibit, and it is unlikely that your black-eyed Susans or wild bergamot are going to march through your neighbor's Kentucky bluegrass.

Plant Descriptions

The technical terminology used in the descriptions of the flowers, leaves, shoots and roots of the species in this book has been kept to a minimum. The knowledge of some botanical terms is essential, however, and relatively painless to acquire.

FLOWERS Illustrated opposite are two typical flowers with all the parts that are usually present. *Complete flowers* have all the parts illustrated, but some of the wildflowers in the book lack one or more of the parts or they may be fused together in different arrangements. The trillium (upper left) is a *simple flower*. The aster (lower left) is a *composite flower*.

In simple flowers, the flower parts are attached to a fleshy pad (the *receptacle*) atop the flower stem or *peduncle*. The outermost parts of the flower are the *sepals*, which are usually small, green, leaflike structures that cover and protect the flower while it is in the bud. Collectively, all of the sepals are called the *calyx*, Latin for "cup." In some species the sepals are fused together to form a tubular calyx, and in other species they resemble petals. Immediately inside the sepals are the *petals*, which may take a variety of forms, some species having petals fused together into a tube, and others having petals that are free and unattached. On some flowers the petal arrangement is radially symmetrical, but on others, the petals take irregular forms. Collectively the petals are called the *corolla*, which means "small crown" in Latin.

In the center of the flower are the sexual parts, the male *stamens* and the female *pistil*. There may be one or several pistils, depending upon the species, but most flowering plants have more than one stamen. The stamen consists of a slender stalk, the *filament*, to which the pollen-bearing sacs, the *anthers*, are attached. The pistil has three major parts whose shapes may vary widely among species. The upper surface of the pistil, which receives pollen grains, is the *stigma*. The stigma is attached to the *ovary* at the base of the pistil by a usually slender tissue known as the *style*. Inside the ovary is a chamber containing the *ovules*, the female sex cells. After the pollen grains are deposited on the stigma, they germinate, sending microscopic tubes down through the style, through portions of the ovary, and finally into the ovules. Following fertilization, the ovules mature into *seeds*, and the ovary matures into the *fruit* of the plant.

The flowers of plants in the aster family, such as New England aster and black-eyed Susan, have a more complex structure. These species usually have two types of small flowers clustered together in a composite *flower head*. These small flowers or *florets* share a broad receptacle, often enclosed from below by many leafy *bracts*. The *ray flowers* usually form a ring around the outside of the head. Each ray flower has a relatively long, strap-like petal which upon close inspection can be seen to be several small petals fused together. Often ray flowers are sterile and lack stamens and pistils entirely. In the center of the flower head are the even smaller *disc flowers*

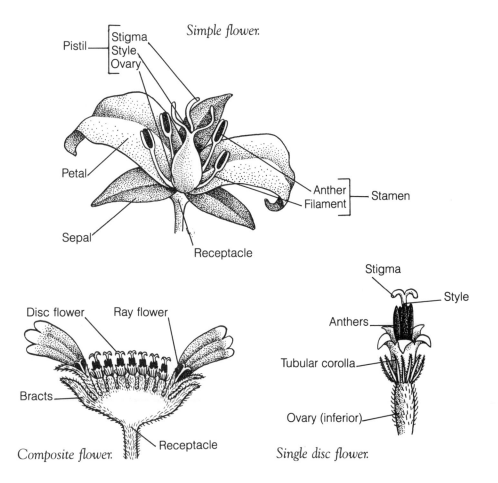

Simple flower.

Composite flower.

Single disc flower.

with minute, tubular corollas. The stamens and the pistils in these flowers are surrounded by the petals, but are usually so small that magnification is required to see them clearly.

COLOR AND HEIGHT

Color of the flower and height of the plant are the gardener's first two concerns in deciding what species to plant. To aid in planning, the 32 species of plants described in this book are listed on page 27 by flower color and page 28 by height. Use the information in these charts as a rough guide only. Keep in mind that some species, such as sharp-lobed hepatica, can appear in a range of colors. Also, the height of the plant depends on the environmental conditions in which it is grown. Further information concerning flower color and plant height is given in the descriptions of individual species.

FRUITS AND SEEDS

Fruits are as intriguing and varied as the flowers that produce them. The main function of fruits, which are formed from ripened ovaries, is to aid in the dissemination of the seeds they contain. The structure of various fruits often gives clues about how the seeds are disseminated. Species that inhabit open spaces, like New England aster and Canada anemone, depend upon the wind to move their seeds away from the parent plants and often have small fruits with tufts of hairs to help keep them buoyed by air currents.

Other wildflowers disseminate their seeds through the air by different means. The capsule fruits of the eastern columbine are borne on long stems. As the stems wave in the wind, the seeds are flung out of openings in the top of the fruit. The fruits of the common blue violet, on the other hand, rupture and eject their seeds up to 12 feet away. Sometimes the fruits make popping sounds as they explode.

Birds, small mammals, and other animals are important agents in dispersing seeds. Birds especially like sweet, fleshy berries. They locate their food by sight rather than smell, and many fruits that are preferred by them, like those of the yellow clintonia, partridgeberry, wintergreen, bunchberry, and Jack-in-the-pulpit, are bright red or dark blue to show up against the green foliage. Often these same fruits are green and have an acid taste before they are ripe, an adaptation that lessens the chance that they will be eaten before the seeds are mature. Most fruits that are eaten by birds are also eaten by small mammals, and frequently the passage of seeds through an animal's digestive system actually enhances germination.

Some wildflowers depend upon ants to carry their seeds about and have evolved specialized seeds to attract them. Species like Dutchman's breeches,

FLOWER COLOR

Species	Page	Brown	White	Pink	Red	Orange	Yellow	Green	Blue	Purple	Lavender
Purple trillium	92	■			■					■	
Jack-in-the-pulpit	126	■						■		■	
Wild ginger	94	■								■	
Groundnut	132		■								
Canada anemone	140		■								
Dutchman's breeches	88		■								
Mayapple	100		■								
Foamflower	98		■								
Bunchberry	112		■								
Shinleaf	118		■								
Partridgeberry	114		■								
Wintergreen	122		■								
False Solomon's seal	108		■								
Bloodroot	84		■								
Wild lily-of-the-valley	104		■								
Turtlehead	134		■	■							
Sharp-lobed hepatica	82		■	■					■		■
Wild leek	116		■					■			
Pasture rose	144			■							
Eastern columbine	96			■	■		■				
Cardinal flower	130				■						
Wood lily	120				■	■					
Black-eyed Susan	146					■	■				
Eastern trout lily	86						■				
Yellow clintonia	110						■				
Solomon's seal	106						■	■			
Closed gentian	136								■	■	
Larger blue flag	128								■	■	
Common blue violet	90								■	■	■
Bluets	142								■		■
New England aster	150									■	
Wild bergamot	148										■

PLANT HEIGHT

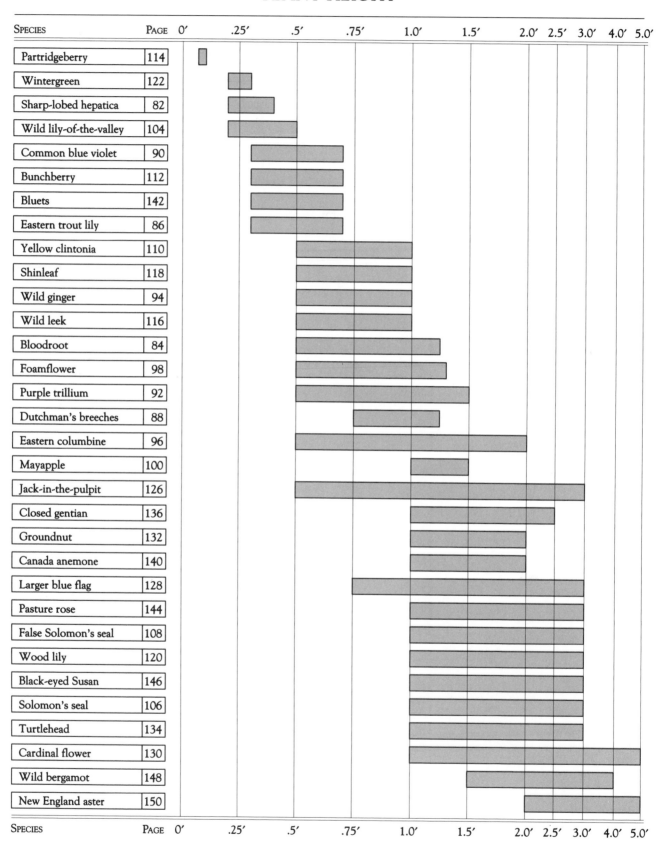

SPECIES	PAGE	0′	.25′	.5′	.75′	1.0′	1.5′	2.0′	2.5′	3.0′	4.0′	5.0′
Partridgeberry	114											
Wintergreen	122											
Sharp-lobed hepatica	82											
Wild lily-of-the-valley	104											
Common blue violet	90											
Bunchberry	112											
Bluets	142											
Eastern trout lily	86											
Yellow clintonia	110											
Shinleaf	118											
Wild ginger	94											
Wild leek	116											
Bloodroot	84											
Foamflower	98											
Purple trillium	92											
Dutchman's breeches	88											
Eastern columbine	96											
Mayapple	100											
Jack-in-the-pulpit	126											
Closed gentian	136											
Groundnut	132											
Canada anemone	140											
Larger blue flag	128											
Pasture rose	144											
False Solomon's seal	108											
Wood lily	120											
Black-eyed Susan	146											
Solomon's seal	106											
Turtlehead	134											
Cardinal flower	130											
Wild bergamot	148											
New England aster	150											

SPECIES   PAGE   0′   .25′   .5′   .75′   1.0′   1.5′   2.0′ 2.5′ 3.0′ 4.0′ 5.0′

bloodroot, trout lily, wild ginger, and purple trillium have a white, oily tissue called an *elaiosome* attached to the surface of the seed. Ants find the elaiosome irresistible and carry the seeds back to their nests. There they chew off the tasty morsels and discard the seeds in their underground compost piles. The ants' rough treatment greatly enhances germination of the seeds and the growth of the young seedlings (see also "Scarification," page 50).

In some cases, water is responsible for moving seeds about. Turtlehead and closed gentian, both wetland wildflowers, have buoyant, waterproof seeds that are frequently transported by water currents.

ROOT SYSTEMS

The forms of the underground portions of the 32 wildflowers described in this book vary greatly and may influence the types of habitats in which they can be grown. The root system also affects how easily a plant can be propagated. Six of the eight most common "root types" illustrated on this and the following page are actually the underground stems, or "rootstocks," of perennials. The remaining two are true roots and lack leaf buds.

Runners and Stolons. Underground stems take a variety of forms. The simplest rootstock has thin horizontal branches, which give rise to new plants. These branches are usually called *runners* if they are above ground, as with strawberries, and *stolons* if they are below ground, as with mint. Partridgeberry and wintergreen are good examples of wildflowers with runners and stolons, respectively.

Tubers. If the tip of a stolon produces a swollen, fleshy storage organ, it is called a *tuber.* The leaf buds of tubers are frequently called "eyes." The potato is probably the most familiar example of a tuber, but wildflowers such as groundnut and Dutchman's breeches also have this type of rootstock.

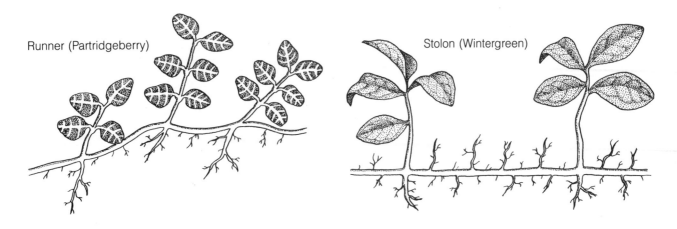

Runner (Partridgeberry)

Stolon (Wintergreen)

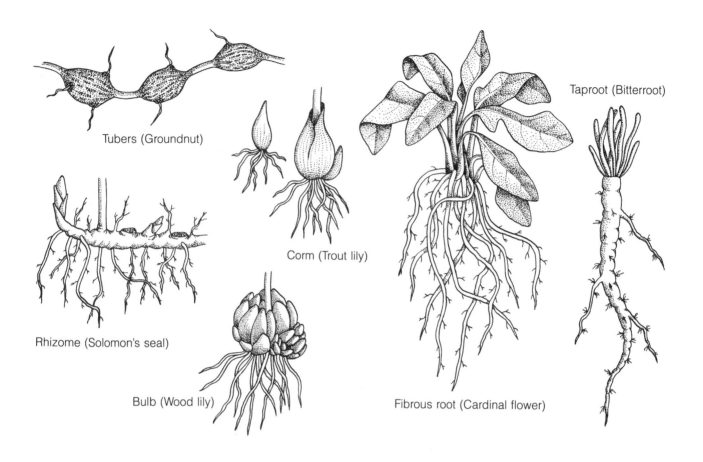

Tubers (Groundnut)

Corm (Trout lily)

Taproot (Bitterroot)

Rhizome (Solomon's seal)

Bulb (Wood lily)

Fibrous root (Cardinal flower)

Rhizomes. Thick, fleshy, horizontal, underground stems with buds on their top surfaces and roots on their bottom surfaces are called *rhizomes.* Rhizomes, like those of larger blue flag and Solomon's seal, store large amounts of starch, which is used to nourish the shoots and flowers of perennials as they emerge from dormancy.

Corms and Bulbs. Rootstocks may also be round and bulbous. A true *bulb* is an actual bud atop a very short stem, surrounded by fleshy leaf scales, as in onions and tulips. *Corms* look like bulbs but are rootstocks formed from the swollen, solid base of the stem itself, as with gladiolus. Jack-in-the-pulpit and trout lily have corms; wood lily has a true bulb. The corms and bulbs of mature plants of some species form small offsets, called "cormlets" or "bulblets" depending on their structure.

True Roots. True roots may be either diffuse and fibrous, as with many garden plants like the cardinal flower, or they may be a strongly vertical, carrotlike *tap root.* The root systems of some wildflowers are intermediate between the two basic types.

THE WILDFLOWER GARDENER'S GUIDE

Flowering Season

A great number of factors, some genetic and some environmental, affect the onset and length of the flowering season of wildflowers. Complex interactions among climatic factors such as amount of sunlight, length of day, moisture, and temperature of air and soil influence exactly when plants start flowering.

Annual species usually have longer flowering seasons than perennials do, and of course they flower in a single growing season. Few annuals, however, flower in the spring in northeastern North America. Perennials, on the other hand, may require several or many years to reach maturity and flower, but once established they generally require little maintenance, and reliably reappear year after year. In general, wildflowers bloom first in the woodlands, in the early spring, and then in fields and meadows, from late spring through fall. Wetlands tend to be in maximum flower during the summer months.

CLIMATE The overall climatic patterns of temperature and precipitation have a considerable effect on the blooming of wildflowers. After a typically cold winter in northeastern North America, spring progresses north at about 20 miles per day, and from the Mississippi River Valley toward the ocean-moderated Atlantic coast at about 65 miles per day. While winters on the Atlantic coast are milder and the growing season much longer than they are inland, the advent of spring is delayed considerably by the cold ocean waters (see frost-free season map on page 59). As one Nantucket native put it, "'Tisn't a lot of difference between winter and spring here, 'cept we know it's spring when the herring start to run."

The emergence of perennials from winter dormancy is often induced by warm temperatures in the spring. For many species the date of emergence or flowering is closely related to "growing degree days." Just like the "degree days" used to calculate the heating and air conditioning needs of buildings, these are a measure of the total accumulation of degrees above or below a critical air temperature. Growing degree days are calculated by adding the average daily temperatures above 40°F for cool season plants or 50°F for warm season plants. These base temperatures appear to be critical to induce plant growth or flowering in the spring.

Perennial species vary widely in the number of degree days required for their emergence and flowering, and there may be as much as a month's difference in the date of flowering of a given species because of year-to-year variation in degree days. Years with an above-average number of cloudy days or heavier than normal precipitation will accumulate growing degree days more slowly than usual. When spring rains are scanty, however, temperatures tend to be higher and the onset of flowering may be markedly early.

Even though exact flowering times frequently vary, the flowering order of wildflower species within the same geographic area tends to be consistent from year to year. The general seasonal progression of flowering of the perennial wildflowers in this book is shown on page 34. The seasons of flowering are given, rather than calendar months, because the number of growing degree days varies from locale to locale and from year to year. The seasons refer to the flowering of a given species near the center of its native range, and the gardener may find that the flowering sequence may be slightly different for plants obtained from different areas.

LOCAL CONDITIONS

The exact time of flowering in your garden may also be influenced by local conditions such as slope, elevation, soil type, and mulches. If your garden slopes to the south, it will be warmer and spring will arrive sooner than if it slopes to the north. The warmest slopes are those on which the sun's rays strike most perpendicularly, but even a 5° south-facing slope may have a microclimate equivalent to that of a flat surface 300 miles farther south. A similar slope facing north would be equivalently cooler. A garden located at the base of a mountain or a hill, on the other hand, may be chilled by the downslope settling of cold air, especially in the spring and fall. Flowering dates may vary by as much as several weeks, therefore, depending on the local topography.

The elevation of a garden will also influence how rapidly growing degree days accumulate. At a given latitude air temperatures generally decrease 3°F per 1,000 feet of rise. For each 100-foot increase in elevation, the air temperature is only three-tenths of a degree cooler, but flowering is delayed by about one day.

Soil conditions may advance or retard the progression of flowering. Sandy soils generally warm up more rapidly in the spring than do peaty or clayey soils. Dark-colored soils will warm more rapidly than light-colored soils will. Heavy mulches, while reducing frost and keeping soils warmer in the winter, provide an insulation layer which may both slow the warming in the spring and maintain cooler soils in the summer.

GENETIC FACTORS

Some plants are genetically programmed to flower in response to specific day lengths or hours of darkness. This characteristic is found in a wide variety of wildflowers, including annuals, biennials, and perennials. Some plants, such as black-eyed Susan, flower only when days are long and nights are short. They are known as "long-day" plants, although they are actually responding to the short nights associated with late spring and early summer. The northern regions of North America, with relatively longer spring and summer day lengths, have a greater proportion of long-day plants than do southern regions. In fact, day length determines the southern limits of some long-day species.

Other species, such as the asters, are "short-day" plants and flower when days are short and nights are long. These species are stimulated to flower by the long nights of early spring, late summer, or fall. When New England asters start to flower, it is a sure sign of summer giving way to fall, regardless of the temperature.

Regional differences in climatic patterns and day lengths have led to the evolution of genetically distinct varieties in some wildflower species. Known as "ecotypes," these varieties are well adapted to local conditions. When individuals of different ecotypes are planted together in the same garden they frequently will flower at different times. For instance, bloodroots from Vermont flower about one week earlier than bloodroots from West Virginia when they are grown together, while hepaticas from southern regions tend to flower sooner than those from northern regions.

EXTENDING THE FLOWERING SEASON

There are several ways in which the flowering season can be prolonged. In some species, such as wild bergamot, trim some of the plants just before they set flower buds. That will delay their flowering by several weeks, and the clipped plants will come into bloom as the flowers on the untrimmed plants are fading. Black-eyed Susans grown from seeds will tend to flower later the first year than in subsequent years. By planting new seeds in the late spring each year, you can have black-eyed Susans flowering into the

FLOWER TIMING

Species	Page	Late Winter	Early Spring	Midspring	Late Spring	Early Summer	Summer	Late Summer	Early Fall	Fall
Sharp-lobed hepatica	82		■							
Bloodroot	84		■	■						
Dutchman's breeches	88			■						
Eastern trout lily	86			■						
Purple trillium	92			■						
Wild ginger	94			■						
Bluets	142			■	■					
Canada anemone	140			■	■					
Common blue violet	90			■	■					
Jack-in-the-pulpit	126			■	■					
Foamflower	98				■					
Wild lily-of-the-valley	104				■					
Mayapple	100				■					
Solomon's seal	106				■					
Yellow clintonia	110			■	■	■				
False Solomon's seal	108				■					
Eastern columbine	96			■	■					
Pasture rose	144				■	■				
Bunchberry	112				■	■				
Larger blue flag	128				■	■				
Partridgeberry	114					■				
Wild bergamot	148					■	■			
Shinleaf	118					■	■			
Wood lily	120					■	■			
Wild leek	116					■	■			
Black-eyed Susan	146					■	■	■		
Wintergreen	122						■	■		
Groundnut	132						■	■		
Cardinal flower	130						■	■	■	
Turtlehead	134							■	■	■
Closed gentian	136							■	■	
New England aster	150								■	■

autumn well after the flowers have withered on plants established in previous years. Many species, both annuals and perennials, will bloom longer if the fading flowers are removed ("deadheaded") before the fruits and seeds start to mature. The only drawback of this technique is that you sacrifice production of seed that could be used for further propagation.

If you have a number of different garden sites with varying slopes and exposures, the differences in microclimates may be sufficient to accelerate flowering in some plants and delay it in others. Another way to extend the flowering season of a given species is to purchase seeds or plants from suppliers in various geographic regions, so that different ecotypes are represented in the garden. The differences in their flowering times may be sufficient to prolong the season even of those species with short-lived flowers.

Wildflower Culture

LIGHT
CONDITIONS

While the vast majority of domesticated horticultural species planted in the garden require full sunlight for optimum growth, native plants have evolved to survive in a wide variety of light conditions, from full sun to deep shade. Therein lies an opportunity in gardening with wildflowers. The light preferences of the 32 species of native plants included in this book are given on page 37.

While some species are successfully grown only in a rather restricted range of light conditions, others can be cultivated in either sun or shade. The form of the plant often changes when grown under different light conditions. Typically when a plant is grown in the shade its leaves will be thinner and larger than when it is grown in the open. Some species, such as shinleaf, are so adapted to shade that they suffer leaf scorching if they have prolonged exposure to the summer sun. Other species, like bunchberry, prefer partial shade and produce smaller plants when grown in full sun. Sun-loving species such as New England aster, however, produce their largest plants in full sun.

The light conditions in deciduous forests change dramatically through the year, and various species of wildflowers have evolved flowering and growth patterns in response to these changes. In the early spring some perennial wildflowers, such as trout lily and Dutchman's breeches, emerge from the soil, grow rapidly, flower, and produce seed in that brief period of warm, sunny weather before the trees overhead have leafed out. As the dense forest shade develops, these plants go into dormancy until the following spring. Although the wild leek's leaves complete their growth and have disappeared by late spring, it waits until early summer to flower. These are all woodland plants, but they need full sunlight for their optimum growth and should be cultivated in sites that are sunny during the spring. Other woodland species, such as shinleaf, are tolerant of deep shade and can even be grown in permanently shaded gardens on the north sides of buildings.

LIGHT CONDITIONS

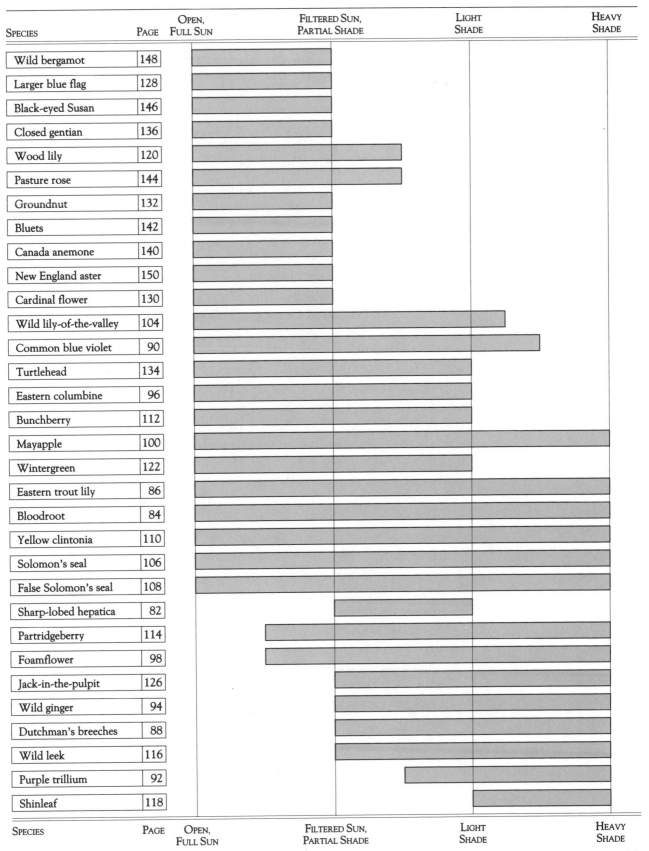

Species	Page	Open, Full Sun	Filtered Sun, Partial Shade	Light Shade	Heavy Shade
Wild bergamot	148	▓▓▓			
Larger blue flag	128	▓▓▓			
Black-eyed Susan	146	▓▓▓			
Closed gentian	136	▓▓▓			
Wood lily	120	▓▓▓▓			
Pasture rose	144	▓▓▓▓			
Groundnut	132	▓▓			
Bluets	142	▓▓			
Canada anemone	140	▓▓			
New England aster	150	▓▓▓			
Cardinal flower	130	▓▓▓			
Wild lily-of-the-valley	104	▓▓▓▓▓▓			
Common blue violet	90	▓▓▓▓▓▓▓			
Turtlehead	134	▓▓▓▓			
Eastern columbine	96	▓▓▓▓			
Bunchberry	112	▓▓▓▓			
Mayapple	100	▓▓▓▓▓▓▓▓			
Wintergreen	122	▓▓▓▓			
Eastern trout lily	86	▓▓▓▓▓▓▓▓			
Bloodroot	84	▓▓▓▓▓▓▓▓			
Yellow clintonia	110	▓▓▓▓▓▓▓▓			
Solomon's seal	106	▓▓▓▓▓▓▓▓			
False Solomon's seal	108	▓▓			
Sharp-lobed hepatica	82		▓▓		
Partridgeberry	114		▓▓▓		
Foamflower	98		▓▓▓		
Jack-in-the-pulpit	126		▓▓▓▓▓▓		
Wild ginger	94		▓▓▓▓▓▓		
Dutchman's breeches	88		▓▓▓▓▓▓		
Wild leek	116		▓▓▓▓▓▓		
Purple trillium	92			▓▓▓	
Shinleaf	118			▓▓	

TEMPERATURE While all of the wildflowers in this book are perennials adapted to cold winters, their northern or southern limits often are determined by winter temperatures. Most gardeners are familiar with hardiness zones, which indicate the relative mildness or severity of winter temperatures. (See page 60, U.S.D.A. Hardiness Zone Map). The higher the hardiness zone number, the milder the winter climate. There is a great deal of similarity between hardiness zones and the length of the frost-free season (see map on page 59). Hardiness zones are based only on the average annual minimum winter temperature, however, and the frost-free season is the average length of time between the last killing frost in the spring and the first frost in the autumn. As you move north through northeastern North America, you will generally encounter shorter frost-free seasons and lower hardiness zone numbers, but this pattern is by no means uniform. The coastline of the Atlantic Ocean, the shores of the Great Lakes, and the valleys of major rivers have significantly milder winters and longer growing seasons than do the peaks of the White, Green, Adirondack, or Catskill Mountains and the Appalachian Range at the same latitude.

Most perennials have a limited range of hardiness zones in which they can survive. The approximate range of hardiness zones for the species of wildflowers in this book is given on page 39 and is shown on the individual range maps. The hardiness ranges indicated are approximate. You can usually cultivate perennials in colder areas if you insulate them with a heavy overwinter mulch to prevent frost penetration in the soil. Be careful to remove the mulch in the spring and to choose a mulching material that will not alter the desired acidity/alkalinity conditions for pH sensitive species, as is explained in the section to follow concerning soils.

Snowy winters are common in much of northeastern North America. The early spring wildflowers of the region are adapted to this condition, so don't despair if late spring snows cover your newly emerged plants. Snow is actually an excellent insulator, and in years when a thick layer of snow blankets the soil before the ground has frozen solid, the soil below usually remains unfrozen. When there is continuous snow cover during the winter, the soil often warms up more rapidly in the spring, and flowering occurs earlier. Snow loses its insulating quality when it becomes compacted, so it is a good idea not to walk in your wildflower garden during the snowy season.

Cold winter temperatures influence not only the northern range of these perennials, but their southern limits as well. Many species in northeastern North America that have evolved to survive harsh winters by becoming dormant in the late summer or fall, when temperatures are relatively mild,

HARDINESS ZONES

Species	Page	Hardiness Zones
Bunchberry	112	1–6
Shinleaf	118	2–6
Canada anemone	140	2–6
Larger blue flag	128	2–7
Wild lily-of-the-valley	104	2–7
Yellow clintonia	110	2–7
Purple trillium	92	2–8
False Solomon's seal	108	2–7
Cardinal flower	130	2–9
Closed gentian	136	3–6
Wild ginger	94	3–7
Black-eyed Susan	146	3–7
New England aster	150	3–7
Sharp-lobed hepatica	82	3–7
Dutchman's breeches	88	3–7
Wintergreen	122	3–8
Bluets	142	3–8
Jack-in-the-pulpit	126	3–8
Eastern columbine	96	3–8
Mayapple	100	3–8
Bloodroot	84	3–8
Turtlehead	134	3–8
Foamflower	98	3–8
Groundnut	132	3–9
Common blue violet	90	3–9
Wild bergamot	148	3–9
Eastern trout lily	86	4–7
Wood lily	120	4–7
Wild leek	116	4–8
Partridgeberry	114	4–9
Pasture rose	144	4–9
Solomon's seal	106	5–7

actually require cold winter temperatures for continuation of their life cycles the following spring. It has long been known that some horticultural fruit crops can be grown only in regions with sufficiently cold winters. For example, peaches require 400 to 800 hours or more of exposure to temperatures below 45°F to break their dormancy, and apple trees require about twice that length of chilling time. Likewise, many northern native wildflowers, such as wild leek and trout lily, enter a dormancy in the summer that is broken by exposure to cold temperatures over the winter months. Without this chilling, they would simply remain dormant or would grow more slowly and not develop flowers properly the following spring.

Many seeds need chilling as well. These seeds require or are enhanced by weeks or even months of exposure to temperatures of 40°F or below to break their dormancy and germinate properly, as is discussed in the following section on propagation.

Some wildflowers are sensitive to summertime temperatures. For example, yellow clintonia and bunchberry require relatively cool temperatures during the summer growing season and cannot be successfully grown in regions with hot summers.

MOISTURE CONDITIONS

Just as wildflowers of the region have adapted to different temperature and light conditions, they have evolved to survive under different moisture conditions, ranging from dry meadows to boggy wetlands. While precipitation in northeastern North America is generally abundant, as you progress toward the Midwest or toward the Laurentian Plateau there is a general decrease in the total amount of precipitation. Rainfall is also more plentiful on the eastern, downwind shores of the Great Lakes than on their western shores, and at higher elevations in the Appalachian Range than in adjacent lowlands (see the map on page 58).

On a local scale, the gardener can choose wildflowers adapted to just about any soil-moisture condition that might be encountered, as is shown in the chart on page 41. Some species, such as larger blue flag, cardinal flower, and turtlehead, thrive in continually wet soils, yet these wildflowers can also be easily cultivated in well-drained soils of moderate moisture — conditions typical of most flower gardens. Other species such as black-eyed Susan and wild bergamot may need moisture while they are becoming established in the garden, but they grow better if the soils are not overly wet. Wildflower gardeners should be judicious with the hose; wild bergamot and other species suffer from leaf mildew if there is too much moisture, and seedlings of most wildflowers are especially sensitive to fungal attack when soils are cold and wet.

MOISTURE CONDITIONS

Species	Page	Wet	Damp	Moist	Moderately or Seasonally Dry	Arid
Turtlehead	134	■	■	■		
Larger blue flag	128	■	■	■		
Groundnut	132	■	■	■		
Cardinal flower	130	■	■	■		
Jack-in-the-pulpit	126	■	■	■		
Bunchberry	112		■			
Bluets	142		■	■		
False Solomon's seal	108		■			
Wintergreen	122	■	■	■	■	
Foamflower	98		■	■		
Closed gentian	136		■	■	■	
New England aster	150			■	■	
Yellow clintonia	110		■	■		
Wild leek	116		■	■		
Wild ginger	94		■	■		
Dutchman's breeches	88			■	■	
Eastern trout lily	86			■	■	
Mayapple	100			■	■	
Wild lily-of-the-valley	104		■	■	■	
Common blue violet	90		■	■	■	
Shinleaf	118			■	■	
Partridgeberry	114			■	■	
Eastern columbine	96			■	■	
Solomon's seal	106			■	■	
Canada anemone	140			■	■	
Sharp-lobed hepatica	82			■	■	
Bloodroot	84			■		
Purple trillium	92			■		
Pasture rose	144			■	■	■
Black-eyed Susan	146			■	■	■
Wild bergamot	148			■	■	■
Wood lily	120			■	■	■

The cultivation of wildflowers is easiest when you match a species' optimal requirements with conditions naturally occurring in the garden, so consider your soil before selecting the wildflowers. If your soil is sandy or gravelly, it will probably drain quickly, and you should plant species that do well in drier conditions. Clayey and peaty soils are often poorly drained, making them hospitable to species preferring plenty of soil moisture.

If your soil conditions do not quite suit a particular species, however, you may be able to add the proper soil amendments before planting. A little extra time and energy invested in site preparation will pay large dividends in the future, so do not rush your wildflowers into soils to which they are ill adapted. Although the root systems of most wildflowers are relatively shallow, soils should be prepared to a depth of several feet for maximum success. Avoid merely piling soil amendments on top of the soil where they will have marginal effect; instead, work them in thoroughly. Organic matter well mixed into the soil will aerate it and increase its water-holding capacity. Organic matter left as a mat on the surface of soils, however, may become excessively dry when rainfall is scant.

If your soil is too dry, the garden not too large, and your hose long enough, it is obviously easy to increase the soil moisture by watering. However, the addition of clay, compost, humus, or even coarse organic matter such as leaves may be a more effective way of assuring the long-term retention of moisture.

If you desire an even wetter habitat for growing wetland species such as larger blue flag and turtlehead in a more natural setting, you can create an artificial wetland. Remove the surface 18 inches of soil, pack the bottom of the depression with a layer of clay several inches thick (or use plastic sheeting), and then fill the depression with the original soil. The clay or plastic liner will slow the downward movement of water, thereby creating a wetland.

If the soil is too wet because of an overabundance of clay, drainage can be improved by the addition of sand or gravel mixed with copious amounts of compost or other organic matter. The organic matter creates additional air spaces in clayey soil and helps to prevent the clay from merely coating the grains of sand. Alternatively, gypsum (calcium sulfate) can be added to clayey soil to improve drainage. Since gypsum is an acidifying agent, it should be used where you will be planting wildflowers that thrive in acid soil, with a pH of 5.5 and below. Gypsum has the additional benefit of helping conserve nitrogen compounds in the soil. It is available at many garden or building-supply centers.

pH AND OTHER SOIL CONDITIONS

The specific soil requirements of 32 native plants are given on the individual species description pages. Some species thrive where nutrient levels are high and humus is abundant in the soil. Other species do best where there is little organic matter and the soil fertility is low.

One of the most important conditions in the cultivation of many wildflowers is the *pH* of the soil. The pH is simply a measure of the relative acidity or alkalinity on a scale from 0 (most acidic) to 14 (most alkaline), with a value of 7 indicating neutral conditions. The pH units are based on multiples of ten, so that a soil with a pH of 4.0 is 10 times more acidic than a soil with a pH of 5.0, and 100 times more acidic than a soil with a pH of 6.0. Likewise, a pH of 9 is 10 times more alkaline than a pH of 8, and so forth.

The pH of the soil is important because it influences the availability of nutrients essential for plant growth. Nutrients such as phosphorus, calcium, potassium, and magnesium are most available to plants when the soil pH is between 6.0 and 7.5. Under highly acidic (low pH) conditions these nutrients become insoluble and relatively unavailable for uptake by plants. However, iron, trace minerals, and some toxic elements such as aluminum become *more* available at low pH. A major concern about acid rain in northeastern North America is the possible increased absorption of these toxic elements by plants.

High soil pH may also decrease the availability of nutrients. If the soil is more alkaline than pH 8, phosphorus, iron, and many trace minerals become insoluble and unavailable for plant uptake.

The availability of nitrogen, one of plants' three key nutrients, is influenced by pH conditions as well. Much of the nitrogen that plants eventually use is bound within organic matter, and the conversion of this bound nitrogen to forms available to plants is accomplished by several species of bacteria living in the soil. When the soil's pH drops below 5.5, the activity of these bacteria is inhibited, and little nitrogen is available to the plants. At about the same pH levels there is a general decline in most forms of bacterial activity and an increase in the activity of soil fungi. This shift in soil biology may further influence which plants can survive and which cannot. In boreal forests, where fungi slowly decompose the thick mat of organic matter, the soils are acidic and nitrogen is relatively unavailable. In deciduous forests, in contrast, bacteria rapidly decompose the thin layer of organic matter and release larger amounts of nitrogen.

The usual pH range of soils is from about 4 to about 8. Typically in northeastern North America over millennia the precipitation has been sufficient to have removed large amounts of potassium, calcium, magnesium

SOIL pH CONDITIONS

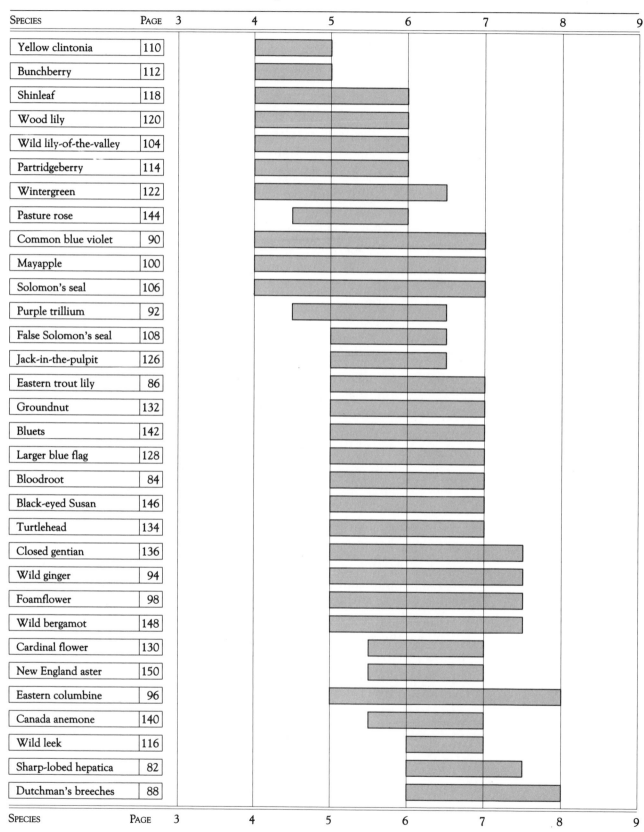

Species	Page	3	4	5	6	7	8	9
Yellow clintonia	110							
Bunchberry	112							
Shinleaf	118							
Wood lily	120							
Wild lily-of-the-valley	104							
Partridgeberry	114							
Wintergreen	122							
Pasture rose	144							
Common blue violet	90							
Mayapple	100							
Solomon's seal	106							
Purple trillium	92							
False Solomon's seal	108							
Jack-in-the-pulpit	126							
Eastern trout lily	86							
Groundnut	132							
Bluets	142							
Larger blue flag	128							
Bloodroot	84							
Black-eyed Susan	146							
Turtlehead	134							
Closed gentian	136							
Wild ginger	94							
Foamflower	98							
Wild bergamot	148							
Cardinal flower	130							
New England aster	150							
Eastern columbine	96							
Canada anemone	140							
Wild leek	116							
Sharp-lobed hepatica	82							
Dutchman's breeches	88							

Species	Page	3	4	5	6	7	8	9

and other alkaline nutrients from the soil. As a result the soils of the region tend to be acidic, with pH values below 7.

Local soil acidity/alkalinity conditions may vary because of differences in bedrock geology or vegetation. In general, alkaline soils develop in locations with limestone or marble bedrock, and acidic soils develop in areas with granite bedrock. Certain species of plants may also increase the acidity of the soil through the addition of organic matter with a low pH. Boreal forests are noted for their acidic soils. The dead foliage of pines, spruce, fir, oaks, and heath plants, deposited on top of the soil, further acidifies the soil as it decomposes. In cool, wet areas, the growth of sphagnum and other mosses may also create locally the acidic conditions so typical of regions with boreal forest.

Some species of wildflowers are relatively insensitive to soil acidity/alkalinity conditions, while others survive only over a narrow pH range. Most often pH preferences are more related to the balance of various nutrients required by particular species, or to changes in the biological activity of soil organisms, rather than to acidity or alkalinity itself. On page 44 is a guide to the pH preferences of those species of wildflowers that have specific soil pH requirements. It is often difficult to grow species close together if they have vastly different pH requirements. It is best to grow acid-loving species, such as yellow clintonia and bunchberry, in a section of the garden that is separate from species such as sharp-lobed hepatica and Dutchman's breeches, which prefer neutral or alkaline soils.

HOW TO MEASURE pH

Before deciding which wildflowers to cultivate and where to plant them, it is essential to know something about the pH of your soils. The measurement is actually quite simple, and there are a number of commercial products readily available from most garden suppliers. The pH is measured by taking samples of soil from the root zone at several different spots in the garden. Using a plastic spoon, place the soil in a small plastic or glass vial, and add an equal volume of water. Shake or stir the sample to mix the soil and water thoroughly, and allow the soil to settle. The pH of the liquid in the top of the vial can then be determined by any one of several means.

The least expensive way to measure pH is with "indicator paper," which can be purchased in short strips or long rolls. This is like litmus paper, but rather than merely showing you whether a solution is acid or alkaline, it produces a range of colors to indicate the pH value. Just stick the strip of paper into the liquid extracted from the soil and compare the color of the dampened paper to the reference chart provided.

A slightly more accurate method, although usually more expensive, is the use of indicator solutions, which are frequently sold in pH kits. A small amount of the liquid extracted from the soil-and-water mix is placed in a ceramic dish, and a few drops of indicator solution are added. As with the indicator papers, the color produced is compared to a pH reference chart.

You can also measure pH with a meter. One type of pH meter operates without batteries and measures pH based on the conductivity of the moistened soil. This type of pH meter is neither more accurate nor faster than the color-indicator methods that use solutions or paper. All provide a rough, but useful, estimate of soil pH.

The most accurate measurements of soil pH use electronic meters with one or several electrodes. These instruments are quite expensive and are used by soil-testing laboratories for determining soil pH. Most state Agricultural Experiment Stations, usually located at land-grant universities, will test soil samples for a nominal charge. To arrange for such pH testing, contact your state's land-grant university or your county's Agricultural Extension Service Agent.

CHANGING THE pH OF SOILS

You may find that the pH of your soil does not suit a particular species, even though all other environmental conditions seem perfect. The acidity or alkalinity of soils can be altered to a limited extent through the addition of various soil amendments. It may take several years to change a soil's pH permanently, however, so be patient.

Pine, spruce, and fir needles can be added to garden soils to lower the pH. If none of these is locally available, peat moss also works well in acidifying soils. Powdered gypsum (calcium sulfate) or sulfur powder can be used to lower soil pH, but these should be used with caution, because they act more rapidly than the organic materials.

Ground limestone is the amendment of choice to raise the pH of the soil. Medium-ground limestone may give better long-term results than very coarse limestone (which may be slow to neutralize soil acids) or very fine limestone (which may be lost too quickly from the soil). Wood ashes can also be used, but keep in mind that they are more concentrated than limestone and may even "burn" wildflowers if too much is applied.

After measuring the pH, add the soil amendment, taking care to mix thoroughly and incorporate it uniformly in the top 6 to 12 inches of soil. Spread the amendment thinly on the ground, and then work it into the soil with a spading fork or shovel. Then add another layer, mixing it into the soil. If you do not mix the amendment evenly you may find pockets of soil with enormously different pH values. Moisten the soil, and then allow it to rest for a day or so before again measuring the pH at several spots. Repeat the process until you have the desired pH conditions.

A very rough rule of thumb is that for a 100-square-foot area of most soils it takes about 2 to 6 pounds of limestone to raise the pH one unit, and 2½ to 7 pounds of gypsum or ½ to 2 pounds of sulfur to lower the pH one unit. Clay soils require more of an amendment to change the pH; sandy soils, less.

It is strongly recommended that organic matter acidifiers be used before resorting to gypsum or sulfur. It is better to change the pH of the soil slowly than to overdo it one way and then the other.

After the appropriate pH is attained, check it periodically. Since the natural processes at work in your garden will be altering the pH through rainfall, bacterial activity, the uptake of nutrients by plants, and climatic factors, you may occasionally have to make further additions of soil amendments. With wildflowers in place, be especially careful to add the amendments in small amounts directly on the surface of the soil, and work them in with minimal disturbance of the plants' roots.

A WORD ABOUT WEEDS AND PESTS

Wildflowers growing in their natural habitats are obviously well adapted for survival under the prevailing local conditions. Gardening, however, involves disturbing the soil and modifying the moisture and light conditions. These changes often invite unwelcome and unwanted plants — weeds. In contrast to many of the desirable native wildflowers, weeds tend to grow quickly, spread aggressively, and set loose copious quantities of highly mobile seeds. Often weeds will accomplish these feats so quickly that they produce many generations in the time it takes to produce a single generation of desired wildflowers. The seeds of weeds tend to be long-lived and may remain dormant, buried in the soil, for many years just waiting for the proper conditions to germinate. Studies have shown that the seeds of some weeds can remain dormant yet capable of germinating for more than forty years. Typically, there are hundreds of weed seeds beneath each square yard of soil surface. Gardening activity frequently brings the weed seeds to the surface and provides ideal conditions for them to thrive.

Weeds are thus inevitable, but do not despair, and *do not resort to the use of herbicides*! Many wildflowers are particularly sensitive to the effects of herbicides, so weeding by hand is the only real choice. You will find that a modest investment of time spent weeding while your wildflowers are first becoming established will pay large dividends. Even natural gardens may need some weeding during the first several years. Once the plants are well established and holding their ground, weeds will have a more difficult time invading, and weeding will be less necessary.

You will find from time to time that various insects will visit your wildflowers, and while some of these may be there for an attractive meal, they usually have an abundance of natural predators which will keep their populations in check so that minimal damage occurs. Wildflowers like turtlehead may look a bit tattered by the end of the season, because the larvae of the Baltimore butterfly and others may have chewed holes in the leaves. The plants have usually suffered little, and *the use of pesticides is unwarranted,* especially if you are trying to attract butterflies or even hummingbirds to the garden. The use of pesticides is also to be avoided because many wildflowers are pollinated by insects, and without the pollinators, there is no fruit and seed production.

When establishing or maintaining a wildflower garden, slugs, household pets and, in rural areas, deer may be more of a problem than insects are. If dogs, cats, or deer become a nuisance, fencing may be the only reasonable solution. Slugs relish certain species of wildflowers, especially those in the lily family. They feed at night when the humidity is high, and can do considerable damage by chewing and stripping leaves. Slugs can be easily and effectively controlled by setting out dishes filled with stale beer. The shallow tubs in which whipped cream cheese or margarine are packaged make ideal slug traps. Fill the tubs three-quarters full with beer and set them about the garden. The slugs much prefer beer to your wildflowers, and once in the brew they drown. Every several days, and after heavy rains, you may have to dispose of the contents and replenish the beer.

Wildflower Propagation

One of the pleasures of growing wildflowers is the opportunity to propagate them and thereby increase their numbers in your garden. As already pointed out, the digging of wildflowers from their native environments is not only unethical, but also frequently illegal. The best way to obtain wildflowers for your garden is to purchase seeds, plants or planting stock from reputable suppliers who sell nursery-propagated material (see Appendix A). Once these wildflowers are established, they can serve as stock for further propagation.

SEEDS   Seeds are by far the cheapest way to propagate large numbers of wildflowers, even though some perennials grown from seeds may take a long time before they are mature enough to flower. Usually seeds are collected when the fruits are mature. Many species have seed dispersal mechanisms which may make it difficult to find plants with the fruits present when you want to harvest them. One way to capture the seeds before they are released from the plant is to cut a foot-long section of a discarded nylon stocking and make a sleeve, tying off one end with a string or twisted wire closure. Slip the sleeve over the developing fruit after the flower petals have withered, but before the fruit is fully ripe. Firmly but gently tie the open end closed so that the seeds can't fall to the ground, being careful not to crush or break the stems in the process. When the fruits are fully ripe, snip the stem just below the nylon bag, put it in a labeled paper sack and bring it indoors for further processing.

Some seeds should be planted fresh and not allowed to dry out, or germination will be delayed. Other seeds will not germinate immediately and have to undergo a process of "after-ripening" before they are ready to sprout. Seeds of fleshy fruits should generally be separated from the pulp prior to storage or planting. If seeds are not the kind that need to be planted immediately and you desire to store them for a while, allow them to air-dry for several weeks and then separate the seeds from the dried remains of the fruit. Gently crushing the dried fruits on a large sheet of white paper will usually release the seeds, which should then be separated from the chaff. The chaff can be removed either by blowing gently across the paper or, if seeds are small enough, by sifting through a strainer. Store the cleaned seeds in small manila coin envelopes or 35mm film canisters.

The seeds of some species will remain dormant unless they undergo certain specific treatments — chilling temperatures, scratching of their seed coats, subjection to light or darkness, or a combination of these. The treatments required to germinate specific seeds are detailed on the descriptive pages following this chapter. These treatments fall into four categories: 1) seed chilling, or *stratification*, 2) seed-coat scratching, or *scarification*, 3) hot-water treatment, 4) light or dark treatment.

Stratification. Many plants that live in northeastern North America have evolved to have seeds that are dormant the first fall after they have been produced. This adaptation prevents tender seedlings from coming up and facing freezing temperatures when they would be only a month or so old. Breaking dormancy requires the seeds to be subjected to a period of cold temperatures (a process called stratification), followed by a period of warm temperatures. These conditions are met with the natural progression of seasons. Usually a temperature of only 40°F is sufficient to break dormancy or enhance germination. The length of stratification varies widely among different species. Germination of some seeds is enhanced if they are stratified under moist conditions in addition to the cold temperatures.

The easiest way to stratify seeds in the Northeast is to plant the seeds outdoors in the late fall. Seeds can be planted directly in the garden where desired or in flats that are left outdoors. If you do not desire to plant the seeds in the fall, it is necessary to place the container or envelope of seeds under refrigeration for the appropriate period of time. If moist stratification is required, the seeds can be placed in damp sphagnum moss or rolled up in lightly dampened paper towels, and placed in an air-tight container or a zip-closure plastic bag for the duration of the stratification.

Scarification. In order for seeds to germinate they have to take up water and oxygen from the outside environment. These substances diffuse through the outer covering of the seed called the "seed coat." Some native species, especially those in the bean family, have seed coats so tough that water and oxygen cannot enter. These seeds remain dormant until the seed coat is scratched, or "scarified." This occurs naturally when seeds are moved around in the soil, especially following rainstorms, nibbled at by ants, or passed through an animal's digestive system. In the home garden best results are obtained if the seeds are scarified by the gardener before planting.

The easiest way to scarify medium-size seeds is to rub the seeds between two sheets of medium-grit sandpaper. You don't want to rub them so hard that you pulverize the seeds, just hard enough to scratch up the surface so that moisture can penetrate to the seed inside. Large seeds can be scarified by nicking the seed coat with a sharp pocket knife.

Hot Water Treatments. Some seeds germinate better after being submerged in hot water prior to planting. Place the seeds in a jar and fill it halfway with tap water that is hot to the touch, but not scalding. Allow the seeds to remain in the water as it cools overnight. The seeds can then be planted the next day.

Light or Dark Treatments. A few species of wildflowers have seeds that are either stimulated or inhibited by light. If the seeds are stimulated by light they should be planted shallowly, so sunlight penetrating through the surface of the soil can have its desired effect. If the seeds are inhibited by light, they should be planted at sufficient depth to prevent light from slowing germination.

PLANTING TECHNIQUES

One of the most efficient ways to propagate wildflowers from seed is to use flats or nursery beds for rearing seedlings for the first year or until they become established. The advantage of flats is that you can transplant seedlings to holding beds and maintain an optimum density of plants more easily than if you plant the seed directly in the desired location. Also, some species have seed that is slow to germinate, and it may take several years for all the viable seeds that were planted to produce seedlings. The soil can be kept in the flats until the seeds have had sufficient time to germinate completely.

If you have only a few seeds, small pots can be used for raising seedlings. If the species is one that thrives in slightly acidic conditions, peat pots are a real convenience. When the seedlings are sturdy they can be transplanted to a nursery bed, where they can grow without competition from other plants, or to permanent locations. Be careful not to disturb the roots or to break off the shoots when removing the seedlings and soil from pots. If you are using peat pots, simply tear off the bottom of the pot and plant the container with its contents so that the surface level of the soil is the same as that inside the pot. (Unlike many gardeners, I tear off the bottom of the peat pot, because I have found the plant makes better contact with the soil that way.)

Soil Mixes and Potting. The soil in which a seed germinates and the seedling starts out is every bit as important as that in which the adult plant grows. A potting soil should have both good drainage and good water-holding capacity. While commercially formulated starting mixes are available from home and garden centers, you can make an inexpensive but effective mix by adding one part milled sphagnum to one part washed builder's sand. The resulting mix is weed-free and sterile. One convenient way to start seeds is to use 4½-by-6¼-inch plastic flats that are 2½ inches deep. Fill the flat to the top with the potting mix and then tamp down the surface with the bottom of another flat, so that the soil surface is just below the rim. Set the seeds on the soil surface, and then cover them with the appropriate depth of additional soil. Moisten the soil with a fine sprinkle, and cover the top of the flat with plastic wrap to help conserve soil moisture. Leave the plastic on the flats until the seeds germinate and the tops of the seedlings are just pushing against the film.

Plugs and Sods. An effective way to grow live plants for transplanting to meadows is to produce wildflower plugs and sods. Plugs are individual live plants that have been grown in small pots or special trays. They can be efficiently transplanted into meadows or gardens because of their compact, dense mass of roots. They are most easily produced in special trays available through greenhouse supply companies and larger garden centers. These trays have cavities up to 2 inches in diameter and 2 inches deep with gently tapering sides so that the plugs can be easily removed.

To produce wildflower plugs, use the larger trays with 2-inch openings, and fill the cavities with potting mix as you would other pots or flats. Allow the seedlings to develop until the roots fully bind the soil in the cavities, a process that may take most of a growing season for some species. Water the plugs by periodically setting the entire tray in a shallow pan and allowing the water to be drawn up from the bottom. The wildflowers can be transplanted into the garden or meadow when a gentle tug at the base of the plant's stem pulls the entire plug, soil and all, out of the cavity.

Wildflower sods are like plugs, only larger. Sods can be made with a number of different wildflowers and grasses grown densely together in flats. You then transplant the entire contents of the flat into a meadow or garden. One way to make sods easier to handle is to line the flat with cheesecloth before adding the potting soil. The seeds are then planted in the soil, and as the seedlings mature their roots will penetrate the cloth liner. When it is time to transplant the sod, you can lift it out of the flat by pulling on the cheesecloth. Once in the ground, the roots of the sod plants will quickly grow through the cheesecloth and after about a year the cloth will simply decompose.

A Special Note on Legumes. Members of the bean family often require the presence of special microorganisms, known as *rhizobia*, in the soil to ensure their survival. These microbes lead a symbiotic existence with leguminous plants, inhabiting nodules formed on the root systems and producing nitrogen compounds that the plants eventually use. Not all soils have abundant populations of these necessary microbes. If you have difficulty in propagating leguminous wildflowers like groundnut, you may need to purchase a commercially produced "inoculant" and add it to the soil when you plant the seeds. Different species require different strains of microbial inoculants, so the addition of "pea" or "soybean" inoculants would not be effective for wildflowers. Make sure you get the right strain of rhizobia for the species you plan to cultivate.

Rhizobia inoculants can be ordered directly from the Nitragin Company, Inc., 3101 W. Custer Avenue, Milwaukee, WI 53209, or Kalo, Inc., P.O. Box 12567, Columbus, OH 43212. You will need to indicate the scientific name of the species to be inoculated and the amount of seed you intend to treat. It may take two to four weeks for these companies to prepare special rhizobia if they are not in stock.

ROOTSTOCK DIVISIONS

One of the quickest ways to propagate perennials is by rootstock division. Rootstocks are best dug up and divided while the plant is dormant, usually in the early spring or fall. In general, perennials that flower in the spring can be most successfully divided in the fall, and those that flower in the fall are best divided in the early spring. For those species like trout lily whose shoots wither and enter dormancy early in the growing season, the location of the plants should be marked with a stake so that the rootstocks can be found later in the fall for propagation. In northeastern North America, the advantage to spring division of summer-flowering perennials is that the plants will then have a chance to establish a more vigorous root system before the next winter. This is especially important in soils prone to frost heaving.

Regardless of the type of rootstock (see illustrations on pages 29–30) the principal technique is quite similar (see illustration on page 54). With a sharp knife (a pocket knife will do splendidly), cut the rootstock so that the divided pieces have at least one vegetative bud or "eye" attached. Since the size of the resulting plant will be determined to a large extent by the size of the divided piece, don't make the divisions too small (unless you want lots of tiny plants).

Runners and stolons are easily divided by cutting the horizontal stem between adjacent rooted plants, which then can be dug up and transplanted when dormant. The division of tubers is also easily accomplished. Cut tubers into pieces, each with a bud or two, and plant them with the buds pointing up (the way you would plant pieces of potato). New shoots and roots will be produced as the plant draws upon the energy reserves of the tuber flesh. Similarly rhizomes can be divided into pieces, each with buds

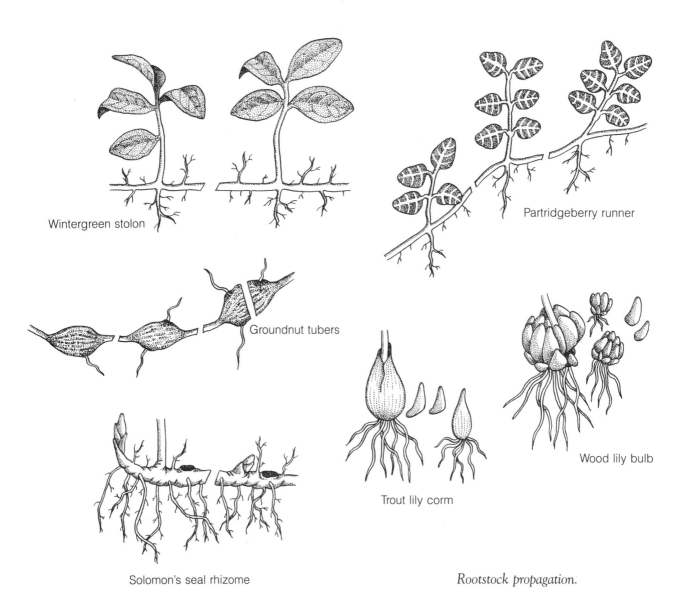

Wintergreen stolon

Partridgeberry runner

Groundnut tubers

Trout lily corm

Wood lily bulb

Solomon's seal rhizome

Rootstock propagation.

and associated roots. Replant the segments at the appropriate depth and spacing.

Corms and bulbs of perennial wildflowers can be divided in a manner similar to other garden perennials. The small offsets that develop on the sides of mature corms and bulbs can be removed with a knife during the dormant season and planted at the appropriate depth. These cormlets and bulblets will usually take several years to develop into plants capable of flowering. If not cut off the parent rootstock, these offsets eventually mature into large, densely crowded plants that may benefit from being divided and given wider spacing.

The fleshy scales of bulbs such as wood lily can be divided and planted like seeds in flats to produce large quantities of "seedlings." Break off the individual scales from dormant bulbs, and in a flat containing potting soil mixture, plant them just below the soil surface, with the tips of the scales pointing upward. Provide light shade and keep the soil moist, but not overly wet, until the resulting small plants are sturdy enough to transplant into a nursery bed or permanent location.

After replanting the rootstock divisions be especially careful not to overwater the soil. The soil should be prevented from thoroughly drying out, but wet soils may invite problems. Rootstocks have carbohydrate-rich stores of energy that the plant draws upon during its period of most rapid growth. If the soil is too wet, bacterial and fungal rots may attack the newly divided rootstock pieces and even kill the plants. For this reason, it is a good idea to plant rootstock divisions in a nursery or holding bed that has well drained soil, and to transplant the stock when dormant the following year.

STEM CUTTINGS

Another successful way to propagate some perennials, like turtlehead, is to make cuttings of stems. These cuttings should be made when the shoots are growing vigorously, usually in June and July, and are most successful if the shoot lacks flower buds. The best time to make a cutting is when the plant has been well watered, by rain or artificial irrigation, especially in the early morning before the sun evaporates the water from the leaf surfaces.

Before making the cuttings prepare a flat with a mixture of coarse compost or sphagnum moss and builder's sand (don't use beach sand from the ocean, as the salt might kill the cuttings). Moisten the soil, poke holes 2 to 3 inches deep and 5 inches apart with your little finger, and take the flat to the garden. Select succulent stems that snap crisply when doubled over. Cut 6-inch pieces of rapidly growing shoots by making a

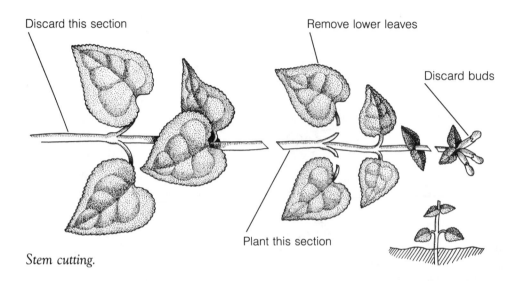

Labels on figure: Discard this section | Remove lower leaves | Discard buds | Plant this section

Stem cutting.

diagonal slice through the stem with a razor blade. To encourage root formation, remove flower buds and leaves from the bottom 6 inches of the stem. Gently place the cutting into the hole and firmly press the soil around the base to assure good contact with the cutting. Then moisten the soil again.

Since the cuttings initially have no root systems, it is difficult for them to take up water. It is essential to keep the flats in the *shade* with the soil *moist* but not wet. Soils that are too wet will prevent oxygen from getting to the developing roots and also encourage rotting diseases. Protect the cuttings from the effects of drying winds, and mist the plants if the humidity is low. To attain ideal humidity control, put the entire flat in a large, *clear* polyethylene bag (available from janitorial supply companies), and tie off the opening. Others have suggested using a clear plastic garment bag to create a mini-greenhouse for starting cuttings. Allow the cuttings to remain in the flat until they go into dormancy at the end of the growing season, and then transplant them to holding beds or permanent locations.

Whether by collecting your own seeds or by dividing or cutting live plants, wildflower propagation can give you satisfactions beyond the considerable cost savings. Many perennials should be divided every several years, and they respond to this treatment by flowering more abundantly and adding even greater beauty to the garden. The surplus divisions can be used to enlarge your plantings, given to other wildflower enthusiasts, or used as material for forcing or container gardens. Perhaps one of the most important benefits of propagating plants yourself is the increased familiarity with wildflowers you gain in the process.

VEGETATION OF NORTHEASTERN NORTH AMERICA

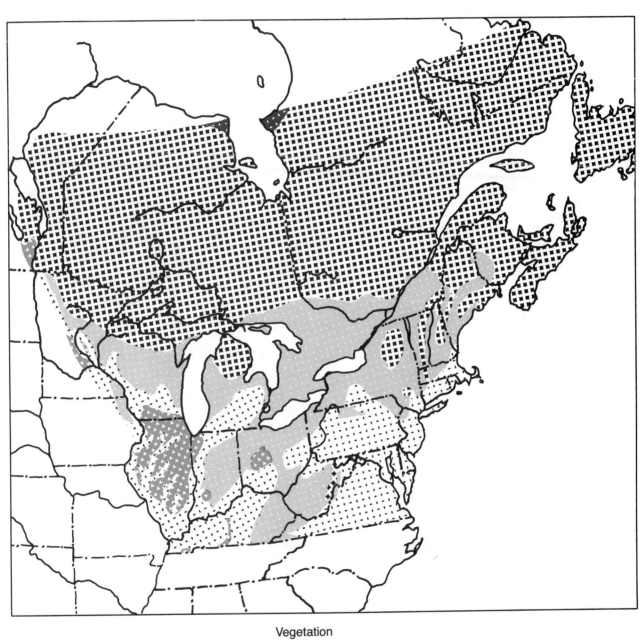

Vegetation

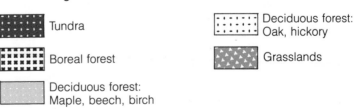

Tundra

Boreal forest

Deciduous forest:
Maple, beech, birch

Deciduous forest:
Oak, hickory

Grasslands

ANNUAL PRECIPITATION OF NORTHEASTERN NORTH AMERICA

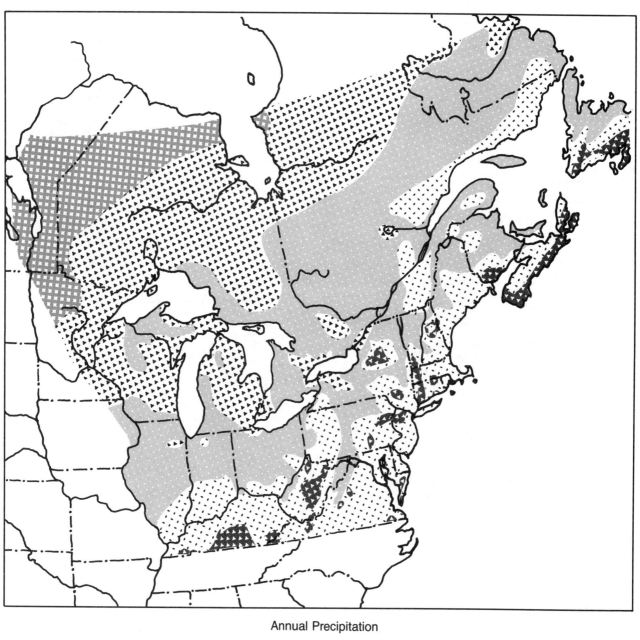

Annual Precipitation

16–24"	40–48"
24–32"	48–56"
32–40"	56–64"

LENGTH OF FROST-FREE PERIOD IN NORTHEASTERN NORTH AMERICA

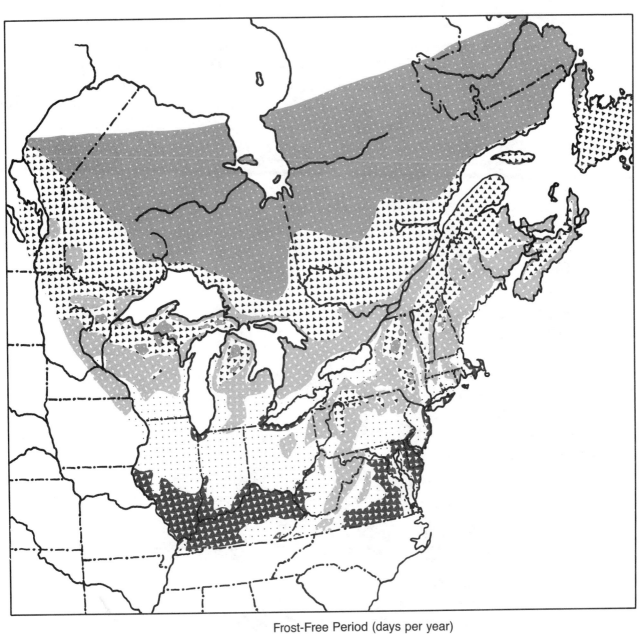

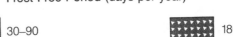

Frost-Free Period (days per year)

30–90		180–210	
90–120		210–240	
120–150		240–270	
150–180			

HARDINESS ZONES OF NORTHEASTERN NORTH AMERICA

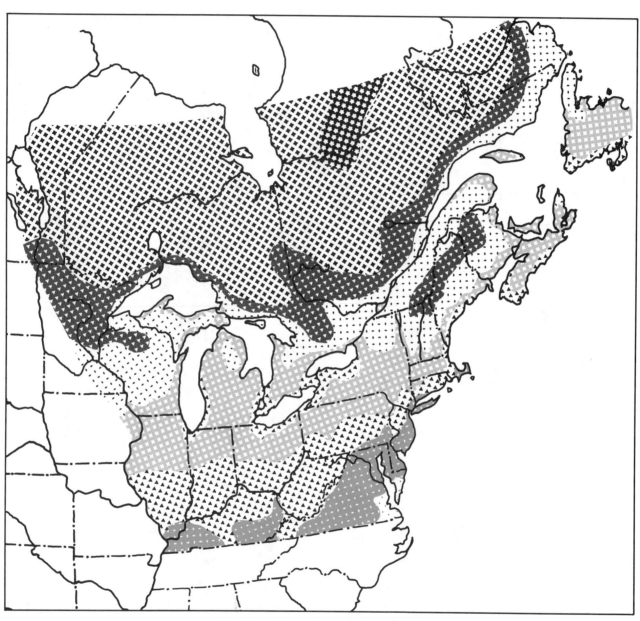

Hardiness Zones/Average Annual Minimum Temperature

Zone 1 Below −50° F

Zone 2 −50°– −40° F

Zone 3 −40°– −30° F

Zone 4 −30°– −20° F

Zone 5 −20°– −10° F

Zone 6 −10°–0° F

Zone 7 0°–10° F

Zone 8 10°–20° F

PART II

A Gallery of
Northeastern Wildflowers

The flowers of the **sharp-lobed hepatica** range in color from white to pink to pale blue. The number of petals and other flower parts is highly variable as well. (See page 82.)

The **bloodroot** blooms before the pie-crust-shaped leaves have fully unfurled. The delicate white flowers are rapidly shed, especially once the flowers are picked. Attached to the seed of bloodroot and some other plants is an oily tissue called an elaiosome (lower right). (See page 84.)

The brown and green mottled leaves give the **eastern trout lily** its common name. The rich brown anthers contrast with the chrome yellow sepals and petals. (See page 86.)

Like miniature pantaloons hung out to dry, the flowers of **Dutchman's breeches** are suspended from its flowering stalk. Both the flowers and the lacy, fernlike foliage die back by early summer. (See page 88.)

Dark lines on the lower petal of the **common blue violet** guide insects toward the sweet nectar inside. These showy flowers are produced in the spring, while small flowers lacking petals are produced later in the summer. (See page 90.)

The nodding, dark red flowers of the **purple trillium** may have the faint odor of rotting meat, a scent that attracts the flies that pollinate this species. (See page 92.)

The broad, heart-shaped leaves of **wild ginger** make it an excellent ground cover. Its ground-level, petalless brown flowers are crawled into and pollinated by beetles. (See page 94.)

The nectar in the 5 spurred lobes of the **eastern columbine** is extracted by hummingbirds. This is an excellent plant for rock gardens, especially if the soils are slightly alkaline. (See page 96.)

Foamflower, a member of the saxifrage family, has compact spikes of white flowers emerging from mounds of heart-shaped foliage. (See page 98.)

In the spring (upper right), **mayapple** leaves emerge like unfurling parasols. The broad leaves rapidly enlarge, forming a fine ground cover (above) and often hiding the creamy white flowers (lower right) from view. The edible fruits, looking like small lemons, mature during the summer (bottom). (See page 100.)

Wild lily-of-the-valley is an adaptable species that makes an ideal ground cover. The tiny flowers have four petals and mature into speckled or red berries over the summer (right). (See page 104.)

Solomon's seal has pairs of bell-shaped flowers dangling below the arching stem. (See page 106.)

The flowers of **false Solomon's seal** are clustered at the tip of the stem. The berries turn first bronze and then red as they ripen during the summer. (See page 108.)

Yellow clintonia, a plant of cool, acid woodlands, has bright yellow or sometimes greenish flowers producing the attractive fruits that give this wildflower its other common name of blue-bead lily. (See page 110.)

Bunchberry makes an attractive ground cover for cool, moist, acid situations. The white-bracted clusters of flowers produce bright red berries in late summer and early fall. (See page 112.)

Partridgeberry forms extensive mats of low, trailing foliage. Pairs of trumpet-shaped white flowers are joined at their bases and produce a single bright red berry. (See page 114.)

In the early spring the succulent leaves of the **wild leek** blanket the ground. The leaves wither before the flower stalk emerges in the summer. (See page 116.)

The waxy white flowers of the **shinleaf** are borne on a shoot arising from the center of a rosette of elliptical leaves. Although the flowers last only a few weeks, the leaves remain green over the winter. (See page 118.)

Wood lily is one of the few lilies whose flowers point upward. The flowers fade to lighter colors after the pollen has been shed, as can be seen above left. (See page 120.)

The perennially green foliage of **wintergreen** makes it an attractive ground cover by itself or where planted with bunchberry, as seen here. The white urn-shaped flowers produce red berries with a wintergreen flavor. (See page 122.)

The unusual flower of **Jack-in-the-pulpit** can be hard to see beneath the leaves. In late summer and fall the stems are adorned only with clusters of bright red-orange berries. (See page 126.)

The purple lines on **larger blue flag** flowers direct bees to the nectar inside and ensure pollination. Butterflies often extract the nectar without pollinating the flower. (See page 128.)

Cardinal flower adds a bright splash to gardens in summer and early fall. The unusual flowers are pollinated by hummingbirds, whose foreheads are dusted with pollen by the white stamens. Cardinal flowers can be planted with **larger blue flag** in a wetland garden for a succession of bloom. (See page 130.)

A wetland garden can make a natural transition between a pond and a lawn or other garden. (See pages 18–19.)

The **groundnut** has clusters of sweet-smelling, pea-like, tan and magenta flowers, and edible tubers. (See page 132.)

Although **turtlehead** is found naturally in wetlands, it can easily be grown in most gardens. Bumblebees are its main pollinator. (See page 134.)

The flowers of the **closed gentian** appear to lack an opening, but even large bumblebees can force their way into the flower through a small hole at the top. (See page 136.)

The **Canada anemone,** a white-flowered member of the buttercup family, can be grown as a bedding plant, in meadows, or even as a ground cover. (See page 140.)

Bluets form clumps of pastel lavender-blue in moist meadows, but also make a fine addition to a rock garden. Their cross-shaped flowers have contrasting yellow centers which attract the attention of insect pollinators. (See page 142.)

The **pasture rose** adds a simple elegance to early summer gardens and meadows. Its bright red "hips" (fruits) are a rich source of vitamin C. (See page 144.)

Black-eyed Susans are synonymous with summer. The photo above shows a roadside meadow planted by the Massachusetts Department of Public Works. The tiny brown disc flowers have bright yellow anthers. (See page 146.)

The lavender flowers of **wild bergamot** attract butterflies and hummingbirds to meadows and sunny gardens in midsummer. The lance-shaped leaves contain a pungent oil and can be used to make herbal tea. (See page 148.)

New England asters fill autumn meadows with their purple and gold flowers. A variety of insects pollinate this progenitor of hardy asters for the horticultural trade. (See page 150.)

PART III

Species of Wildflowers

The following pages give detailed information about 32 species of wildflowers. The plants are grouped by their natural habitat and appear in the order of their flowering. Wildflowers within the groups can grow together as companions, but many of the species can grow in more than one habitat. Each habitat group is introduced by general comments, a wildflower garden plan, and suggestions of additional species not in this edition of *The Wildflower Gardener's Guide* that make appropriate companions. Further information on these companions can be found in *A Garden of Wildflowers* or other books listed in Appendix D.

Each of the 32 wildflowers included in this book is listed by its most frequently used common name as well as by its Latin scientific name. Other common English and French Canadian names are also given. The individual wildflower description starts with general information about the species and its ecology. A discussion of culture and growth requirements follows, with specific directions for the plant's propagation. A few companions that grow under similar conditions are listed.

Each species is illustrated. A scale shows the approximate size of the plant, and a quick reference box shows plant family, flower color, flowering and fruiting time, growth cycle (annual, biennial, or perennial), habitats where the species naturally occurs, and hardiness zones where the species can be grown. The page numbers of color photographs of the species in Part II are also given. The map shows the wildflower's native distribution, but most species can be grown over a much wider area.

WOODLAND SPECIES
Early Spring

The wildflowers in this section start flowering before the trees have fully expanded their leaves. The order of the species in this section follows their flowering sequence.

Early spring woodland gardens often don't look much like ornamental gardens, since the flowers usually emerge through a layer of last winter's leaf mulch. In addition to insulating the plants' roots from spring frosts, the old leaves provide a neutral backdrop for the display of their bright flowers.

Although these species grow in habitats that are deeply shaded during the summer, when they are growing rapidly during the spring they need direct sun. A shady garden border is a good place to plant many of these species. The north edges of clearings will generally have more sun than will the shaded south edges. North sides of buildings are generally not as well suited because they may not get enough sun during the spring flowering period.

It is easier to establish an early woodland garden under large, mature trees than among dense undergrowth and young trees which might provide too much competition. Be careful when planting near evergreen trees: select wildflowers that tolerate acidic soils, and plant them in gaps where sunlight can reach them.

COMPANIONS Many of these wildflowers can be grown together in a garden, but there are other native species described in *A Garden of Wildflowers* and other books listed in Appendix D that you might want to consider. **Spring beauty** (*Claytonia virginica*) is a petite wildflower with delicate pink and white flowers that appear in the very early spring. It likes humusy soils and disappears when the tree leaves overhead are fully expanded. **Yellow fawn lily** (*Erythronium grandiflorum*), a western relative of the eastern trout lily with large, showy flowers, can easily be grown in northeastern gardens as long as the soils are moist. **Virginia bluebells** (*Mertensia virginica*) is an

Woodland garden, early spring.

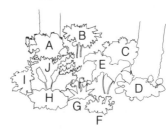

A. Eastern columbine
B. Mayapple
C. Bloodroot
D. Common blue violet
E. Purple trillium
F. Sharp-lobed hepatica
G. Eastern trout lily
H. Foam flower
I. Wild ginger
J. Dutchman's breeches

adaptable wildflower, hardy to zone 3. Its light blue, tubular flowers fade to pink several weeks before its leaves die back to the ground in late spring or early summer. Virginia bluebells can be grown wherever the soils are moderately moist to wet. **White trillium** (*Trillium grandiflorum*) is larger than the purple trillium and has white flowers that turn pink as they wither. It is one of the handsomest and easiest trilliums to grow in gardens. The **early yellow violet** (*Viola rotundifolia*) flowers in the very early spring about the same time that the sharp-lobed hepatica is in bloom. Its large, round, velvety leaves form a low rosette. **Round-lobed hepatica** (*Hepatica americana*) is a close relative of the sharp-lobed hepatica. If your soils are too acidic for the sharp-lobed hepatica, which prefers pH 6–8, try the round-lobed hepatica — it prefers soils with pH 4–6.

Low-growing ferns can add a natural touch to early spring woodland gardens. **Christmas fern** (*Polystichum acrostichoides*) is easily grown in woodland gardens. It remains green throughout the winter and its fiddleheads arise in the early spring. **Maidenhair fern** (*Adiantum pedatum*) with its lacy fronds and **common polypod** (*Polypodum vulgare*), which forms low mats, are also good choices.

SHARP-LOBED HEPATICA   *Hepatica acutiloba*

Sharp-lobed liverwort, sharp-lobed liverleaf, *Trinitaire*

The hepaticas are about the earliest of the spring wildflowers in the woodlands of northeastern North America. The common names of this hardy perennial refer to the 3-lobed, somewhat leathery leaves, which look to some like a piece of liver. Ancient herbalists took the shape of the leaf to be a sign that hepaticas could cure liver diseases. The Cherokee people, on the other hand, used the plant to banish nightmares of snakes. About 2 inches long and 4 inches broad, the leaves remain a dark brownish green over the winter, and then wither as new leaves emerge in the spring. The 3–4-inch leaf stalks and flower stalks are both covered with silky, downward-pointing hairs. The flowers have 3 small, unlobed leaves at their bases, and 5 to 18 petal-like sepals, ranging in color from light blue to pink to white. Bees and flies visit the numerous pistils and stamens in the centers of the flowers. The flowers open with the morning sun but close and droop in the evening, in cloudy weather, and on cold days. The ⅛-inch-long, green-brown, seedlike fruits of hepatica are covered with hairs which allow them to float away on the wind.

CULTURE

Hepaticas are found growing naturally in woods with calcium-rich soils. In the garden they should be provided with ample amounts of compost and planted in lightly shaded areas where the soil remains moist, but not wet, throughout the summer. They are ideal plants for shady rock gardens. Sharp-lobed hepaticas prefer slightly acidic to slightly alkaline soils, so adjust the soil pH to between 6 and 7.5 by adding ground limestone if necessary. The plants also benefit from a light overwinter mulch of *calcium-rich* leaves, such as sugar maple, ash, birch, or basswood. Do not plant them in the same soil with the round-lobed hepatica, which requires acidic soils.

PROPAGATION

Hepaticas can be propagated either from root divisions or from seed. Divide rootstocks in the fall, being careful not to break the attached leaves, which contain nutrient and energy reserves for next spring's flowers. Plant the divisions with the buds at the soil surface and the leaves above the soil. Mulch lightly for the winter. Seeds may be sown as soon as ripe in the spring or in the fall and should be kept moist. They require cold treatment for optimal germination, so give collected seeds moist stratification if they are stored over the winter. Sow seeds ¼ inch deep in well-composted loam of the appropriate pH, and mulch lightly to conserve moisture. If flats are used, place them in shady locations and keep them out over the winter. Some germination may occur by fall in spring-sown seeds, but most seeds require overwintering. Remove some of the mulch from the seedbed in the spring. Plants from seed generally blossom the second year.

COMPANIONS

Bloodroot, Jack-in-the-pulpit, eastern columbine, wild ginger, eastern trout lily, Dutchman's breeches.

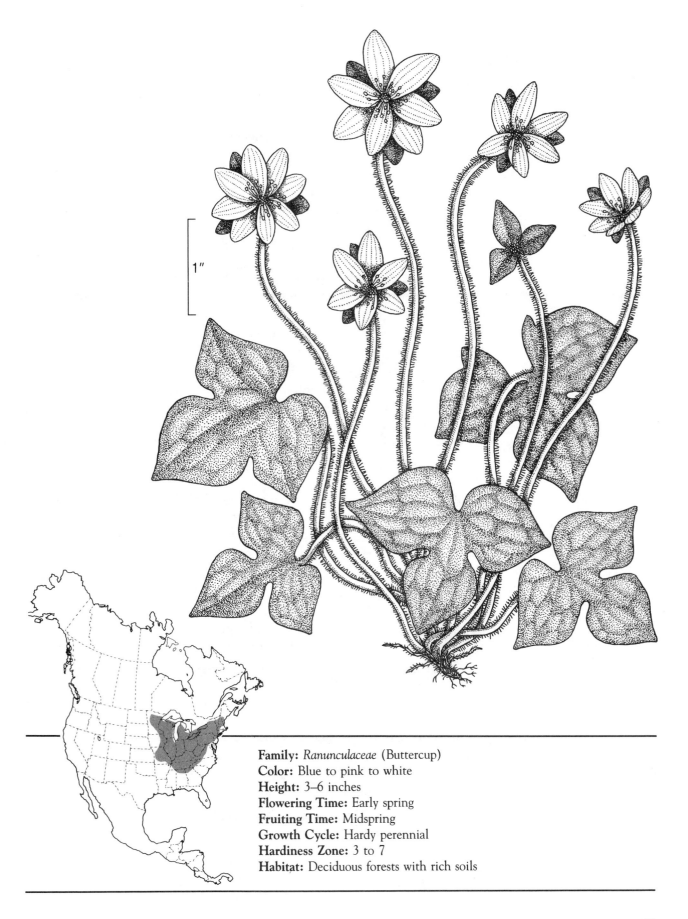

Family: *Ranunculaceae* (Buttercup)
Color: Blue to pink to white
Height: 3–6 inches
Flowering Time: Early spring
Fruiting Time: Midspring
Growth Cycle: Hardy perennial
Hardiness Zone: 3 to 7
Habitat: Deciduous forests with rich soils

SHARP-LOBED HEPATICA *(Hepatica acutiloba)*

BLOODROOT

Sanguinaria canadensis

Sanguinaire, sang-dragon

Both the common and scientific names of this plant refer to the carmine-colored juice in its rhizomes, roots and stems. This fluid contains a toxic, opiumlike alkaloid, sanguinarine, which if taken internally causes nausea, irritation of mucous membranes, and nerve poisoning, yet the sap has anti-cancer and antiseptic qualities as well. Bloodroot has long been used in combination with oak bark to make a natural red dye. The leaves and flowering stem arise from the rhizome in early spring. At first the leaves are wrapped around the flower bud, and then the daisylike flower expands above them as they unfurl. The 8–16-inch flowering stems bear a single flower about 2 inches in diameter, which usually has 8 (but sometimes 6 to 12) white petals surrounding the many yellow stamens. The flowers, which close at sunset, are too fragile to be picked. Individual flowers last only a few days and the entire flowering season lasts but a week or two. After the flowers have withered, the rounded, shallow-lobed, 4–8-inch, pale green leaves continue to grow and remain green until late summer. The fruit is a cigar-shaped capsule containing glossy, brown, ⅛-inch seeds with prominent elaiosomes.

CULTURE

Bloodroots can be grown in locations from full sun to full shade, as long as they have sun in the early spring when they emerge from the ground, flower, and do most of their growing. If grown in full sun to light shade, bloodroots spread rapidly and make an excellent ground cover. Although bloodroots grow best when the pH is 5–7, ample amounts of humus and moisture and good but not excessive drainage are more important. Mulch the plants with a thin layer of deciduous leaves during the winter, north of hardiness zone 5.

PROPAGATION

Bloodroots can be easily propagated from both rhizome divisions and seed. Dig the rhizomes in the late summer when the leaves have just finished yellowing. Wear gloves and wash your hands after handling the roots of this plant. Plant horizontally ¾ inch deep with the buds near the soil surface, and mulch with a thin layer of leaves. Plants from rhizome divisions may flower the following spring. Alternatively, collect freshly ripe seeds from the fruits as they split open in mid- to late spring. Remove the elaiosomes and then plant the seeds immediately, before they dry out. Keep the seeds moist and give them a cold treatment for 2 to 3 months over winter. Place them directly where you want the plants to become established or on the surface of flats filled with loam. Add a ½-inch top dressing of compost mixed with peat moss. Since bloodroot seeds are eaten by mice, cover the flats with hardware cloth or screening for the winter. Seedlings can be transplanted the following summer and take about 3 years to flower.

COMPANIONS

Purple trillium, wild ginger, foamflower, false Solomon's seal, eastern columbine, Dutchman's breeches, sharp-lobed hepatica.

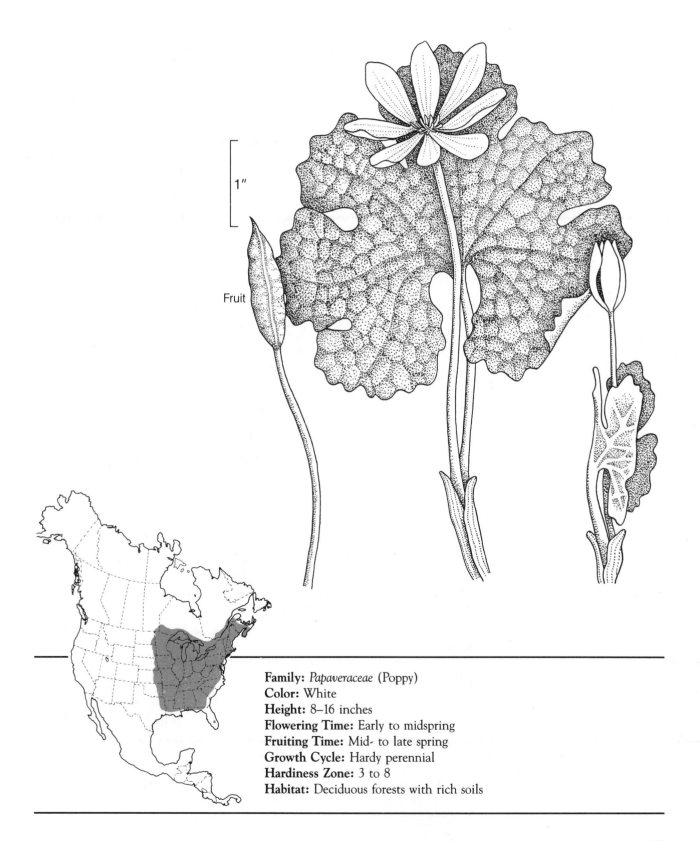

1"

Fruit

Family: *Papaveraceae* (Poppy)
Color: White
Height: 8–16 inches
Flowering Time: Early to midspring
Fruiting Time: Mid- to late spring
Growth Cycle: Hardy perennial
Hardiness Zone: 3 to 8
Habitat: Deciduous forests with rich soils

BLOODROOT *(Sanguinaria canadensis)*

EASTERN TROUT LILY　　*Erythronium americanum*

Dogtooth violet, yellow adder's tongue, fawn lily, *ail doux*

One of the early spring wildflowers of the East, trout lilies are visible only for about one month of the year. In the fall the shoot emerges from the ¾-inch bulb, which may be as much as a foot deep, and grows toward the soil surface. Sometimes the rolled leaves can be seen above the ground as the snow melts in the spring. Young plants send up a single, fleshy, light green leaf, mottled with tan spots. The common name trout lily refers to the speckled leaf pattern. Mature plants have 2 leaves 3–6 inches long. The 3–8-inch flower stalk bears a single, nodding, 1–1½-inch flower with 3 petals and 3 petal-like sepals, all of which are a rich chrome yellow. The petals and sepals are bent backwards fully exposing the 6 brown (or sometimes yellow) stamens. The fruit, an oblong capsule containing ⅛-inch kidney-shaped seeds with prominent elaiosomes, ripens in the late spring or early summer. At about the same time, plants too young to flower sometimes produce white runners.

CULTURE

In order to germinate and to flower, this hardy perennial requires cold treatment, and to resume growth every spring, its bulb requires about 4 months of night temperatures below freezing or 5 months below 40°F. Trout lilies do all their growing for the year in the spring, and start to go into dormancy as the deciduous trees overhead fully expand their leaves. Plant them where they will get ample sun in early spring. The bulbs are easily dehydrated, so plant them where the subsoil is moist but not wet throughout the year. Trout lilies thrive in rich soils that are moderately to slightly acidic (pH 5–7). They naturalize well in lawns, but wait to mow the grass until the leaves have withered. They will colonize to make an attractive seasonal ground cover.

PROPAGATION

The easiest way to propagate this plant is to buy mature bulbs from a reputable grower. If planted 5 inches deep in late summer or fall, they will eventually seek their own level. Once established, trout lilies spread by seeding and by root offsets. Mark plant locations in the spring, dig offsets in the late summer, and then set the small bulbs at least 3 inches deep, mulching well. Propagation from seed takes a long time. Collect seed as it ripens in the late spring, removing the elaiosomes to prevent ants and small mammals from digging them up. Immediately plant the seeds where wanted or ¼ inch deep in flats filled with a mixture of sandy loam and compost, keeping the soil moist. Although some seeds may germinate by fall, many wait until the second year. The first year a single small, narrow leaf emerges from a small bulb. After 4 to 7 years, when trout lilies are finally ready to flower, they will produce a pair of leaves.

COMPANIONS

Sharp-lobed hepatica, purple trillium, Dutchman's breeches, common blue violet, yellow clintonia, bluets.

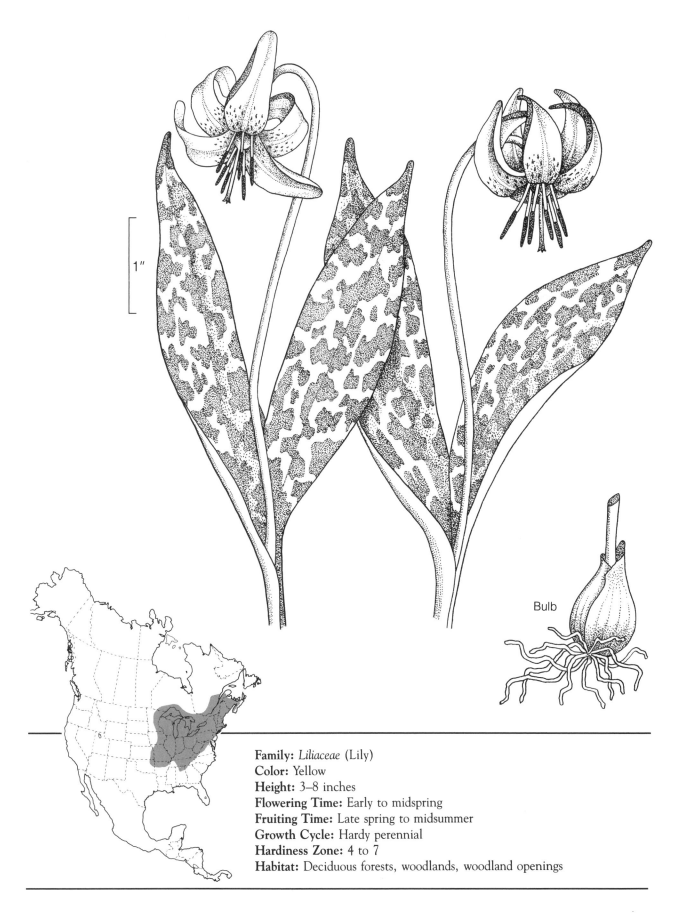

Family: *Liliaceae* (Lily)
Color: Yellow
Height: 3–8 inches
Flowering Time: Early to midspring
Fruiting Time: Late spring to midsummer
Growth Cycle: Hardy perennial
Hardiness Zone: 4 to 7
Habitat: Deciduous forests, woodlands, woodland openings

1"

Bulb

EASTERN TROUT LILY *(Erythronium americanum)*

DUTCHMAN'S BREECHES

Dicentra cucullaria

Dicentre à capuchon

The creamy white flowers of this plant, attached to a foot-tall stalk, look like clusters of miniature pantaloons hung upside down to dry. A fleshy stalk bears from 4 to 10 fragrant flowers, each with a yellow-cream opening and 2 white spur petals pointing into the air. The Latin name *Dicentra* refers to the two spurs. The flowers last a week or two, but should not be picked because they wilt quickly. They are pollinated by queen bumblebees, which emerge from hibernation just as the pollen is ripe. Some bumblebees don't bother to enter the flowers to obtain the sweet nectar but instead chew holes in the tips of the spurs. The highly divided, gray-green foliage dies back in late spring or early summer, and the nutrients and carbohydrates it contained are stored in clusters of white, grainlike tubers. The high sugar content in the tubers of this perennial makes it frost-hardy. The leaves and tubers contain a morphinelike alkaloid, cucularine, which is poisonous. The fruit is an oval-shaped capsule containing many tiny, black, glossy seeds with elaiosomes that attract, and are carried off by, ants.

CULTURE   Although Dutchman's breeches are generally found in forests and woodlands in the wild, they do well under cultivation, especially in humus-rich soil that is slightly acidic to slightly alkaline (pH 5.5–8). Plant in shade to partial shade, preferably under sugar maples or other deciduous trees whose leaves form humus rapidly. Moisture should be available, especially in the spring flowering season, but the soil should not be waterlogged.

PROPAGATION   The easiest way to propagate this plant is by division of the scaly tubers in the early summer to fall. Plant large tubers about 1 inch deep and smaller ones ½ inch deep, mulching with deciduous tree leaves over the winter. It may take several years for the new plants to reach maturity and flower. Propagation from seeds requires 2 to 3 months of moist chilling for germination. As soon as seeds are ripe in the summer, remove their elaiosomes, plant them outdoors at a depth of ¼ inch, mulch lightly, and let them overwinter. Since it may take more than a year for the seeds to germinate, let them go for 2 years in the flats before you throw out the soil. Expect to wait 3 to 4 years before seedlings reach maturity.

COMPANIONS   Wild ginger, eastern trout lily, wild leek, eastern columbine, bloodroot, sharp-lobed hepatica.

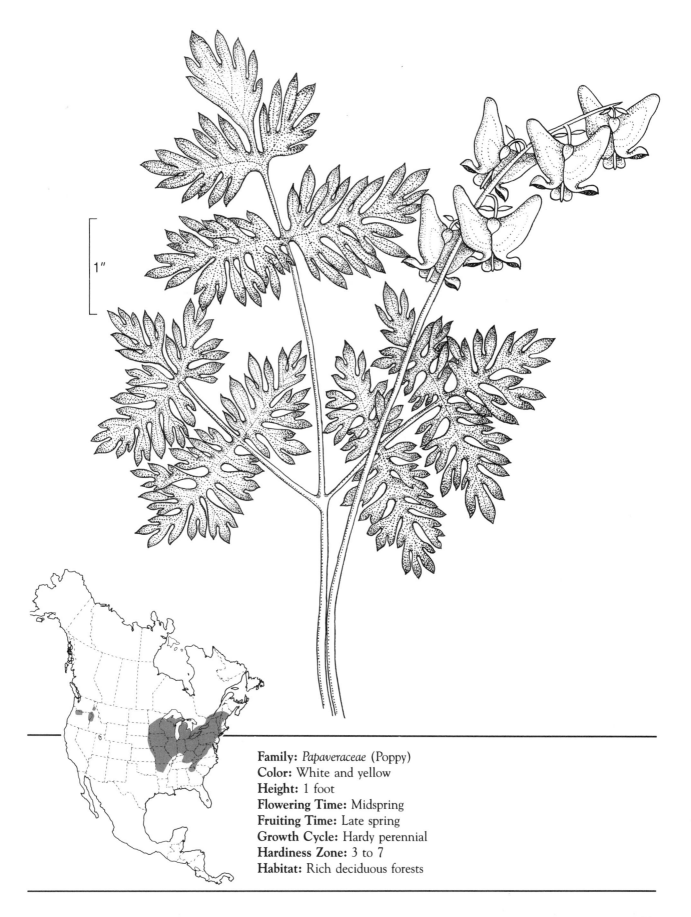

Family: *Papaveraceae* (Poppy)
Color: White and yellow
Height: 1 foot
Flowering Time: Midspring
Fruiting Time: Late spring
Growth Cycle: Hardy perennial
Hardiness Zone: 3 to 7
Habitat: Rich deciduous forests

1″

DUTCHMAN'S BREECHES (*Dicentra cucullaria*)

COMMON BLUE VIOLET

Viola papilionacea

Confederate violet, *violette papilionacée*

The English translation of this wildflower's scientific name is "violet that looks like a butterfly," a reference to its delicate, winglike, purple-blue, or gray-blue petals. This violet is unusual in that it produces two kinds of flowers. In the spring the familiar 5-petaled flowers are borne on 6-inch-long leafless stems. The upper pair of side petals have small, fuzzy "beards," and the broad bottom petal is marked with purple stripes that guide pollinating bees to the nectar concealed in the spur at the base. In the white center of the ¾-inch flower is a single pistil, surrounded by 5 stamens bearing bright orange anthers. In late spring and summer different flowers with closed buds lacking petals appear on short, horizontal stems hidden beneath the leaves. These flowers produce seeds without the aid of insect pollinators. The fruits of both kinds of flowers are 3-part capsules that open explosively when mature, often making a popping sound and flinging the small, round seeds up to 12 feet away. The seeds are dispersed even farther by ants, which carry them off to their nests, chew off the tasty elaiosomes, and discard the seeds in underground refuse heaps. The germination and early growth of seedlings is enhanced by this treatment. Common blue violets are "stemless" — both their flower stalks and 3–8-inch-high, heart-shaped leaves arise directly from a branching, gnarly rhizome just below the soil surface. Violet leaves are the favorite food of fritillary butterfly caterpillars, which feed on the leaves at night, and their rhizomes are frequently eaten by wild turkeys. Violets are also edible by humans, and rich in vitamin C. Use the leaves and flowers to make an elegant salad.

CULTURE

This wildflower isn't choosy about the environment in which it grows, a reason, perhaps, why this is the most common violet found in the region. It grows in shady forests, sunny meadows, edges of lawns, and even railroad embankments. The common blue violet is easy to grow in gardens and may become aggressive if given ample sun, moisture, and space. To keep it in check, grow it in a garden with a fairly dense planting of taller species that can provide shade and competition. The common blue violet is also easy to force into bloom by bringing it indoors in January.

PROPAGATION

Common blue violet is easy to propagate by seeds or rhizome division. Collect the seeds in the early summer as the fruit capsule starts to turn tan. You can capture the seeds using a nylon sack as mentioned on page 49. The seeds require stratification (4 weeks at 40°F), so it is best to plant them in the fall in the desired location. Divide the gnarly rhizome in the fall, spacing the crowns about a foot apart and ½ inch below the soil surface.

COMPANIONS

Purple trillium, eastern trout lily, eastern columbine, foamflower, Solomon's seal, false Solomon's seal, wood lily.

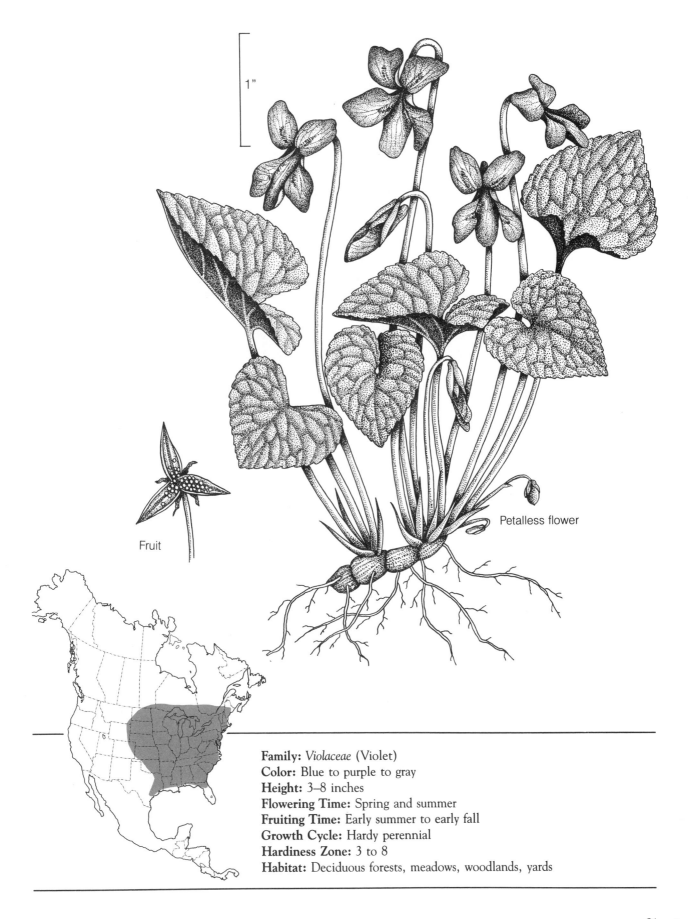

1"

Fruit

Petalless flower

Family: *Violaceae* (Violet)
Color: Blue to purple to gray
Height: 3–8 inches
Flowering Time: Spring and summer
Fruiting Time: Early summer to early fall
Growth Cycle: Hardy perennial
Hardiness Zone: 3 to 8
Habitat: Deciduous forests, meadows, woodlands, yards

COMMON BLUE VIOLET (*Viola papilionacea*)

PURPLE TRILLIUM

Trillium erectum

Wakerobin, stinking Benjamin, red trillium, *trille dressé*

The purple trillium is one of the most common yet most striking of the trilliums in northeastern North America. This hardy perennial has a single whorl of 3 diamond-shaped leaves clasping its 6–18-inch-high stem. Perched above the leaves is a single nodding flower on a 1–4-inch stem. One of purple trillium's other familiar names is stinking Benjamin; indeed some of its flowers smell like rancid meat (or a wet dog), which attracts its major pollinator, the big green fleshfly. The 3-petaled flowers are usually crimson to maroon, although there are yellow to white forms as well. The petals arch slightly backward and alternate with the 3 green sepals. In the center of the 1–2-inch flower are 6 stamens with yellow anthers. The petals wither after 2 to 3 weeks as the fleshy, oval, berrylike fruit develops. When the fruit is fully ripe it is ½–1 inch long, dark red, and filled with many small (1/10-inch) brown seeds. Birds and mammals eat many of the berries, and the seeds of unconsumed fruits are usually carried off by ants. The root system of purple trillium is a stout, brown, bulbous rhizome with many stringy roots, which run deep beneath the soil surface. Native Americans used cooked roots as an aphrodisiac, emetic, and anti-spasmodic.

CULTURE

Purple trillium is a plant of rich woods and thrives in deep leafmold. Plant it in areas that receive sun in early spring and light to heavy shade once the trees have leafed out. Work plenty of compost into the top 6–12 inches of the soil and mulch the plants over winter with deciduous tree leaves. The soil should be moist, but not excessively so. Purple trillium will grow in a variety of soil conditions between pH 4.5 and 6.5.

PROPAGATION

Purple trillium is easy to propagate by seeds or root division. Seeds should be collected as soon as the fruit is ripe and dark red. Separate the seeds from the fruit pulp, removing the elaiosomes, and immediately plant them ¼ inch deep in humus-rich loam. Keep the seeds moist and give them a thin mulch of deciduous tree leaves. Alternatively, the seeds may be planted in flats containing a mixture of loam and compost and left outdoors for the winter. Proper germination requires stratification, and even then it may take longer than you desire. Be patient: some seeds may not germinate until the second year, and it will take several years for these plants to reach maturity and flower. Seedlings will have only a single leaf the first year and may be transplanted to permanent locations late the following summer. Propagate by rhizome division during midsummer when the small new rhizome extensions can be carefully cut from the parent and planted about 2 inches deep in the desired location. This method may be only slightly quicker than from seed.

COMPANIONS

Wild leek, Jack-in-the-pulpit, eastern trout lily, bloodroot, wild ginger, Solomon's seal, yellow clintonia, partridgeberry, common blue violet, foamflower.

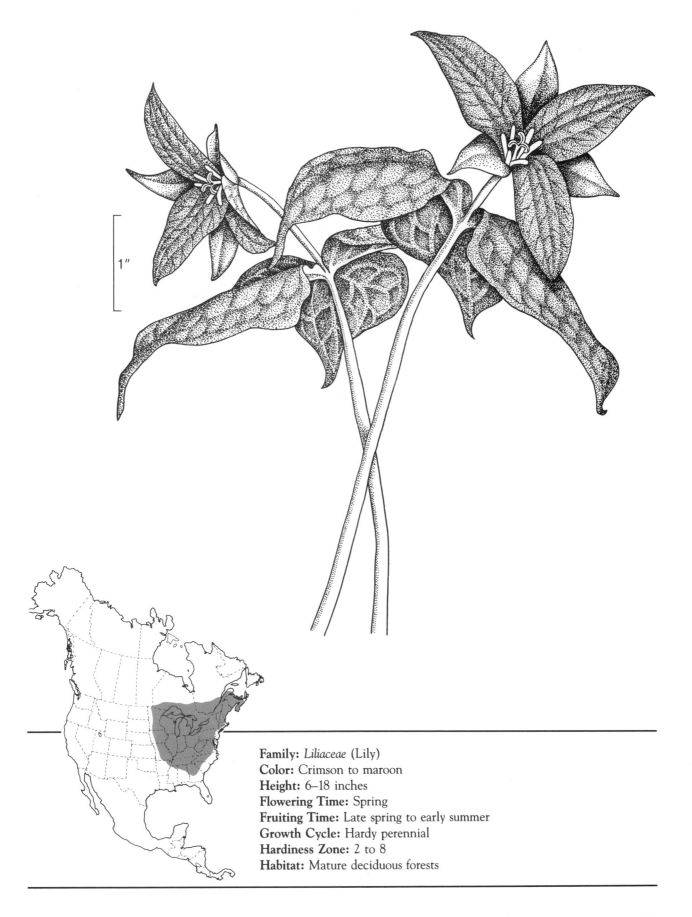

1″

Family: *Liliaceae* (Lily)
Color: Crimson to maroon
Height: 6–18 inches
Flowering Time: Spring
Fruiting Time: Late spring to early summer
Growth Cycle: Hardy perennial
Hardiness Zone: 2 to 8
Habitat: Mature deciduous forests

PURPLE TRILLIUM (*Trillium erectum*)

WILD GINGER

Asarum canadensis

Gingembre sauvage, asaret du Canada

This hardy, stemless perennial gets its name from the pungent ginger flavor of its edible roots. Wild ginger is far more valued as an ideal ground cover, however, than as an ingredient for making candy. The heart-shaped, medium green leaves persist throughout the summer. The velvety leaves are quite broad, 7 inches at maturity under ideal conditions, and stand 6–12 inches high. The flowers of wild ginger are quite unusual in that they lack petals. The 3 purple-brown, bud-covering sepals open before the leaves have unfurled. Each plant has a single flower, which lies horizontally along the soil surface. Beetles and flesh flies crawl along the ground and into the throat of the blossom to deposit pollen on the stigma and pollinate the flower. The fleshy fruit that develops contains several ¼ inch, oval, gray-brown seeds with prominent elaiosomes. Ants often carry the seeds away, nibbling off the elaiosomes before burying the seeds. Native Americans used wild ginger as a birth-control agent and as a pleasant-tasting medicine for a variety of ailments. The roots do contain a substance, aristolochic acid, which has antimicrobial and antitumor properties.

CULTURE

Wild ginger is usually found growing in rich woods and on limestone ledges. It grows best in partial to full shade in soils that remain moist, but not wet, through the growing season. Wild ginger is easily cultivated on a wide range of soils from moderately acidic to alkaline (pH 5–7.5). It can be brought indoors and forced, but requires cold treatment to break the dormancy it enters in the fall.

PROPAGATION

Although wild ginger can be raised from seed, it is often difficult to locate the fruits and seeds among the leaf litter. If you are successful in finding the fruits, collect the seeds as the fruits mature and start to split open. Remove the elaiosomes and immediately plant the seeds ½ inch deep where you desire the plants to become established. An easier way to propagate wild ginger is by dividing the creeping, forking rhizomes. In the fall after the leaves have withered, plant pieces of rhizomes about ½ inch deep with the bud tips just below the surface of the soil. Mulch with deciduous leaves. Rhizomes can also be divided in the spring, if you can remember where the plants are.

COMPANIONS

Bloodroot, wild leek, sharp-lobed hepatica, eastern columbine, purple trillium, Dutchman's breeches.

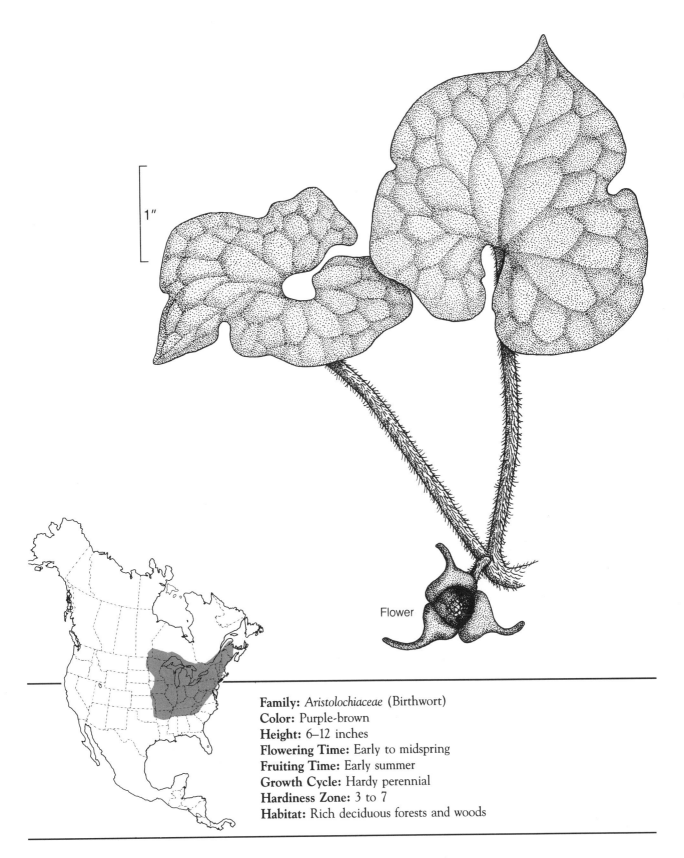

1"

Flower

Family: *Aristolochiaceae* (Birthwort)
Color: Purple-brown
Height: 6–12 inches
Flowering Time: Early to midspring
Fruiting Time: Early summer
Growth Cycle: Hardy perennial
Hardiness Zone: 3 to 7
Habitat: Rich deciduous forests and woods

WILD GINGER *(Asarum canadensis)*

EASTERN COLUMBINE

Aquilegia canadensis

Wild columbine, meetinghouses, *gants de Notre Dame*

The eastern columbine is one of the easiest and most beautiful plants to grow in a native-plant garden. A slender, hardy perennial, it reaches up to 2 feet in height. The attractive, rounded, compound leaves are dull grayish green and divided into threes. The showy, nodding flowers, up to 2 inches across, are borne atop leafy stems and have 5 spurred scarlet petals covering the yellow centers. The French name means "Our Lady's gloves," referring to the flower's 5 "fingers," and the common name "meetinghouses" refers to the congregation of spurs in the center. Inside the spurs are drops of sweet nectar, extracted by bumblebees as they hang upside-down pollinating the flowers. Hummingbirds also frequent eastern columbine. Some naturally occurring varieties of the species have salmon, pink, or yellow flowers. The fruit is a 5-chambered capsule that becomes erect as it matures and then opens, flinging away the many small, glossy, black seeds as the plant sways in the wind. The gnarled rootstocks of the eastern columbine tend to be deep seated. Native Americans had many medicinal uses for columbine seeds, roots, and leaves.

CULTURE Eastern columbine is an ideal plant for rocky slopes and a variety of light conditions from full sun to full shade. Columbine can be grown in prairies and grasslands if the grass is not too thick, although it is usually grown in woodland situations. The plant is frequently found growing in limestone-rich soils in the eastern U.S., but it can also be successfully grown in moderately acid soils; soil pH between 8 and 5 is acceptable. Although moisture is needed for seedlings to become established, the deep rootstock of mature plants enables the eastern columbine to endure dry spells well. It is an attractive plant for rock gardens, especially where the winters are relatively mild and the foliage remains green.

PROPAGATION Eastern columbine is most easily propagated from seed, because mature rootstocks are difficult to divide and transplant. For seeds to germinate properly they must have moist stratification for 3–4 weeks at 40°F or below. Germination will then occur in 3–4 weeks if seeds are held at 70–80°F temperatures. Clear a small area where you want the plants to become established, and scratch the seed into the soil with a garden rake. Then cover the area with a light mulch of maple, birch, ash or other deciduous leaves. Alternatively, in the fall, sow the seeds ¼ inch deep in flats, cover with a thin layer of light soil and mulch, and then leave outdoors for the winter. After seedlings have become sturdy the following spring, they may be carefully transplanted to permanent locations. Plants will usually produce flowers the second year. Once established, columbine self-seeds readily and requires little further care.

COMPANIONS Bloodroot, wild ginger, sharp-lobed hepatica, wild leek, common blue violet, Dutchman's breeches, false Solomon's seal, bluets.

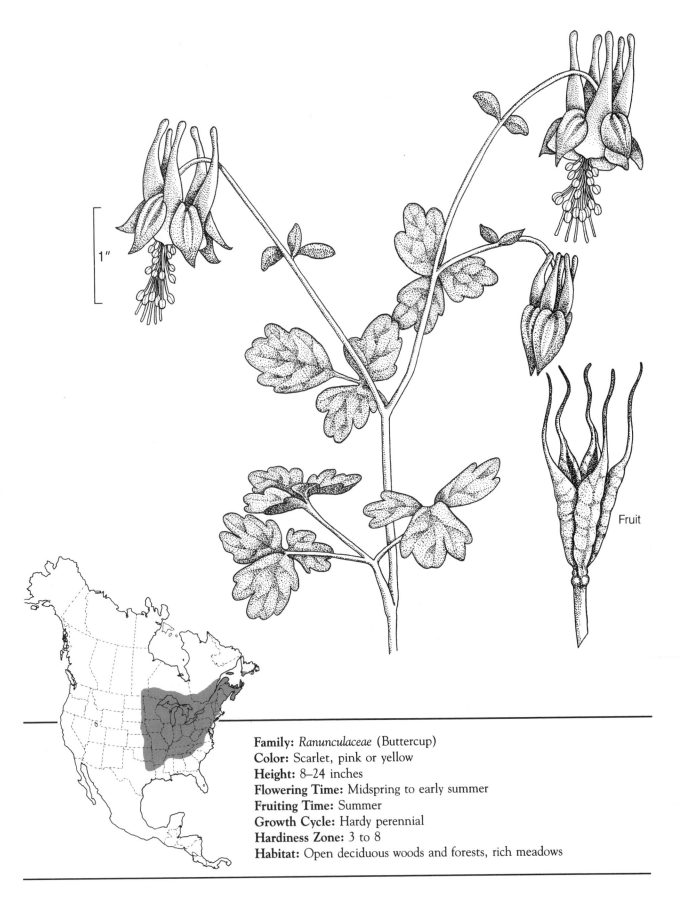

1"

Fruit

Family: *Ranunculaceae* (Buttercup)
Color: Scarlet, pink or yellow
Height: 8–24 inches
Flowering Time: Midspring to early summer
Fruiting Time: Summer
Growth Cycle: Hardy perennial
Hardiness Zone: 3 to 8
Habitat: Open deciduous woods and forests, rich meadows

EASTERN COLUMBINE *(Aquilegia canadensis)*

FOAMFLOWER

Tiarella cordifolia

False miterwort, *tiarelle cordifoliée*

Long, slender stamens give foamflower's spikes of white flowers the frothy appearance referred to by its common name. Each of the 5-petaled, ¼-inch-wide flowers is surrounded by a white 5-lobed calyx. In the centers of the flowers are 10 stamens and a single pistil, whose shape gives the species its Latin name, *Tiarella* ("small tiara"). By midsummer the fruit capsules are mature and contain finely pitted, shiny black, elliptical seeds. Like other members of the saxifrage family, the 8–12-inch-high spikes of flowers arise from a mound of attractive foliage. The flower stalks lack leaves in the northeastern part of foamflower's range, but do have leaves in the South. The heart-shaped leaves are sharply toothed and, like the flower stems, covered with dense hairs. During mild winters the leaves often remain green until they wither the following spring, when new leaves start to grow. In early summer, just as the fruits are forming, mature plants send out runners that produce new plants nearby. With time, sizeable colonies may develop.

CULTURE

Foamflower is an excellent plant for rock gardens, borders, or even ground cover if planted densely. It grows naturally in cool, moist, deciduous forests, but is easily grown in shady gardens as long as the soil is moist throughout the growing season. Soils with pH 5–6 are ideal, but foamflower can be grown in soils with pH 4.5–7. Slugs are fond of its leaves, so have the beer traps ready (see page 48). Foamflower is easy to force into winter bloom by bringing it indoors in mid-January.

PROPAGATION

The easiest way to propagate foamflower is to divide the runners in the fall or spring. Simply cut the runner and gently dig up the new plants, being careful not to disturb the newly formed white roots. Plant the divisions about a foot apart and set the crowns even with the soil surface. Keep the new plants well watered until they become fully established. Foamflower is also easy to propagate from seeds collected from mature fruits. Immediately plant the seeds ¼ inch deep in a mixture of peat moss, sand, and compost, kept continually moist. If seeds are planted in flats, keep them outside for the winter. Transplant the seedlings the following fall to desired locations.

COMPANIONS

Bloodroot, common blue violet, purple trillium, false Solomon's seal, Jack-in-the-pulpit.

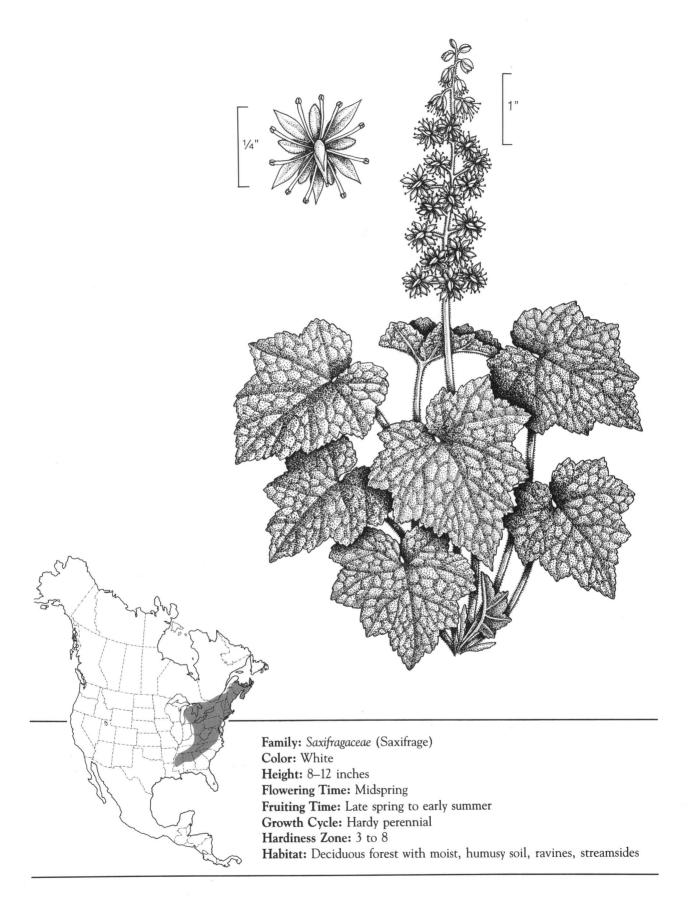

¼"

1"

Family: *Saxifragaceae* (Saxifrage)
Color: White
Height: 8–12 inches
Flowering Time: Midspring
Fruiting Time: Late spring to early summer
Growth Cycle: Hardy perennial
Hardiness Zone: 3 to 8
Habitat: Deciduous forest with moist, humusy soil, ravines, streamsides

FOAMFLOWER (*Tiarella cordifolia*)

MAYAPPLE

Podophyllum peltatum

Mandrake, *pomme de Mai*

Mayapple, a natural ground cover, carpets eastern woodlands with colonies of up to a thousand plants growing together. The 12–18-inch-high shoots are of two kinds — the nonflowering stem, bearing a single broad leaf with 5 to 9 deeply cleft lobes, and the flowering stem, bearing a pair of leaves. As the shoots emerge in the spring the leaves expand, looking like parasols rising from the ground. The flower buds emerge from between the pairs of leaves 2 to 3 weeks later. The 3 green sepals fall off as the 2-inch, nodding, fragrant flowers start to unfurl their 6 to 9 waxy white petals. Bumblebees are the main pollinators of mayapple, whose flowers last about a week. In late spring or early summer the sweet, lemon-shaped, 1–2-inch fruit ripens, turning from green to yellow. Then in midsummer the foliage withers back to its creeping, branched rhizomes and fibrous roots. The eastern box turtle eats mayapples and disperses their seeds to new locations. Germination of the ¼-inch, light brown, elliptical seeds is enhanced by passage through the turtle's digestive system. To humans, however, all parts of the mayapple except the flesh of fully ripe fruits are poisonous, as they contain the bitter resin podophyllin. The ingestion of as little as 5 grains of podophyllin can cause death; yet processed extracts are used in modern cancer treatments.

CULTURE

Mayapple makes an attractive ground cover and is easy to cultivate. Given ample moisture and sunlight it may even have to be contained to keep it from crowding out other plants. Mayapple makes its best growth in the spring just before the leaves of deciduous trees are fully expanded. Although it blooms most vigorously where it is sunny in the early spring, mayapple can tolerate fairly dense shade during the summer. In the garden, the plant does well in full sun and in shady borders. It is not choosy about soils, as long as they are relatively moist and have moderately acidic to neutral conditions (pH 4–7). An overwinter mulch of deciduous leaves is preferable to pine needles.

PROPAGATION

The easiest way to propagate mayapple is by dividing the rhizomes. Wear gloves or wash your hands immediately after handling the rhizomes, since some people may develop a rash after touching them. The nonflowering shoots produce buds on the rhizome before withering in the late summer. Divide the rhizomes in the fall, with at least one bud on each piece. Plant the divisions 1 inch deep with the buds pointing up, and mulch them with an inch or so of deciduous leaves. Seed germination is enhanced by moist stratification for 2 to 3 months. Remove the seeds from the fruit as soon as they are ripe in the fall, and plant them thickly, ½ inch deep in flats that are left out for the winter. The seedlings that emerge in the spring will have a single unlobed leaf the first year, and in several years will reach maturity and flower.

COMPANIONS

Solomon's seal, false Solomon's seal, wood lily.

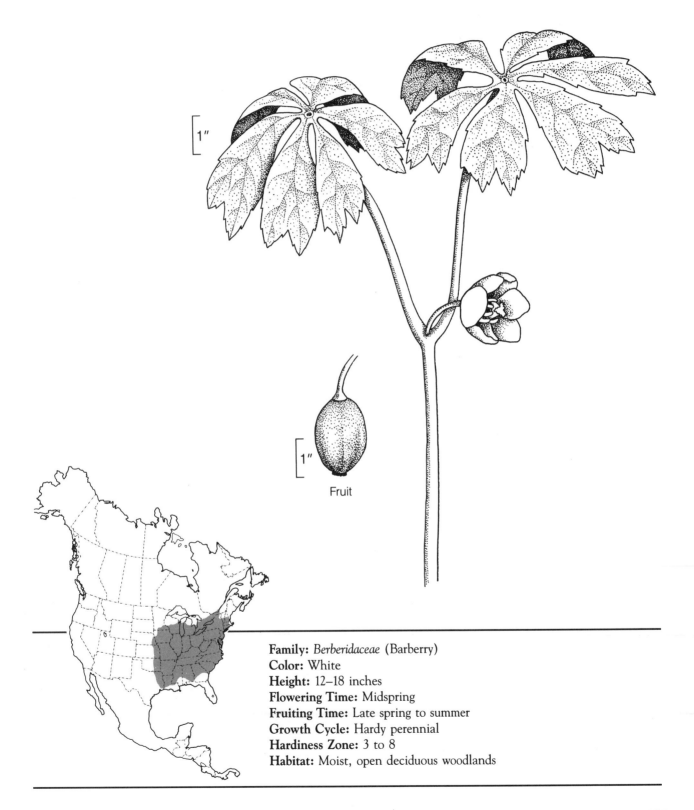

1"

1"

Fruit

Family: *Berberidaceae* (Barberry)
Color: White
Height: 12–18 inches
Flowering Time: Midspring
Fruiting Time: Late spring to summer
Growth Cycle: Hardy perennial
Hardiness Zone: 3 to 8
Habitat: Moist, open deciduous woodlands

MAYAPPLE *(Podophyllum peltatum)*

WOODLAND SPECIES
Late Spring to Summer

This section presents wildflowers that bloom in the late spring and summer, when the forest trees cast a deep shade. Many of these plants, however, can also grow in sunny locations. In laying out a woodland garden, be careful to group plants with similar pH preferences together. Plants that prefer acidic soils, like wood lily, wintergreen, bunchberry, partridgeberry, and yellow clintonia, should be grown apart from plants that prefer neutral or only slightly acidic soils, like wild leek, sharp-lobed hepatica, eastern columbine, wild ginger, and bloodroot.

When you design the garden, be sure to create paths so that you can tend the plants and enjoy them close up without trampling them. A thick layer of pine needles makes an attractive path for areas with acid soil. Also take advantage of the visual interest provided by rocks, logs, and stumps. These materials are a natural part of the woodland habitat and can become convenient landmarks separating sections of the garden.

COMPANIONS These wildflowers can be grown together with the early spring wildflowers described on pages 80–101, but keep their pH preferences in mind. Select species that will provide a succession of bloom, and plant clusters that will bloom sequentially to fill the garden with color.

Other species that should be considered include **Colorado columbine** (*Aquilegia caerulea*), a hardy perennial with large blue and white flowers, which prefers neutral soils and light shade. It is an excellent selection for woodland rock gardens. The **American bellflower** (*Campanula americana*) has a terminal spike of light blue, flat, inch-wide flowers. It is one of the taller (2–6 feet high) wildflowers growing in woodland and forest openings of the region. In midspring **white baneberry** (*Actaea pachypoda*) produces delicate white flowers in clusters atop its 1–3-foot high stems. The most striking feature of this wildflower, however, are the white "doll's-eye" fruits borne on thick pink stalks lasting through the summer and into the fall. **Wild geranium** (*Geranium maculatum*) punctuates late spring woodlands with splashes of laven-

Woodland garden, late spring.

A. Yellow clintonia
B. False Solomon's seal
C. Wood lily
D. Solomon's seal
E. Wild leek
F. Shinleaf
G. Wild lily-of-the-valley
H. Partridgeberry
I. Wintergreen
J. Bunchberry

der. During the summer "crane's-bill" fruits develop, typical of members of the geranium family. The plant's broad, deeply lobed, dark green foliage makes an attractive ground cover. In midsummer the **thimbleberry** or **purple-flowering raspberry** (*Rubus odoratus*) produces 2-inch-wide, 5-petaled, magenta flowers. While not an herbaceous wildflower, this native 3-foot-high shrub should be considered for its attractive maple-like foliage as well as for its striking flowers. Thimbleberry lacks prickles and has rather dry, tasteless, inch-wide, flattened raspberries.

Medium-sized ferns add an element of contrast to the woodland wildflowers of late spring and summer. **Spinulose woodfern** (*Dryopteris spinulosa*) is one of the most common in the region and is adaptable to a variety of garden settings. The *intermedia* variety of this 2-foot-high, lacy-cut fern remains green throughout the winter, while the fronds of other varieties wither in the fall. **Lady fern** (*Athyrium filix-femina*) and **New York fern** (*Dryopteris noveboracensis*, sometimes listed as *Thelypteris noveboracensis* in catalogs) are slightly smaller, yet have equally attractive, finely divided fronds.

WILD LILY-OF-THE-VALLEY · *Maianthemum canadense*

False lily-of-the-valley, Canada mayflower, two-leaved Solomon's seal, beadruby, *muguet, maïanthème du Canada*

Wild lily-of-the-valley frequently blankets woodlands with its 3–6-inch-high, spear-shaped leaves. The leaves arise from extensive, forking, white rhizomes that grow about an inch below the soil surface. While individual shoots live only for a few years, the underground rhizomes continue to produce new ones each year. Young shoots have a single leaf, but when they reach the flowering stage, the zigzag stem produces 2 or occasionally 3 leaves. Although this species and the true lily-of-the-valley are both in the lily family, their flowers are quite different. Rather than 6-lobed, bell-shaped flowers, wild lily-of-the-valley has a 1–2-inch-long plume of quarter-inch flowers, each with 2 petals and 2 identical-looking sepals. The flowers have 4 stamens, unlike the typical 6 found in most other members of the lily family. After being pollinated by bumblebees, the sweetly fragrant flowers produce berries containing several $\frac{1}{10}$-inch, round white seeds. The berries turn from speckled green to ruby red as the foliage yellows near summer's end. The berries don't last long; mice, chipmunks, grouse, and many other birds quickly consume them. Although the fruits are edible, they should be eaten in moderation because of their purgative properties. The common name Canada mayflower is a literal translation of the plant's scientific name, although it is in a different family than the mayflower (trailing arbutus).

CULTURE

Wild lily-of-the-valley is one of the most adaptable wildflowers in the region. It prefers mildly acidic soils (pH 4–6.5) with abundant organic matter, but grows well in full sun or in shade. When grown in sunny locations, the shoots tend to be more densely packed and they flower more abundantly, but the leaves tend to be smaller than when grown in the shade.

PROPAGATION

The easiest way to propagate wild lily-of-the-valley is from divisions of the rhizomes, although propagation from seed is not difficult. It takes several years, however, for plants propagated from seeds to flower, while rhizome divisions usually flower the next spring. In the fall, after the leaves have yellowed, divide the rhizomes into 2-inch pieces, making sure that each segment has at least one of the greenish buds. Set the divisions about 6 inches apart and about ¾ inch deep, moisten the soil, and mulch for the winter. Collect the fruits in the late summer and separate the seeds from the pulp. Immediately plant the seeds ⅓ inch deep in the desired location or in flats that are left outdoors for the winter. Once established, wild lilies-of-the-valley will spread rapidly.

COMPANIONS

Bunchberry, yellow clintonia, wintergreen, shinleaf, Solomon's seal, false Solomon's seal.

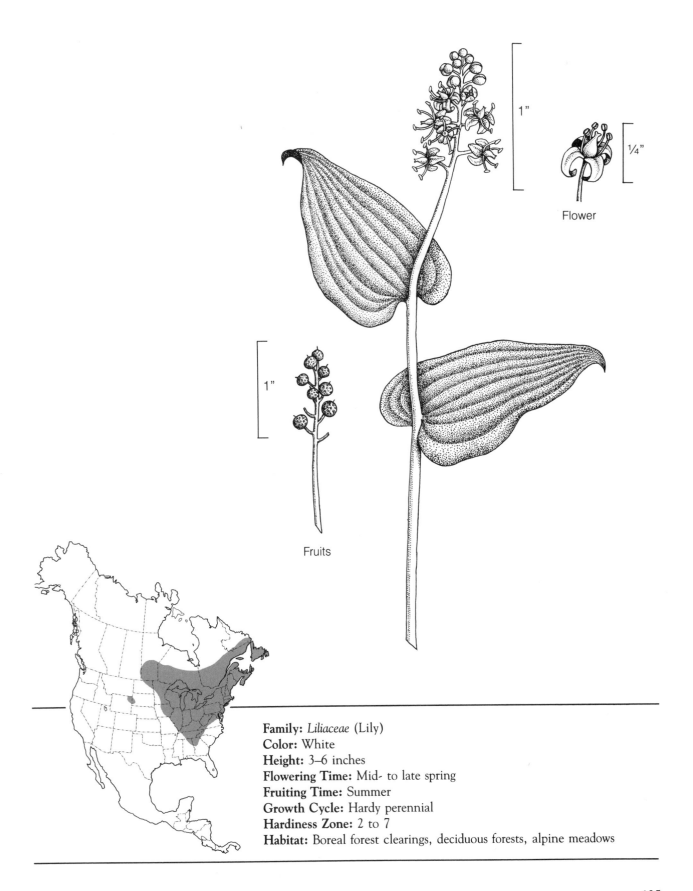

1"

1/4"

Flower

1"

Fruits

Family: *Liliaceae* (Lily)
Color: White
Height: 3–6 inches
Flowering Time: Mid- to late spring
Fruiting Time: Summer
Growth Cycle: Hardy perennial
Hardiness Zone: 2 to 7
Habitat: Boreal forest clearings, deciduous forests, alpine meadows

WILD-LILY-OF-THE-VALLEY (*Maianthemum canadense*)

SOLOMON'S SEAL   *Polygonatum biflorum*

Sceau-de-Salomon à deux fleurs

There are several theories concerning how this hardy perennial got its common name. Some suggest that the circular scars caused by the shedding of the previous year's shoots from the gnarled, fleshy, underground rhizome are reminiscent of King Solomon's governmental seals. Others think that the reference to Solomon is related to the 6-pointed star pattern evident when the rhizome is cut in cross section. Regardless of which interpretation is correct, Solomon's seal is an attractive addition to a garden of wildflowers. The arching stems are 1–3 feet high with 2 rows of flat 3–5-inch lance-shaped leaves clasping the stem. The yellow-green flowers, usually in pairs, hang down from the axils of the leaves. The ½–1-inch-long tubular flowers have 6 short, rounded lobes. Many birds and small mammals consume the ¼-inch, round, blue-black berries as they ripen in the summer. Germination of the small, elliptical seeds seems to be enhanced by passage through these creatures' digestive systems.

CULTURE
Solomon's seal can be grown in a wide variety of environments. Although it appears naturally in shady habitats, it can planted in open sun. It grows best where soils are moist and the pH is 4.5–5.5, but it is tolerant of variable moisture conditions and soil acidities from pH 4 to 7.

PROPAGATION
Solomon's seal can be propagated by rhizome divisions or by seed. Divide the rhizomes in the spring or fall when the plants are dormant. Cut pieces of the rhizome with at least one bud on each segment and set them horizontally with the buds pointing up, 18 inches apart and 1 inch deep. Alternatively, collect seeds after the fruits are mature and have turned black, but before they dry out. If the seeds dry out their germination may be delayed. Remove the seeds from the fruit and plant them ½ inch deep in outdoor beds or flats to be left out over winter. Keep the seedbed moist. It is essential that the seeds be given a moist, cold treatment (2 months at 40°F) for germination to occur. Solomon's seal seeds germinate better in the dark than in the light, so a top dressing of compost and a thin layer of leaf mulch may further enhance their germination in the spring. Be patient — it often takes 3 to 4 years for seedlings to reach flowering size.

COMPANIONS
Purple trillium, mayapple, false Solomon's seal, foamflower, wild lily-of-the-valley, common blue violet, wood lily.

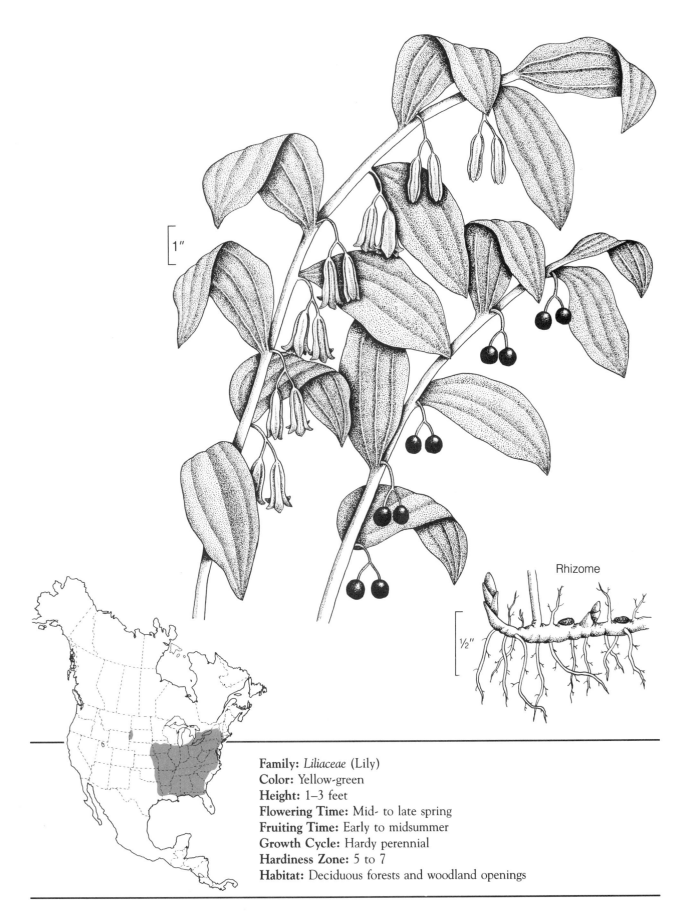

Rhizome

1"

½"

Family: *Liliaceae* (Lily)
Color: Yellow-green
Height: 1–3 feet
Flowering Time: Mid- to late spring
Fruiting Time: Early to midsummer
Growth Cycle: Hardy perennial
Hardiness Zone: 5 to 7
Habitat: Deciduous forests and woodland openings

SOLOMON'S SEAL (*Polygonatum biflorum*)

FALSE SOLOMON'S SEAL

Smilacina racemosa

Solomon's zigzag, Solomon's plume, *smilacine à grappes*

Like the Solomon's seal, the false Solomon's seal has a thick, knotted rhizome and 5 to 12 leaves in 2 rows along the stem. Although both plants have arching stems 1–3 feet long, the stem of the false Solomon's seal has a slight zigzag to it. The leaves of false Solomon's seal tend to have wavier edges and bases that clasp the stem more than do those of the true Solomon's seal. The most obvious difference between the two species, however, is the flowers. In striking contrast to the bell-shaped flowers of Solomon's seal, which bloom a week or so earlier, the numerous creamy white flowers of false Solomon's seal are clustered in a 6–12-inch plume at the end of the stem. Each of the ¼-inch flowers has 6 petal-like parts. The fruits, ⅛-inch berries, contain 1 to 2 round seeds and turn from green to speckled pink to a translucent ruby red as they ripen. They are fragrant and edible, but have a bitter aftertaste. They disappear rapidly as birds and small mammals consume them.

CULTURE   The best situation for this hardy perennial is partial to full shade in soils that are moist and rich in humus. Although they will grow in full sun or in drier environments, they tend to be somewhat stunted under those conditions. False Solomon's seal does best in moderately acidic soils with a pH 5–6.5.

PROPAGATION   False Solomon's seal can be propagated by either rhizome division or seed. The plant spreads naturally by extension of its rhizomes and is easy to establish. Divide the rhizomes when the plant is dormant in the fall. Space rhizome divisions, each with at least one bud, a foot or more apart, and set them horizontally at a depth of 1½ inches. A thin layer of deciduous leaf mulch will help retain moisture. Plants from rhizome divisions will generally flower the second year. For optimal germination, seeds should be gathered as soon as the fruits ripen in the summer and should not be allowed to dry out. Germination of the seeds is greatly enhanced by cold, moist stratification (40°F for 3 to 4 months) and by darkness, since light inhibits the process. To ensure that the seeds are in darkness, leave an inch-thick mulch of deciduous leaves through the spring. Even under the best of conditions the seeds are slow to germinate, frequently taking 2 years, so be patient. If you plant them ¼ inch deep in flats that are left out over the winter, let them go through a second spring before you discard the soil. Have patience also as you wait for false Solomon's seal to flower once the seeds have germinated — it may take 5 years.

COMPANIONS   Mayapple, Solomon's seal, eastern columbine, bloodroot, common blue violet, wood lily, larger blue flag.

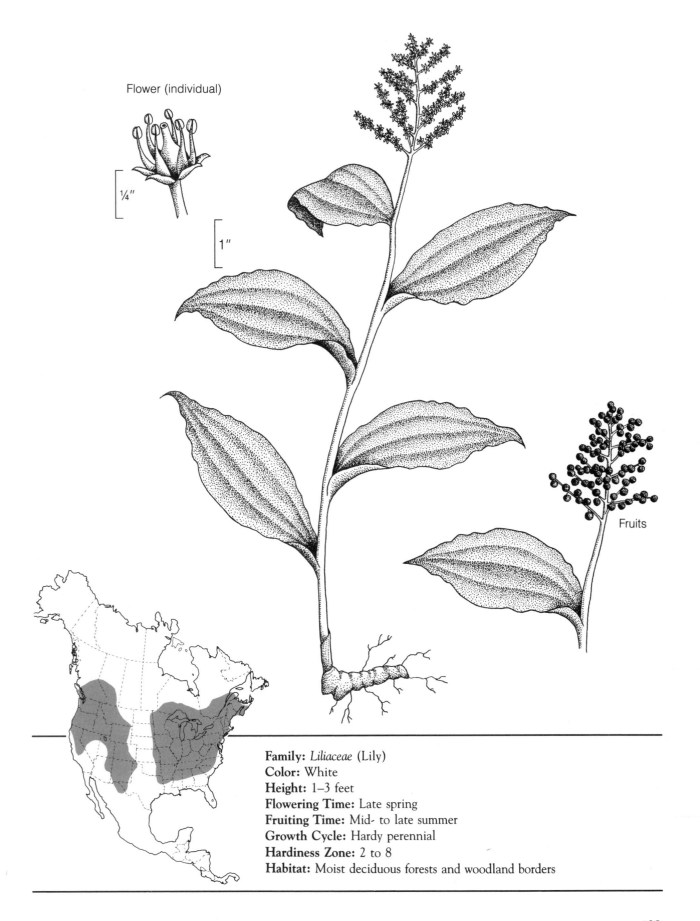

Flower (individual)

¼"

1"

Fruits

Family: *Liliaceae* (Lily)
Color: White
Height: 1–3 feet
Flowering Time: Late spring
Fruiting Time: Mid- to late summer
Growth Cycle: Hardy perennial
Hardiness Zone: 2 to 8
Habitat: Moist deciduous forests and woodland borders

FALSE SOLOMON'S SEAL (*Smilacina racemosa*)

YELLOW CLINTONIA

Clintonia borealis

Corn lily, bluebead lily, *clintonie boreale*

Named in honor of DeWitt Clinton, an avid naturalist and former governor of New York, this perennial has attractive features from spring until fall. Once established it makes a stunning ground cover, punctuated by yellow flowers in the late spring and iridescent blue fruits in the summer. Yellow clintonia has 2 to 4 oval leaves which are usually 6 inches long but may reach 10 inches under optimal conditions. Clusters of lustrous leaves arise from creeping rhizomes that branch out each summer as they grow along just under the soil surface. The leaves remain green until they wither in midfall, when next year's shoots extend to the surface of the soil. Clusters of 1 to 8 flowers are borne on a 6–15-inch stem overtopping the leaves. Each flower has attractive brown anthers and 6 yellow, lilylike divisions. The flowers last for about 2 weeks, after which the developing berry fruit matures to a brilliant cobalt blue, inspiring the common name bluebead lily. Although the young leaves, which taste like cucumber, are edible, the berries are not — except by chipmunks and birds, which relish them.

CULTURE   Yellow clintonia is difficult to grow at elevations below 1000 feet or where summer temperatures are substantially above 75°F. They require cool, moist, acid (pH 4–5) conditions in order to flourish. They thrive in partial to full shade at lower elevations, although in mountain environments they are frequently found growing in full sun. Apply a heavy mulch of mixed pine and deciduous leaves in the fall and leave it on during the spring.

PROPAGATION   The easiest method of propagating clintonia is from seed. Collect ripe fruit in the late summer or early fall and separate the ⅛ inch, glossy brown, elliptical seeds from the pulp. Plant the seeds ¼ inch deep in permanent locations or in flats that are left outdoors over winter. Seeds must be stratified to germinate. Although some seeds may take more than one year to germinate, most should germinate the first spring. Seedlings will have a single leaf at first, but with time leaves will increase in number and size. It takes several years for the young plants to mature and produce flowers. Root division should be done in the early summer as soon as flowering has been completed or in the late fall after the next season's shoots have formed. Be careful when handling the rhizomes and roots, because they are brittle. Plant the root section about 1 inch deep with the new shoot tip just at the surface of the soil.

COMPANIONS   Purple trillium, eastern trout lily, bunchberry, wintergreen, shinleaf, partridgeberry.

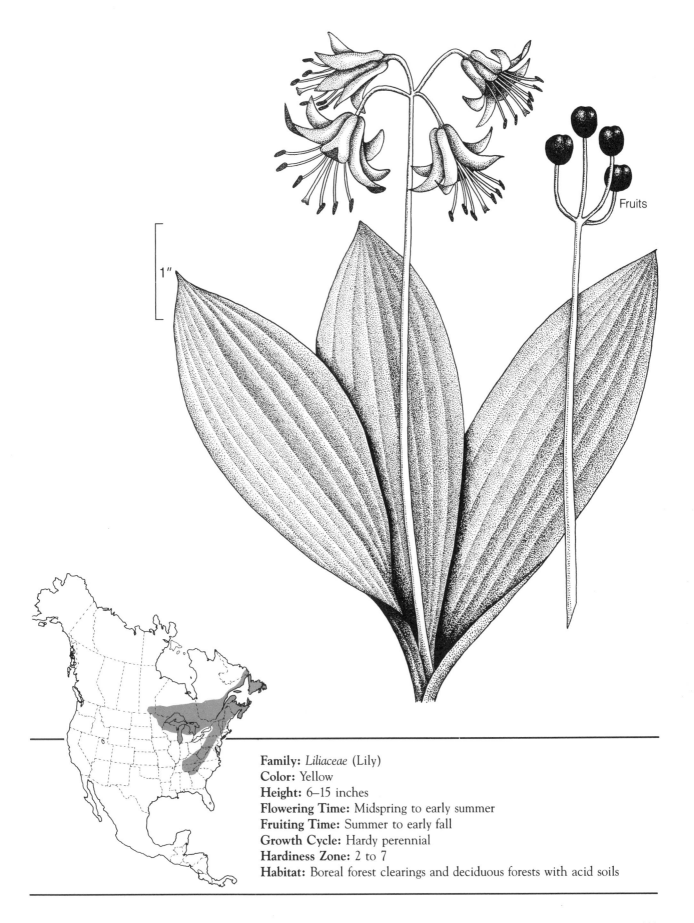

Fruits

1"

Family: *Liliaceae* (Lily)
Color: Yellow
Height: 6–15 inches
Flowering Time: Midspring to early summer
Fruiting Time: Summer to early fall
Growth Cycle: Hardy perennial
Hardiness Zone: 2 to 7
Habitat: Boreal forest clearings and deciduous forests with acid soils

YELLOW CLINTONIA (*Clintonia borealis*)

BUNCHBERRY

Cornus canadensis

Dwarf cornell, crackerberry, puddingberry, *quatre-temps, rougets*

This relative of the flowering dogwood tree attains a height of only 4–8 inches. Bunchberry spreads by slender, forking woody rhizomes, which creep along just under the ground litter and give rise to attractive colonies, forming dense carpets over time. Whorls of 3 to 9 but usually 4 thick, lustrous 1–3-inch-long leaves are overtopped by a cluster of small, greenish white flowers. What appear to be four creamy white petals are actually bracts, which fall away as the fruits develop. The bright red, ¼-inch, berrylike fruits, each with a 2-seeded, light brown stone, are clustered in spectacular bunches. The fruits, often persisting into winter, are edible but unrewarding except to birds such as grouse, vireos, and thrushes, which relish them.

CULTURE

Bunchberry grows best in cool, damp, even wet locations in regions that do not have excessively hot summers. It is an ideal ground cover where there is partial shade and the soils are acid (pH 4–5) with ample conifer mulch and organic matter. In the sun the plant will do well, but its leaves tend to be much smaller, thicker, and not as deep green.

PROPAGATION

Bunchberry may be propagated by seed or divisions of the rhizomes. Harvest mature fruit in the fall, remove the stones from the pulp, and plant them ½ inch deep in a mixture of peat moss and sand. Keep the soil moist. Seeds require moist stratification in order to germinate, and if planted in flats, they should be left outdoors for the winter. Germination of some of the seeds will occur 1 to 3 months into the spring, and the seedlings can be transplanted to permanent locations in the fall. You might want to add new seeds to the flats at this time and leave them out a second winter, because many of the seeds planted the first year may not have germinated. Flowering usually occurs in the third year. You can divide the rhizomes in the early spring or late fall. Cut 6-inch segments of the rhizome, each with at least one bud. Set the divisions ¼ inch deep, mulch them with conifer needles, and keep moist.

COMPANIONS

Yellow clintonia, wintergreen, wild lily-of-the-valley, partridgeberry, shinleaf.

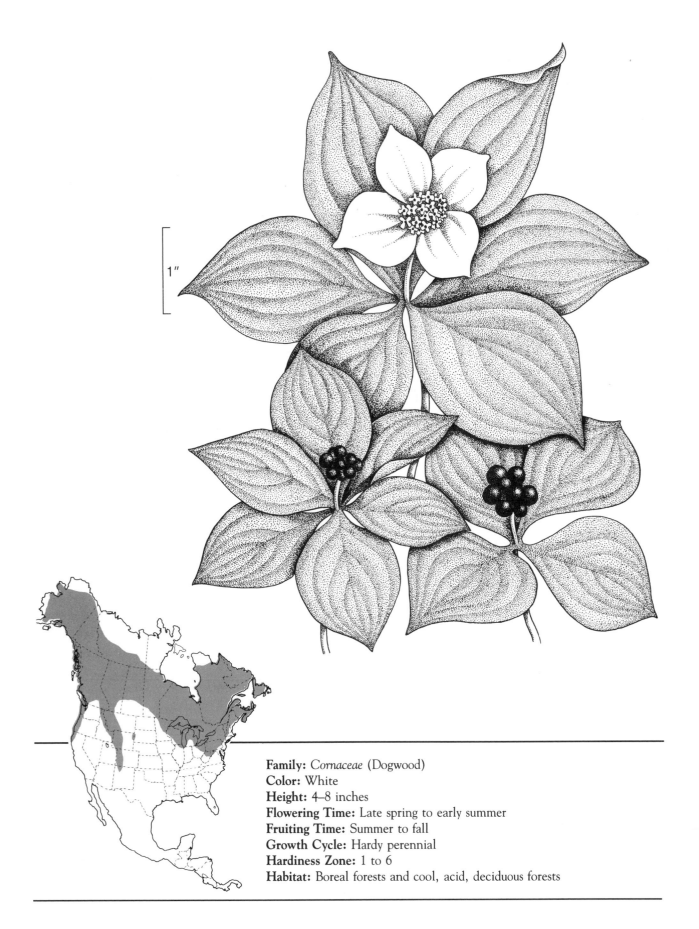

1"

Family: *Cornaceae* (Dogwood)
Color: White
Height: 4–8 inches
Flowering Time: Late spring to early summer
Fruiting Time: Summer to fall
Growth Cycle: Hardy perennial
Hardiness Zone: 1 to 6
Habitat: Boreal forests and cool, acid, deciduous forests

BUNCHBERRY *(Cornus canadensis)*

PARTRIDGEBERRY

Mitchella repens

Twinberry, two-eyed-berry, squawvine, running box, *pain de perdrix*

A favorite for indoor terraria, partridgeberry is even more effective outdoors as a ground cover in cool, shady locations. The stems of this hardy perennial trail over the ground, barely reaching an inch in height. Its pairs of small, round, dark green, glossy leaves are evergreen and frequently variegated with white. The flowers, like the leaves, come in pairs, and are usually white or very light pink, fragrant, and shaped like small trumpets with 4 pointed lobes. Different partridgeberry plants may produce different types of flowers, some with stamens longer than the pistil and others with the pistil longer than the stamens. These two flower types increase the likelihood that insects will transfer pollen between different plants as they search for nectar. After pollination the 2 paired flowers fuse, and their 2 ovaries produce a single red, berrylike, edible fruit. The fruits, which have a slight pepperminty taste, contain 4 to 8 bony gray nutlets, and persist through the winter, or until grouse, quail, or other ground-foraging birds find them. The common name "squawvine" arose from the plant's use by Native Americans to ease childbirth.

CULTURE

Partridgeberry grows best in cool, moist, shaded and, especially, humus-rich soils. It has its maximum growth when temperatures are below 60°F in the spring before the deciduous trees have leafed out. It can be grown on dry to moist soils but prefers the latter. Partridgeberry will also tolerate a range of soil acidity conditions from pH 4–6. A light mulch of pine or hemlock needles can supply the proper organic matter and acidity conditions.

PROPAGATION

The easiest way to propagate partridgeberry is by dividing or cutting the trailing stems. One method is to cut a 6–12-inch piece from the leading tip of the plant in spring, carefully uprooting the section to avoid breaking off the small roots. Plant the section in well-drained soil into which you have worked compost and peat moss. Keep the cuttings moist and they will take root with ease. The cuttings will eventually spread, and generally bear flowers the second year. Propagation from seed is usually much slower. The seeds require moist stratification (40°F for at least 6 weeks) for proper germination. Gather the fruits in the fall and remove the nutlets from the pulp. Plant the seeds ¼ inch deep in flats containing a mixture of sand, compost and peat moss. Cover the flats with a ¼-inch-thick layer of pine needles and leave out for the winter. Germination in the spring generally takes 2 to 3 weeks once the temperature has risen above 60°F. Transplant the seedlings to permanent locations in the fall.

COMPANIONS

Wintergreen, purple trillium, yellow clintonia, shinleaf, bunchberry.

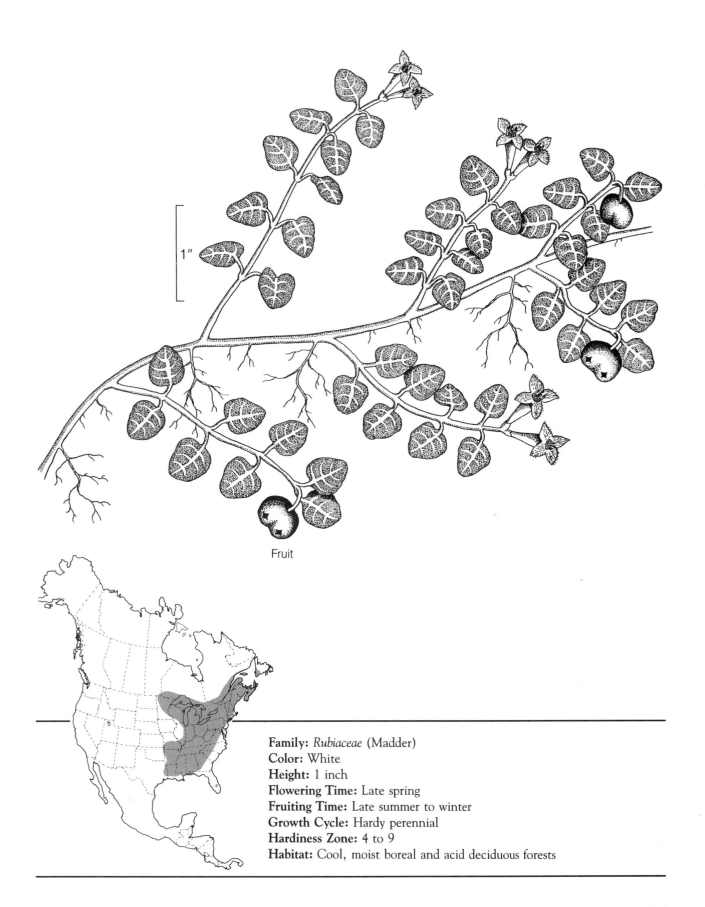

Fruit

Family: *Rubiaceae* (Madder)
Color: White
Height: 1 inch
Flowering Time: Late spring
Fruiting Time: Late summer to winter
Growth Cycle: Hardy perennial
Hardiness Zone: 4 to 9
Habitat: Cool, moist boreal and acid deciduous forests

PARTRIDGEBERRY *(Mitchella repens)*

WILD LEEK

Allium tricoccum

Ramp, *ail des bois*

Wild leek is a favorite of edible-wild-plant fanciers, but not of dairy farmers whose cows produce ill-flavored milk when they graze upon it. Groups of 2 to 3 fleshy, spatula-shaped leaves, some up to a foot long, emerge in the early spring. Often one encounters dense carpets of wild leeks covering the forest floor. The leaves, which like the 1–2-inch edible bulbs have a strong onion flavor, remain green for only about a month and then yellow and wither as flowering begins. As the leaves disappear, a hooded flower stalk emerges from the ground and reaches 6–12 inches in height. A hemispherical cluster of small, greenish white, 6-petaled flowers, each with 6 stamens, bursts forth at the top of the stalk. The fruit of the wild leek is a ⅓-inch papery capsule containing 3 shiny black ⅛-inch seeds. Birds disseminate the seeds, apparently mistaking them for berries. Native Americans ate baked wild leeks and used them as a condiment for soups.

CULTURE — Wild leek is a plant of rich woods and thickets. Although it is adapted to survive in shady conditions, with leaves that go into dormancy as the forest trees overhead are leafing out, wild leek grows best where it is sunny at least during the early spring. Plant in humus-rich soil or work ample amounts of compost to a depth of at least 6 inches. Wild leek thrives in neutral to mildly acidic soil, so adjust the pH to 6–7. The soil should be moist during the spring and early summer when wild leeks are in leaf and flower.

PROPAGATION — Wild leek are easily propagated from seeds and divisions of bulb offsets. The hard black seeds should be collected as they become exposed during the summer. Plant the seeds ½ inch deep in outdoor flats containing a mixture of loam and compost. Carefully transplant the small bulbs the following summer, setting them 1–1½ inches deep. Bulbs more than 1 inch in diameter frequently produce small offset bulbs which can be divided in the summer as the fruits are maturing. Since the conspicuous leaves will have disappeared by the time you divide the offsets, it is a good idea to mark the location of choice plants before the leaves wither. Plant the offsets 1½ inches deep and give them a good top dressing of compost.

COMPANIONS — Purple trillium, wild ginger, Dutchman's breeches, eastern columbine.

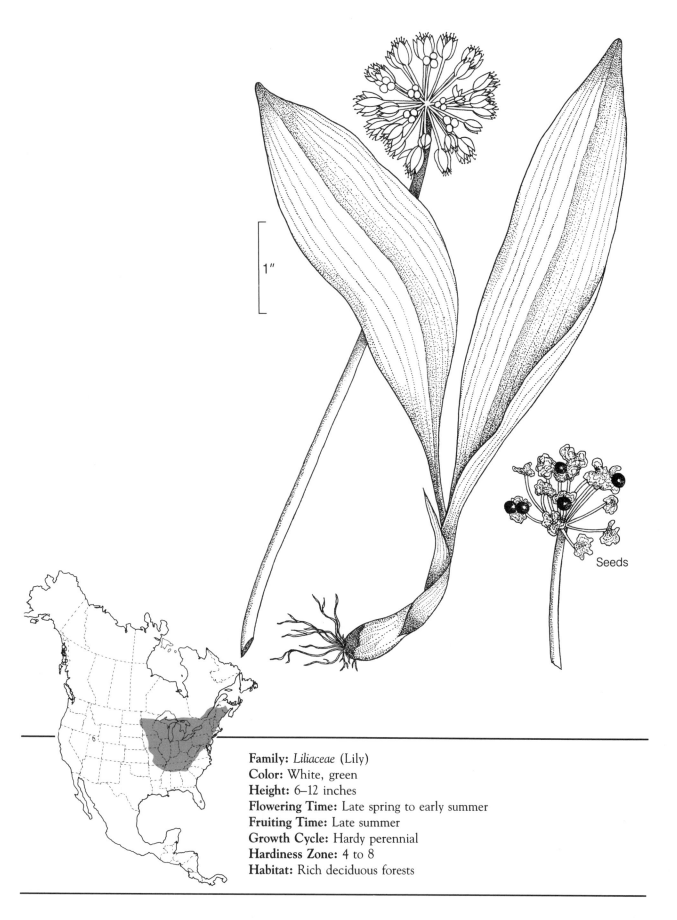

Family: *Liliaceae* (Lily)
Color: White, green
Height: 6–12 inches
Flowering Time: Late spring to early summer
Fruiting Time: Late summer
Growth Cycle: Hardy perennial
Hardiness Zone: 4 to 8
Habitat: Rich deciduous forests

1″

Seeds

WILD LEEK *(Allium tricoccum)*

SHINLEAF

Pyrola elliptica

Pyrole elliptique

Shinleaf is not easy to bring into the garden, but it is one of the few eastern woodland plants that flower in midsummer in deep shade. It is worth the effort, therefore, if you desire a prolonged succession of flowering hardy perennials. The dull green evergreen leaves are about 3 inches long and cluster in a rosette arrangement at the ground surface. They resemble pear leaves and are elliptical, as the scientific name indicates. The flower stalk is 4–12 inches high and bears 3 to 21 nodding white flowers, frequently tinged with pink or veined with green. Bees and flies pollinate the fragrant flowers. Each of the 5-petaled flowers is about ⅓ inch across and has a long, pendant pistil. The fruit is a small capsule with many elongated brown seeds so fine they are blown away like dust in the wind. Shinleaf has a creeping underground root and stem system, and frequently small colonies of the plant can be found growing together. The common name of the plant refers to its use as a shin plaster for wounds.

CULTURE

Shinleaf is a plant of deep shade. It can be grown in either moist or relatively dry soils, but has a definite preference for acidic soil conditions (pH 4.5–5.5). It also grows best where there is ample organic matter in the soil. Liberal additions of compost, adjusted to the appropriate acidity by the addition of peat moss and conifer needles, aid in the establishment and maintenance of the species.

PROPAGATION

Shinleaf is difficult to propagate from seed because it is slow to germinate. The seeds should be planted where they can overwinter and receive cold treatment. Prepare a seedbed or flat with a mixture of sandy loam, compost, and peat moss. Sprinkle the seeds on top and gently scratch them into the soil or cover them with a dusting (⅛ inch) of finely milled peat moss. Keep the soil moist and be patient. An alternative is to propagate shinleaf by dividing the runners in the early spring or midfall, replanting the divisions about 18 inches apart with the buds just at the surface of the soil.

COMPANIONS

Partridgeberry, wintergreen, wild lily-of-the-valley, bunchberry, yellow clintonia.

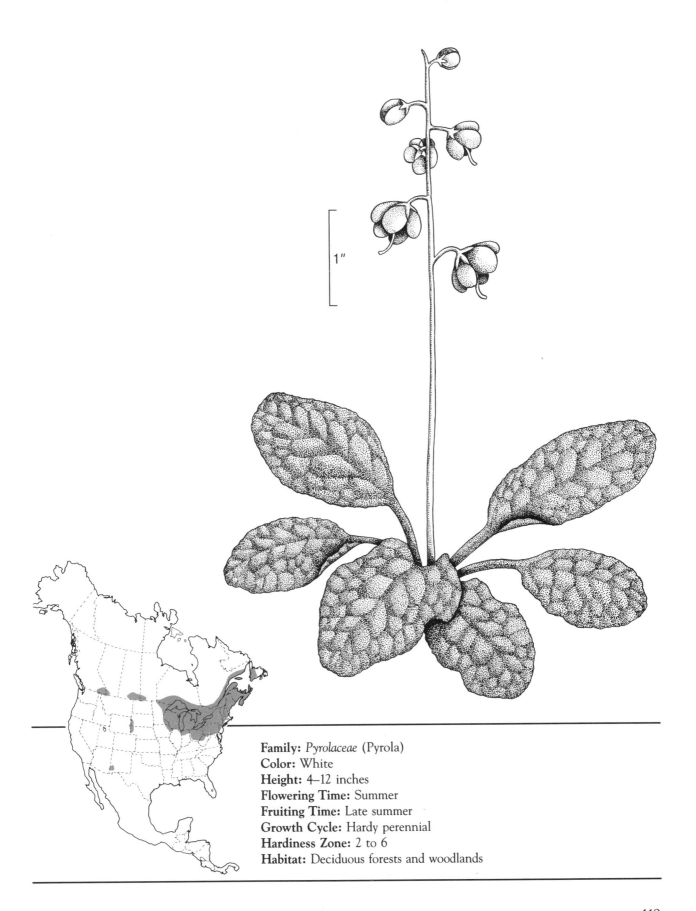

Family: *Pyrolaceae* (Pyrola)
Color: White
Height: 4–12 inches
Flowering Time: Summer
Fruiting Time: Late summer
Growth Cycle: Hardy perennial
Hardiness Zone: 2 to 6
Habitat: Deciduous forests and woodlands

1″

SHINLEAF *(Pyrola elliptica)*

WOOD LILY

Lilium philadelphicum
(Lilium umbellatum)

Wild red lily, flame lily, *lis de Philadelphie*

This attractive lily grows both in open woodlands of eastern North America and in grasslands from western Canada to New Mexico. One of the few lily species with flowers that point upward, wood lilies have gaps between the bases of the petals and sepals, which allow rainwater to drain out. The 6 large brown anthers open and release pollen in dry weather but close when it rains. Flower colors range from bright red in the West to orange in the East, but all varieties have purple spots on the petals and petal-like sepals. As the flowers age, their colors subtly fade. Flowers occur singly or in clusters atop an 8–36-inch stem. The leaves in the eastern variety are arranged in whorls around the stem, but in the western variety they are scattered along the stem. The roots of this hardy perennial arise from a deep-seated, white, scaly bulb an inch or so in diameter. New bulbs are formed at the sides of the mature bulb each year. The fruit of the wood lily is a 1–2-inch capsule densely packed with flat, ¼-inch seeds with papery wings.

CULTURE

While one variety of wood lily will grow in swamps, most grow in relatively dry prairies. One of the most drought-tolerant lily species, it generally grows best in well-drained soils. Although wood lilies grow in the light shade of open woodlands, they should be planted where they can get full sun for at least part of the day. They do best in humus-rich soils that are moderately acidic (pH 4–6).

PROPAGATION

Propagation is easiest from divisions of the scaly bulb which can be dug as soon as the lily goes into dormancy and the seed is ripe in the late summer. Be careful when digging the bulbs not to damage the roots of the mature plant. Plant the small offset bulbs about 3 inches deep and mulch with pine needles and oak leaves. Alternatively, plant individual bulb scales of the mature bulb ½ inch deep in flats filled with light sandy soil mixed with peat moss and leave out over winter. Replant the old bulb about 5 inches deep. When seedlings become dormant the next year, transplant the small bulbs 3 inches deep in the desired location. It will take several years for the plants to reach maturity and flower. Propagation from seed is slower, but generally successful. Plant seeds in outdoor flats as in bulb scale propagation, keeping the seedbed moist but not wet. The seeds will generally germinate in the fall, overwinter as tiny bulbs, and resume growth the following spring. Transplant the small bulbs when they are dormant the following summer. Seedlings from seeds will generally produce a single leaf the first year and take 3 to 5 years to reach maturity and flower. Since cross-pollination is necessary for wood lily to produce seeds, plant several bulbs in your garden.

COMPANIONS

Bluets, Solomon's seal, mayapple, common blue violet, false Solomon's seal, pasture rose, black-eyed Susan.

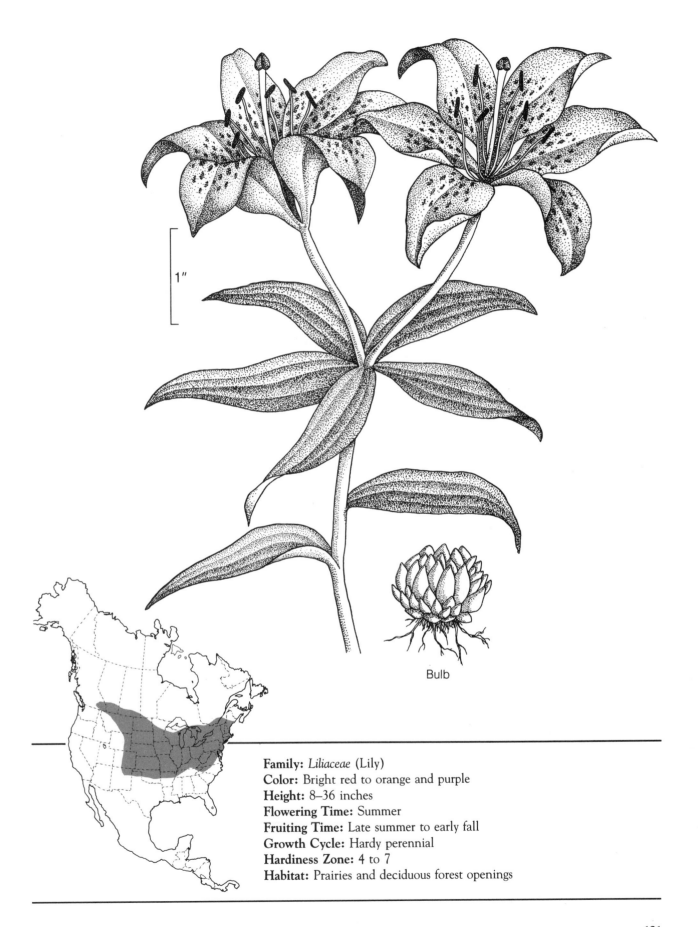

1"

Bulb

Family: *Liliaceae* (Lily)
Color: Bright red to orange and purple
Height: 8–36 inches
Flowering Time: Summer
Fruiting Time: Late summer to early fall
Growth Cycle: Hardy perennial
Hardiness Zone: 4 to 7
Habitat: Prairies and deciduous forest openings

WOOD LILY *(Lilium philadelphicum)*

WINTERGREEN

Gaultheria procumbens

Teaberry, checkerberry, *petit thé des bois, gaulthérie couchée*

Wintergreen is as desirable to grow for its foliage as for its red berries and white flowers. Both the fruits and the leathery evergreen leaves contain the aromatic oil of wintergreen. Although the leaves and fruits of wintergreen or "teaberry" are frequently used in herb teas, oil of wintergreen is toxic if consumed internally in a concentrated form. The young leaves, not as leathery as the old ones, are a light shade of green and refreshing to chew. Wintergreen spreads from creeping stolons just below the surface of the soil. Tiny, slender, semi-woody stems rise to a height of 2–4 inches and in summer bear 1 or 2 nodding white flowers less than ½ inch long. The urn-shaped, 5-lobed flowers dangle below the ¾-inch leaves. The fruits are red, pulpy berries with many small brown seeds. The flesh of the berry becomes mealy and pink with age, and sometimes it remains attached to the plant until the next spring. Chipmunks, grouse, mice, black bears, and birds eat the fruits, and deer eat the leaves during the winter. Wintergreen has long been used as a folk medicine cure for toothaches. The plant contains methyl salicylate, a compound that is similar to aspirin.

CULTURE Wintergreen is quite tolerant of shade, but it grows and flowers best in sunny openings with light shade during midday. It is not choosy about soil conditions as long as the soil is acid (pH 4–6.5) and has abundant organic matter. It can be grown on soils ranging from dry sands to wet peats, and is found growing naturally in piney woods, oak forests, and bogs.

PROPAGATION Wintergreen is relatively easy to grow even though it may spread only 4 to 6 inches a year. Make cuttings of the stems and runners in the early summer before they become woody, and plant them in a flat with a moistened mixture of sand and peat moss. Transplant the cuttings to an appropriate location the following spring. The seed of wintergreen requires moist stratification (40°F) for 1 to 2 months in order to germinate. Collect the fruits in the fall, sow the seeds thickly on a mixture of sand and fine-milled peat moss, and cover the seeds with a thin layer of peat moss. Germination may be slow, so don't give up for at least two springs. It is wise to cover the overwintering flats with hardware cloth or screen to prevent rodents from eating the seeds. Remove the screen in the spring and provide light shade. Transplant to permanent locations in the fall or the following spring.

COMPANIONS Partridgeberry, bunchberry, wild lily-of-the-valley, yellow clintonia, shinleaf.

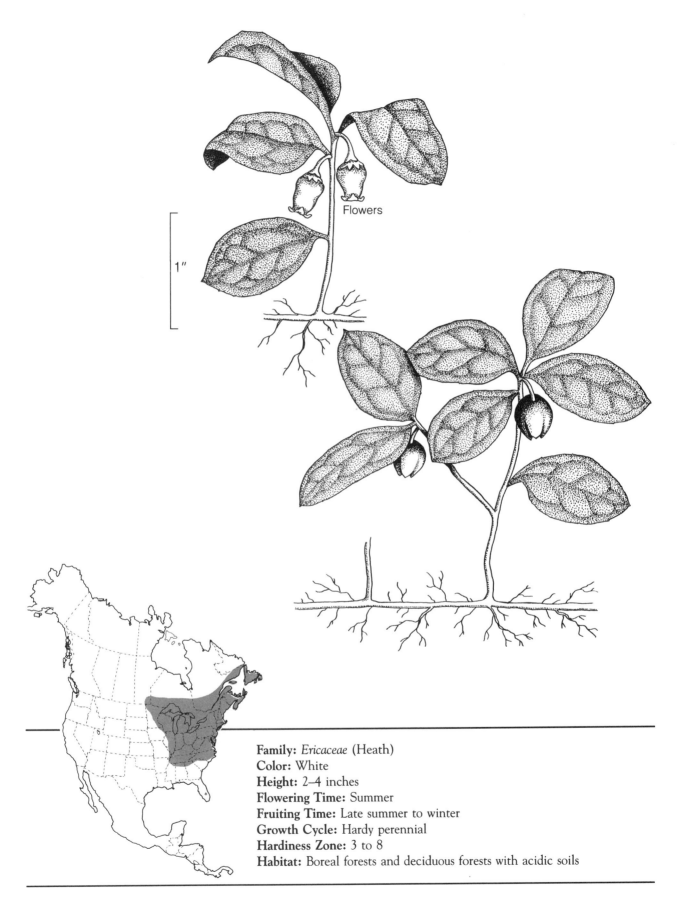

Flowers

1"

Family: *Ericaceae* (Heath)
Color: White
Height: 2–4 inches
Flowering Time: Summer
Fruiting Time: Late summer to winter
Growth Cycle: Hardy perennial
Hardiness Zone: 3 to 8
Habitat: Boreal forests and deciduous forests with acidic soils

WINTERGREEN *(Gaultheria procumbens)*

WETLAND SPECIES

The plants included in this section are ideal for poolside, stream bank, or even swamp forest gardens. They grow naturally in damp or even waterlogged soils, but can also be grown in any garden as long as the soils are moist.

You should be very cautious about introducing certain species into a wetland garden. **Spiked** or **Purple loosestrife** (*Lythrum salicaria*), a European species that unfortunately is sometimes included in commercial wildflower mixes, has 2–3-foot-high spikes of magenta flowers that appear in midsummer. Although attractive, the species is overly aggressive, often crowding out other native wetland species. The common **reed** (*Phragmities communis*) is a dramatic wetland grass that can grow 10–15 feet high. Its foot-long plumes of fruits are radiant white in the autumn sun, but too quickly it will force aside other native species. Once established, reeds spread rapidly by very deep, inch-thick rhizomes, making them exceedingly difficult to eradicate.

COMPANIONS There are numerous companion species that should be considered when planning a wetland garden. **Foamflower** (page 98) and **common blue violet** (page 90) grow naturally on stream banks and shady damp areas, and **bluets** (page 142) can even be found in the crevices of boulders in brooks. **Bunchberry** (page 112) growing among streamside mosses creates a striking scene both in spring when the white-bracted flowers are in bloom, and later in the year when the cluster of bright red berries appears.

Consider the nature of the wetland in selecting companion species. If your wetland garden is sunny and open, there are many species that you can choose. **Sweet flag** (*Acorus calamus*) has an irislike leaf with a prominent vein running down the center, but its cob-shaped spadix of yellow flowers looks nothing like an iris. Although sweet flag is edible, iris is poisonous. **Swamp milkweed** (*Asclepias incarnata*) has round clusters of rose and magenta flowers atop its 2–3-foot-high stems. It produces the familiar milkweed pod fruits, but is not as weedy as its relative, the common milkweed. The **rose mallow** (*Hibiscus palustris*) is a spectacular wildflower of coastal areas in this region. The 3–6-

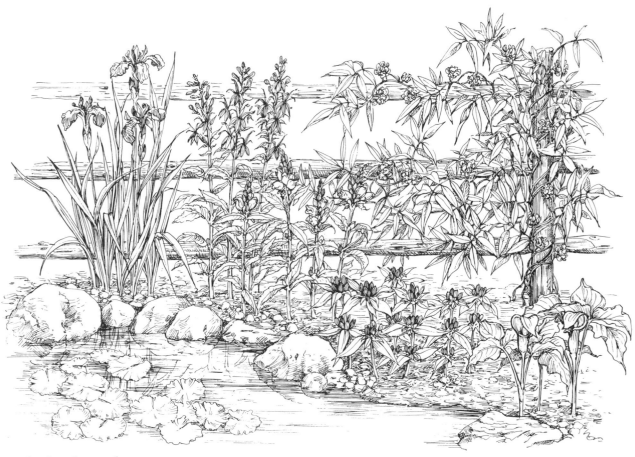

Wetland garden, early summer.

A. Larger blue flag
B. Cardinal flower
C. Groundnut
D. Jack-in-the-pulpit
E. Closed gentian
F. Turtlehead

foot-high stems bear several bright pink, hollyhock-like flowers up to 6 inches across.

Other species grow better in shady environments. **Virginia bluebells** (*Mertensia virginica*) with its loose coil of light blue flowers, and **cowslip** or **marsh marigold** (*Caltha palustris*) with its large, yellow buttercup flowers, are excellent choices for shady wetlands. Both of these species flower in the spring and their foliage withers just after the leaves come out on the trees overhead. The **sweet white violet** (*Viola pallens*), with its fragrant, twisted-petaled flowers, blooms about the same time, and has foliage that persists through the summer.

Ferns are a natural addition to the wetland garden, and they come in all sizes. **Ostrich fern** (*Matteuccia struthiopteris*) and **royal fern** (*Osmunda regalis*) will grow to 6 feet under optimal conditions. **Interrupted fern** (*Osmunda claytoniana*) and **cinnamon fern** (*O. cinnamomea*) usually grow to 3 feet, and **marsh fern** (*Dryopteris thelypteris* or *Thelypteris palustris*) is usually only a foot or so high.

JACK-IN-THE-PULPIT

Arisaema triphyllum

Indian turnip, *oignon sauvage, petit prêcheur*

Jack-in-the-pulpit not only has a most intriguing flower, but it also bears a spectacular cluster of bright red-orange fruits. With adequate shade and moisture, this perennial may reach a height of 3 feet, although 6–24 inches is more common. The flower consists of a central column, commonly called a "Jack," but referred to botanically as a *spadix*. Bearing small male flowers toward the top or small female flowers at the base, the spadix is enveloped by a purple-and-white-striped, hooded petal called a *spathe*. The spathe looks like a pulpit in which the spadix or "Jack" is standing, inspiring the plant's common name. Jack-in-the-pulpit flowers sometimes change sexes, as mentioned on page 5, depending upon the growing conditions of the previous year. As the fruits start to develop, the spathe withers and frequently enshrouds them. The fruits turn from a bright summer green to red-orange as they mature in the late summer and early fall. Pheasants, wild turkeys, and other fruit-eating birds and mammals usually consume them before winter. The rootstock of the Jack-in-the-pulpit is a 1–2-inch corm that looks like a gladiolus bulb. Some botanists divide Jack-in-the-pulpit into three distinct species according to differences in the sizes of mature plants and the colors of the flowers and leaves. The Chippewa called this plant "bite-the-mouth" from the painful irritations that result from eating raw corms. The corms are edible only after drying and processing to remove the toxic compound calcium oxalate; however, the use of Jack-in-the-pulpit corms as a food by Native Americans inspired its common name, Indian turnip.

CULTURE   Jack-in-the-pulpit will grow most vigorously in moist, shady locations, in soils that are seasonally wet. When grown in full sun the plants tend to be small and stunted. Best results are attained by growing this species in moderately to slightly acidic soils (pH 5–6.5). If you desire female plants, which produce the attractive fruits, keep the soil moist and annually top-dress the plants with compost.

PROPAGATION   Jack-in-the-pulpit is successfully propagated both from seed and by root divisions. Collect fruits in the fall when the berries are red. Remove the ⅛-inch brown seeds from the pulp and plant them ½ inch deep where plants are desired or in flats to be left out over winter. For proper germination the following spring, the seed must be moist-stratified for 6 to 12 weeks at temperatures below 40°F. Seedlings will mature and produce flowers the second year. Root divisions can be made in the fall and the segments planted about 6 inches apart at depths 2 to 3 times their diameters. It is prudent either to wear gloves or to wash your hands immediately after handling the corms, since people with sensitive skin may develop rashes upon touching them.

COMPANIONS   Larger blue flag, turtlehead, foamflower, purple trillium.

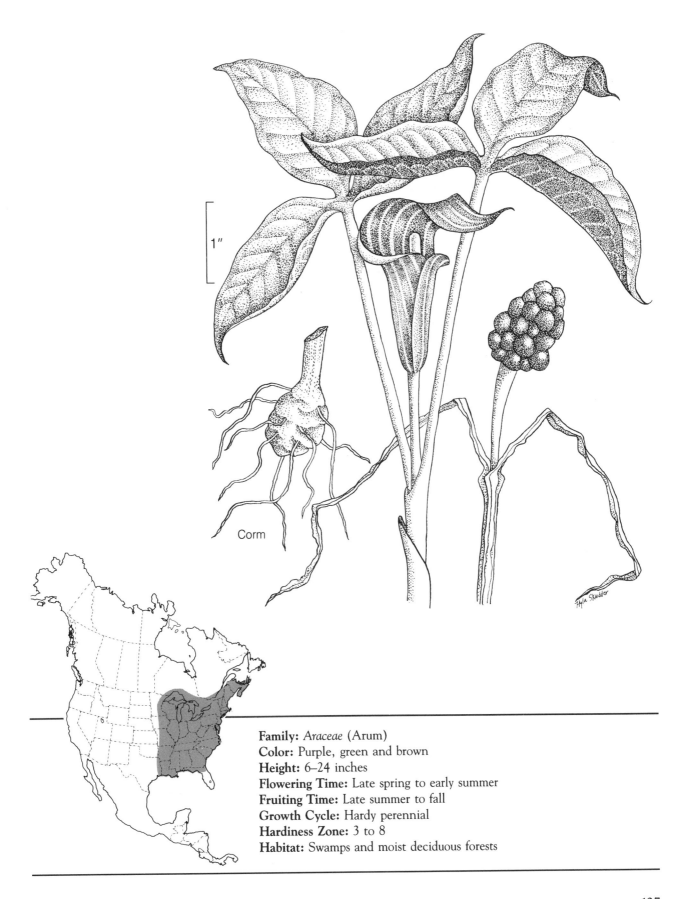

Corm

Family: *Araceae* (Arum)
Color: Purple, green and brown
Height: 6–24 inches
Flowering Time: Late spring to early summer
Fruiting Time: Late summer to fall
Growth Cycle: Hardy perennial
Hardiness Zone: 3 to 8
Habitat: Swamps and moist deciduous forests

JACK-IN-THE-PULPIT (*Arisaema triphyllum*)

LARGER BLUE FLAG

Iris versicolor

Wild iris, blue flag, *clajeux*

The larger blue flag strongly resembles its domesticated relatives which, like it, derive their Latin name from the goddess of the rainbow. The firm sword-shaped leaves, sometimes purplish at the base, are 8–36 inches long and generally overtopped by a flower stalk or scape. Each stalk bears 1 or 2 blue flowers which look like slightly scaled-down versions of the garden irises. As with other irises, the flowers emerge from a papery spathe and have a distinctive 3-part arrangement. The 3 true petals point skyward, and the 3 petal-like sepals, sometimes called "falls," droop down and flutter in the breeze, giving the plant the common name blue flag. Between the petals and the sepals are 3 arching, blue, petal-like styles ending in thin stigma lips. Hidden beneath the styles are the stamens. This unusual arrangement of floral parts ensures cross-pollination. When a bee lands on a flower, it is guided to the nectar by the dark purple lines on the sepals, a route that takes it first past the stigma, which is dusted by pollen from the bee's back, and then past the stamens where the insect inadvertently picks up another load of pollen. The flowers last for 3 to 6 days and shrivel as the oval 3-part fruit capsule starts to develop. The seeds are glossy, brown, and disc-shaped. The stout, light-colored, creeping rhizomes contain a poisonous substance, iridin.

CULTURE
The larger blue flag is a plant of wet meadows, stream banks and marshes. Even though it can tolerate complete submergence, it is not necessary to have the soil constantly wet, and the plant can be easily grown in most gardens. Full sun or light shade and a soil with a pH anywhere between 5 and 7 are the only other requirements. This is not a demanding plant.

PROPAGATION
Propagation of blue flag is similar to the division of most garden iris. People with sensitive skin may develop a skin rash upon touching iris rootstocks, so wear gloves or wash your hands immediately after handling the rhizomes. Once flowering is over in the summer, cut the leaves back to about 6 inches and divide the rhizomes with a sharp knife. Plant each piece of rhizome with its attached clump of leaves so that the root system lies horizontally just below the soil. Many of the divisions will flower the next year. Seeds can be collected as the fruits turn brown and split open. Immediately plant the seeds ⅓ inch deep in the desired location or in flats containing a mixture of peat moss and loam. Keep the seeds moist and leave them outdoors over winter to enhance their germination the following spring. Seedlings can be carefully transplanted from the flats in the spring. It takes about three years for plants from seeds to mature and flower. Once established, larger blue flag will spread by self-seeding and extension of its rhizomes.

COMPANIONS
Cardinal flower, Jack-in-the-pulpit, turtlehead, false Solomon's seal, closed gentian.

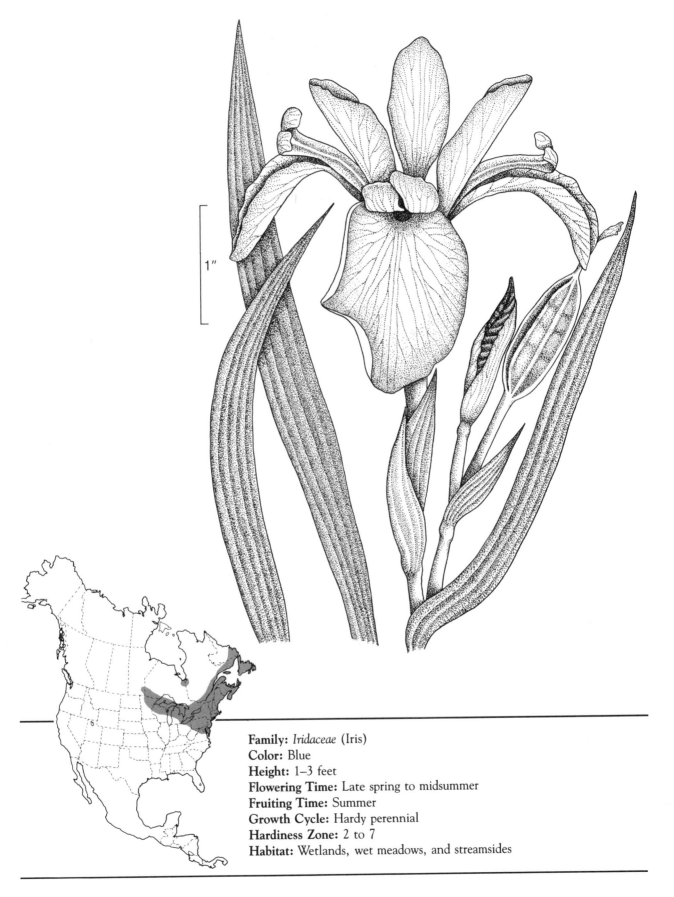

1"

Family: *Iridaceae* (Iris)
Color: Blue
Height: 1–3 feet
Flowering Time: Late spring to midsummer
Fruiting Time: Summer
Growth Cycle: Hardy perennial
Hardiness Zone: 2 to 7
Habitat: Wetlands, wet meadows, and streamsides

LARGER BLUE FLAG (*Iris versicolor*)

CARDINAL FLOWER
Lobelia cardinalis

Lobélie cardinale

One of the least subtle of wildflowers, cardinal flower is a beautiful addition to any sunny, moist location. As early as 1626, it was introduced by colonists to Old World gardens. Queen Henrietta Maria of England is alleged to have remarked that its bright red flowers reminded her of a cardinal's vestments, and thereby gave the plant its common name. Usually 1–3 feet high, the plants may reach 5 feet under optimum conditions. The scarlet to deep red, inch-long flowers, borne in open clusters at the top of the stem, are tubular with 2 erect lobes on the upper lip and 3 pointed lobes on the lower lip. The fused stamens and style protrude from between the lobes of the upper lip and have a hairy white "beard" that looks like a water droplet. Pollen is shed from the anthers before the flower's stigma is mature, and dusts the heads of hummingbirds, the main pollinators, as they drink the sweet nectar. Actually, not all cardinal flowers produce nectar, but those that do sometimes have holes chewed through the base of their tubes by bumblebees taking a shortcut. The fruit is a 2-part capsule containing many small (1/20-inch), elliptical, shiny brown seeds with fluted projections.

CULTURE
Cardinal flower is a plant of moist, wet, or even submerged soils that are partially exposed to the sun, but is quite adaptable to normal garden conditions. It grows well in slightly acidic to neutral soils (pH 5.5–7) but soil pH is not as important as maintenance of soil moisture. This perennial is hardy to zone 4, but should be mulched for the winter in areas prone to frost heaving.

PROPAGATION
Cardinal flower is easily propagated by seed, division, or layering. Germination is enhanced by moist stratification and requires exposure of the seed to light. In the fall, sprinkle the seeds on top of humus-rich soil in flats, moisten, and cover them with a thin layer of mulch. Leave the flats outdoors over winter and remove the mulch in the spring. Cover the top of the flat with a sheet of transparent plastic film. Germination should occur after 3 to 4 weeks of warm spring weather. Allow the seedlings to grow the first summer in the flat and then transplant them to their permanent locations in the fall or following spring. Plants from seed will usually flower the second year. Root division is also an option. The best time to make root divisions is in the early spring. Set the rootstocks 6–12 inches apart with the buds just at the soil surface, and keep them moist. To propagate by "layering," in midsummer, carefully bend the stem over so it is lying on the ground, stake the tip, cover the stem with 1/4 inch of soil, and keep moist. Along the buried stem new roots will form and new shoots will emerge. In the fall the stem segments between the new shoots can be cut and the new plants can be transplanted.

COMPANIONS
Larger blue flag, turtlehead, closed gentian, New England aster.

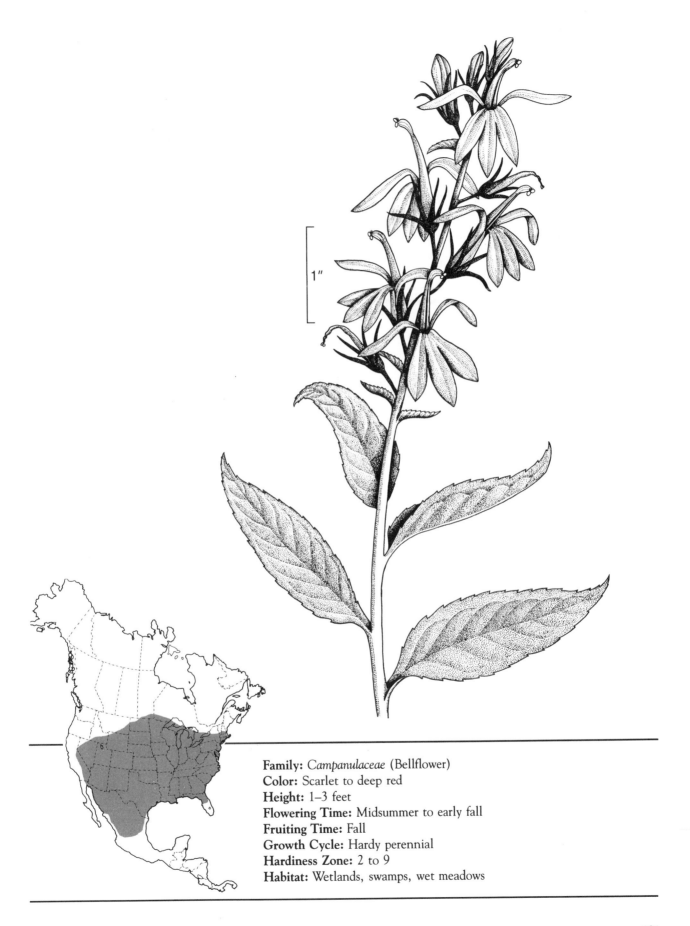

Family: *Campanulaceae* (Bellflower)
Color: Scarlet to deep red
Height: 1–3 feet
Flowering Time: Midsummer to early fall
Fruiting Time: Fall
Growth Cycle: Hardy perennial
Hardiness Zone: 2 to 9
Habitat: Wetlands, swamps, wet meadows

CARDINAL FLOWER (*Lobelia cardinalis*)

GROUNDNUT

Apios americana

Wild bean, Indian potato, potato bean, *pénacs, patates en chapelet*

The groundnut, a member of the pea family, is a hardy perennial climbing vine. It has been grown in Europe since the 1600s for food and as a foraging crop for bees, but is infrequently cultivated in its native North America. The stems are long and twining and may reach a height of 1–2 feet as they climb along the ground or over shrubs in their path. Groundnut has compound leaves with 5 to 7 leaflets and compact clusters of fragrant, nectar-rich, pealike, brownish purple flowers. The flowers develop into 2–3-inch pod fruits which contain ¼-inch, black, rectangular seeds. Since in New England and to the north this species tends to have three sets of chromosomes rather than the usual pair, it does not produce viable seeds in the northern part of its range. In this region it reproduces vegetatively from its tubers which are frequently transported by rivers. The chains of walnut-sized tubers may extend for 20 feet or more. These tubers, which give this plant its common names, are edible and taste like green peas. In the autumn the top of the plant dies back as the tubers enlarge.

CULTURE

Groundnut's habit of quickly climbing over low shrubs makes it an ideal plant for the edges of clearings, trellises, or areas that need to be covered in a hurry. It spreads rapidly from underground stems and you may need to contain its root system if it encroaches on other plants. If the plants become too aggressive, dig up some of the tubers and eat them! Groundnut prefers open locations and has more controllable growth in the shade, although there it flowers less. Groundnut will grow under a variety of soil conditions ranging from moderately acidic to neutral (pH 5–7) as long as moisture is abundant during the growing season.

PROPAGATION

The best way to propagate groundnut is from divisions of the tubers in the fall. Dig up underground stems and separate the tubers, or obtain nursery planting stock. Plant two or three tubers together in holes that are 3–4 inches deep and spaced 2 feet apart. Seeds can be planted in either fall or spring, about ¾ inch deep in desired locations. Since the seeds from the northern part of the range are sterile, make sure the seed you obtain is from plants grown south of New York. Plant the seeds in clusters of 4 to 5, and keep them moist until the seedlings become established. Groundnut usually forms nitrogen-producing nodules easily when propagated by division. If inoculation of seeds is required, use cowpea (*Vigna*) rhizobia (Nitragin-type EL).

COMPANIONS

Not for this one!

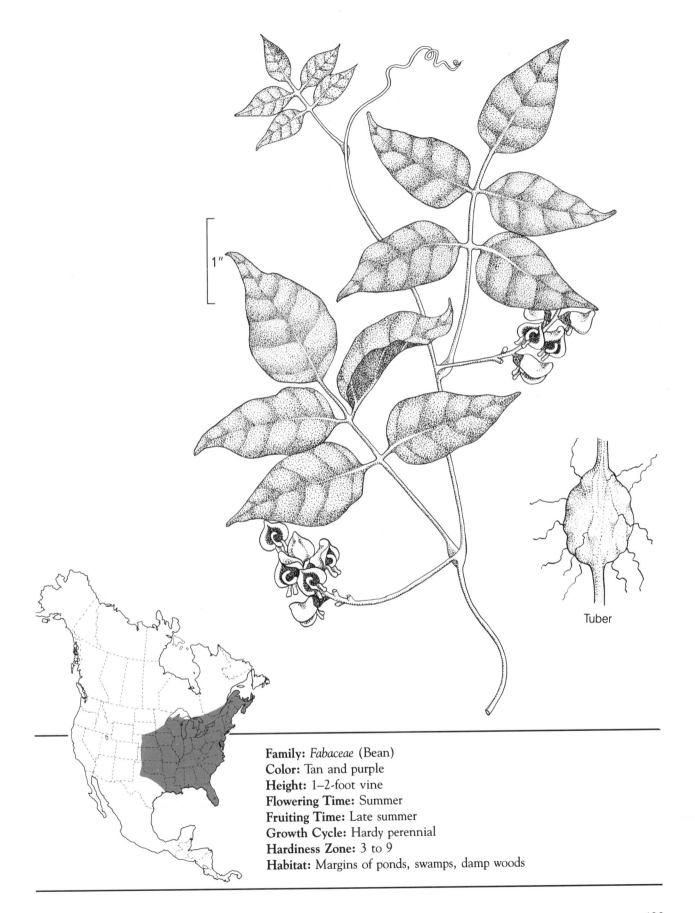

1"

Tuber

Family: *Fabaceae* (Bean)
Color: Tan and purple
Height: 1–2-foot vine
Flowering Time: Summer
Fruiting Time: Late summer
Growth Cycle: Hardy perennial
Hardiness Zone: 3 to 9
Habitat: Margins of ponds, swamps, damp woods

GROUNDNUT (*Apios americana*)

TURTLEHEAD

Chelone glabra

Balmony, snakehead, *tête de tortue*

The name turtlehead refers to the terminal spike of puffy-lipped white flowers, which look like the gaping mouths of turtles. Hardy perennials, turtleheads generally grow 1–3 feet high, but may reach 4 feet with ample light and moisture. Pairs of 5-inch-long, lance-shaped leaves clasp the smooth stem. Turtlehead leaves are the favorite food of black and orange Baltimore butterflies, which feed in communal webs during the summer and fall. The 1-inch white flowers, sometimes tinged with pink or yellow-green, are long lasting, and the flowering season frequently lasts into fall. Bees and bumblebees pollinate the flowers, disappearing inside in search of the very sweet nectar. The flowers wither late in the season, revealing a ½-inch capsular fruit. This fruit turns from green to tan as it splits open, shedding the many small, flattened, winged seeds with dark centers. The seeds can float on either wind or water. The root system is quite fibrous. Native Americans made a bitter black tonic from turtlehead leaves to cure tumors and liver diseases.

CULTURE

In the wild, turtlehead is usually found growing in wet meadows and on the sides of ditches where the soil is moist or wet. This species makes a nice addition to any garden, however, if soils are not excessively dry. Ample applications of compost or rotted manure to the soil around the plant will provide needed nutrients and conserve moisture during the summer flowering period. Turtleheads are adaptable to a variety of light conditions, ranging from full sun to partial shade. The plant is not especially particular about soil conditions, but grows best in moderately to slightly acid soils (pH 5–7).

PROPAGATION

Seeds, root divisions, and cuttings are all successful ways to propagate turtlehead. Seeds need cold, damp stratification in order to germinate. Collect seeds in the fall, place them in a plastic bag with moistened peat moss, and refrigerate them for 4 months before planting in the spring. Direct seeding or seeding in flats in the fall is preferred. Plant about ⅛ inch deep, cover with ⅛ inch of sifted compost, and moisten. Seeds will germinate in the spring and plants will bloom the second year. Turtleheads self-seed if the soil is moist. The best time to divide roots is in the early spring or late fall while the plants are dormant. With care, however, the rootstocks can be divided even in early summer. Space root divisions about 18 inches apart and about 1 inch deep with the buds at the soil surface. Make stem cuttings in the summer prior to flowering, being careful to prevent the slip from drying out. If flower buds have formed, remove them from the stem, place a 6-inch cutting in moist sand, and provide support and moisture until the top withers in the fall. Then transplant the newly formed rootstock to a permanent spot.

COMPANIONS

Cardinal flower, larger blue flag, closed gentian, Jack-in-the-pulpit, New England aster.

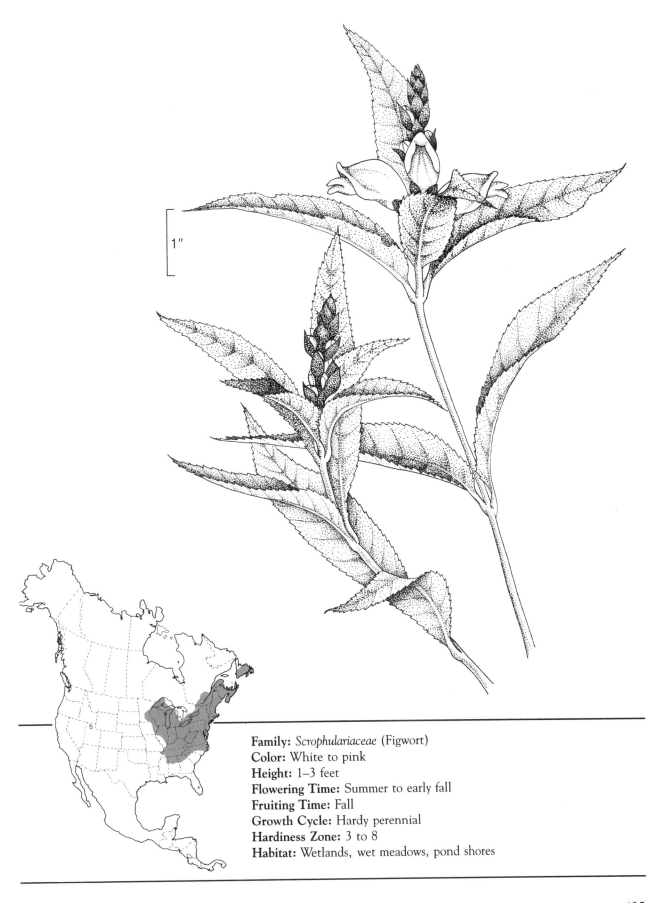

1″

Family: *Scrophulariaceae* (Figwort)
Color: White to pink
Height: 1–3 feet
Flowering Time: Summer to early fall
Fruiting Time: Fall
Growth Cycle: Hardy perennial
Hardiness Zone: 3 to 8
Habitat: Wetlands, wet meadows, pond shores

TURTLEHEAD *(Chelone glabra)*

CLOSED GENTIAN

Gentiana andrewsii

Bottle gentian, blind gentian, *gentiane d'Andrews*

Not only is the closed gentian one of the easiest of the gentians to cultivate, but it has unusual and interesting flowers as well. The clusters of 2 to 5 flowers are borne at the bases of the upper leaves of this 1–2-foot hardy perennial. Robust plants may have 2 whorls of flowers. The 1½-inch flowers have 5 petals, ranging in color from intense navy blue to blue-violet and even white, attached to one another by petal-like pleats that form a tube. The tube appears to lack an opening, inspiring the plant's common names of closed, bottle, and blind gentian, but pollinating insects such as bumblebees force their way into the flower with ease. Surrounded by the petals and unseen from outside the flower are the 5 stamens, their anthers fused together. The reddish stems are clasped by pairs of 2–4-inch leaves, whose size increases toward the top of the stem. The fruit of the closed gentian is a papery, tan capsule containing ⅛-inch, light tan, winged seeds, and the root system is a root crown with many white, fibrous roots.

CULTURE

An excellent garden plant, closed gentian is adaptable to a wide variety of conditions, from full sun to light shade, in soils that range from dryish to damp and from neutral to slightly acidic (pH 5–7.5). It grows best in a sandy or even gravelly loam, rich in humus and *moist* throughout the growing season.

PROPAGATION

Closed gentians can be propagated by either seed or divisions of the root crown. Root crown division should be done in the fall or early spring. Divide crowns into pieces, each with at least one bud, and plant 1 foot apart with the buds at the top of the crown about 1 inch below the soil surface. Mice love to eat gentian buds, so protect the plants with hardware cloth or screen. Germination requires stratification (3 months at 40°F) and is enhanced by exposure to the light, so lightly scatter the seeds just on the surface of a flat containing a mixture of loam and compost. Do not scratch the seeds into the soil, but moisten and give them a light covering of peat moss. Leave the flats out for the winter so the seeds can be chilled, or artificially refrigerate moistened seeds and then plant them in flats indoors in early spring, keeping the surface of the soil moist. The seeds will germinate in 1 to 4 weeks following spring temperatures above 65°F, but the process may be slow. The first year the seedling will form only a rosette of leaves, and should be provided with light shade and moisture. Leave seedlings in the flat for the first growing season, transplant them to a holding bed for the second year, and then move them to a permanent location the following year. Plants from seed will usually flower in the third or fourth year.

COMPANIONS

Cardinal flower, New England aster, turtlehead, larger blue flag.

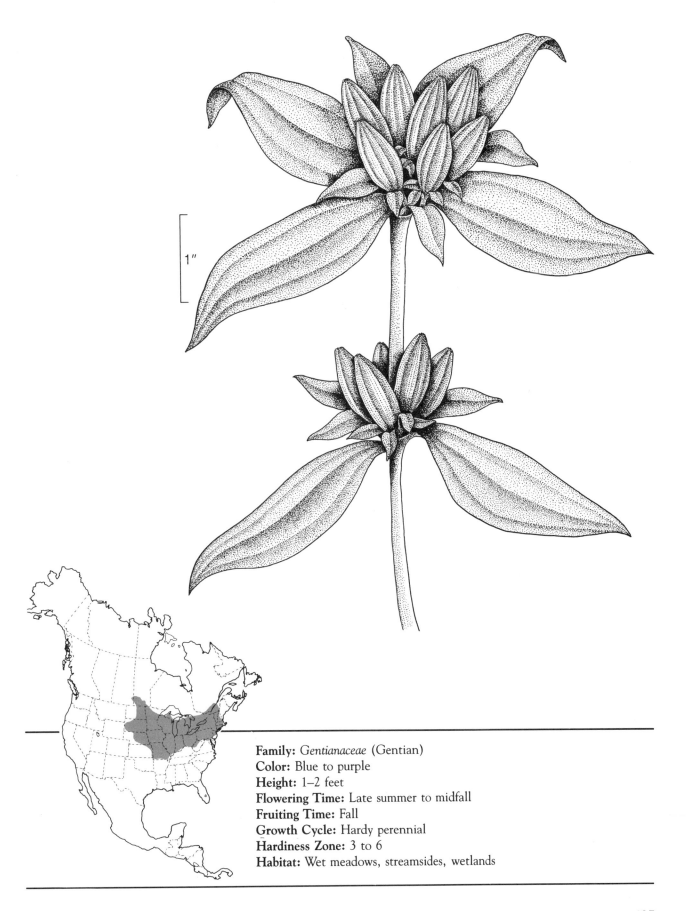

Family: *Gentianaceae* (Gentian)
Color: Blue to purple
Height: 1–2 feet
Flowering Time: Late summer to midfall
Fruiting Time: Fall
Growth Cycle: Hardy perennial
Hardiness Zone: 3 to 6
Habitat: Wet meadows, streamsides, wetlands

CLOSED GENTIAN *(Gentiana andrewsii)*

MEADOW SPECIES

The species in this section all grow best in sunny locations and are ideally suited for wildflower meadows. Remember that grasses are a necessary ingredient for the wildflowers to grow straight and tall, and without annual mowing or burning shrubs and trees may take over (see pages 19–23).

Take advantage of variations in the site when you plan a wildflower meadow. Many of the wetland species such as **larger blue flag** (page 128), **turtlehead** (page 134), and **cardinal flower** (page 130) are ideally suited to damp depressions in meadows, and complement **black-eyed Susan** and **wild bergamot** planted on drier ridges and hilltops. **Wood lily** (page 120) and **pasture rose** are excellent choices for the partially shaded borders of meadows.

COMPANIONS

There are a large number of species native to North American prairies that are well suited to meadows in the Northeast. **Butterfly weed** (*Asclepias tuberosa*), true to its name, draws many species of butterflies to its clusters of bright orange flowers. It is quite drought tolerant and grows well where the soil is dry, as does **blanketflower** (*Gaillardia aristata*). Blanketflower is a very cold-hardy perennial and has yellow and deep red composite flower heads that look like 2-inch-wide pinwheels. **Lance-leaved coreopsis** (*Coreopsis lanceolata*) establishes itself easily in meadows and has a long season of bright yellow flower heads. It provides a pleasing contrast when interplanted with **purple coneflower** (*Echinacea purpurea*), which has drooping, lavender to crimson ray flowers and spiny, golden-purple disc flowers. **Nodding wild onion** (*Allium cernuum*) grows naturally in wet prairies. Its pendant clusters of pale lavender flowers contrast well with the upright spikes of light magenta flowers of the **false dragonhead** (*Physostegia virginiana*), which grows in the same habitat. The false dragonhead has a long blooming period and makes an ideal cut flower. If the meadow has wet, acid soil, you should consider **meadow beauty** (*Rhexia virginica*). In midsummer meadow beauty has delightful deep rose-crimson flowers with bright golden stamens. Later in the season copper red, urn-shaped fruits are produced.

Meadow garden, summer.

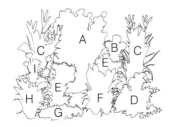

A. New England aster
B. Wild bergamot
C. Big bluestem
D. Pasture rose
E. Black-eyed Susan
F. Northern dropseed
G. Bluets
H. Little bluestem
I. Canada anemone

Although you should be cautious about using commercial wildflower mixes and planting weedy exotic species, there are some alien species worthy of consideration, unless you are attempting to restore a native landscape. **Deptford pink** (*Dianthus armeria*), a 6–18-inch-high wildflower with European origins, has shocking pink flowers with delicate petals. It enlivens dry fields and roadsides throughout the region. **Ragged robin** (*Lychnis flos-cuculi*), another exotic in the pink family, prefers wet meadows and its flowers, which appear in the spring, have 5 lavender-pink petals so deeply clefted that they appear to be shredded. The **orange hawkweed** (*Heiracium aurantiacum*) produces small dandelion-like flowerheads that are deep orange near the edges and yellow-orange at the center. Its flowering season lasts most of the summer. Perhaps the most popular exotic meadow wildflower is the **ox-eye daisy** (*Chrysanthemeum leucanthemum*) which can be found in fields and by roadsides. Its lovely flowers attract many species of butterflies in midspring. If planted in dryish sites it is usually well behaved, but it can become aggressive if given ample moisture and sun.

CANADA ANEMONE

Anemone canadensis

Anémone du Canada

This is one of the easiest of the northeastern wildflowers to grow and an excellent plant to fill in open or partially shaded areas. Canada anemone, a member of the buttercup family, is a hardy perennial which grows 1 to 2 feet tall. The flower stems look as if they have grown through the pairs of stalkless leaves that surround them. The long-stemmed single flowers have 5 white, unequal-sized petal-like sepals surrounding the rich yellow stamens and pistils. When the pollen is ripe and ready to be released, the sepals protect the anthers by closing at night and on cloudy days. The flowers are usually 1 to 2 inches in diameter and produce burrlike clusters of flattened, ¼-inch fruits with long beaks. Hairs on the fruits help them float on the wind. The plant's extensive root system was used medicinally by Native Americans.

CULTURE

Canada anemone grows best in open, sunny locations or partial shade. Although it grows most robustly in soils with moderate moisture and neutral conditions (pH 6–7), it is not at all choosy about soils and can even be found growing along roadsides. When Canada anemone is grown in the open, it will often naturalize too easily and quickly crowd out other wildflowers in the garden. It is usually prudent to confine the plant with 6-inch plastic or metal edging strips buried at the soil surface. Canada anemone is less aggressive when grown in partial shade. As clumps of anemone become crowded, flowering may decrease. If this occurs, divide the plants in the fall.

PROPAGATION

Canada anemone has no difficulty propagating itself once established. The easiest way to start the plant is to obtain a division of the rhizome in the early spring or fall when it is dormant. Each piece of rhizome should be several inches long and have good roots and buds visible. Plant the segments a foot apart and no more than ½ inch deep with the bud just at the soil surface. Seeds should be gathered when mature in the summer and planted where you desire plants to become established. Usually the seedlings will mature and produce flowers within two years.

COMPANIONS

Grow it alone or in meadows where it will get sufficient competition from grasses and other wildflowers.

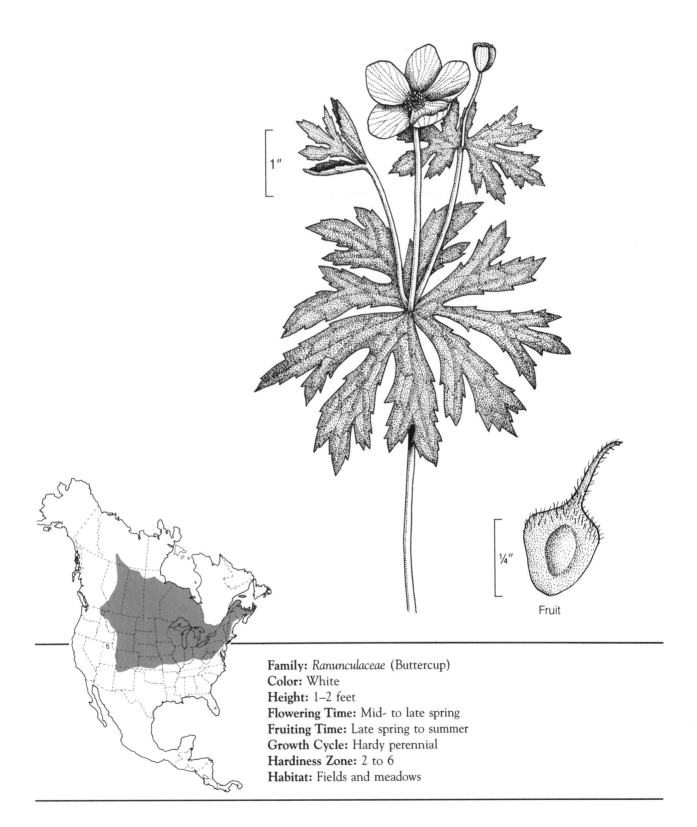

1"

¼"

Fruit

Family: *Ranunculaceae* (Buttercup)
Color: White
Height: 1–2 feet
Flowering Time: Mid- to late spring
Fruiting Time: Late spring to summer
Growth Cycle: Hardy perennial
Hardiness Zone: 2 to 6
Habitat: Fields and meadows

CANADA ANEMONE (*Anemone canadensis*)

BLUETS

Houstonia caerulea

Quaker ladies, innocence, *houstonie bleue*

These small, delicate plants are found growing both in compact tufts and in broad expanses in grassy fields, thickets, and streamsides. Bluets grow as hardy perennials or "winter annuals," with seeds germinating in the fall and flowering in the spring. The yellow centers of the tiny (¼–½-inch) trumpet-shaped flowers contrast pleasantly with the 4 pointed, blue to lilac lobes, which form a cross. Bluets require cross-fertilization to produce seeds and have two different kinds of flowers, which facilitates the transfer of pollen between plants. Some plants produce flowers with long pistils and short stamens, and others produce flowers with long stamens and short pistils. Insect pollinators most frequently transfer pollen from the flowers with long stamens to the flowers with long pistils. The thin leaf stems are short, only 2–8 inches high, with a pair of narrow, tiny leaves, while the leaves at the base of the flower stem are broader and more numerous. The fruit is a small capsule with many minute seeds. Bluets tend to grow in clumps, spreading from seed or short rhizomes that send up clusters of shoots. Several species of butterfly, including the clouded sulfur and the painted lady, are attracted to bluets.

CULTURE

Bluets thrive in open sunny locations, woodland openings, on the margins of brooks, and in very light shade. They do well when grown among the grasses of lawns and fields, but care should be taken not to mow them too early in the spring before they have had an opportunity to set seed. Bluets require a soil that is both acidic (pH 5–7) and somewhat moist. They are an exceptional plant for rock gardens.

PROPAGATION

Bluets are easy to propagate from both divisions and seed. Dig the plants either in the spring, before or after flowering, or in the fall. Carefully divide the plants and replant with the basal leaves just above the surface of the soil. Bluets are most conspicuous when they are in flower, so mark their location when you can easily spot them in the grass. If you collect seeds in the summer for planting the following spring, refrigerate them over the winter, since germination is enhanced by moist stratification. Seeds should be sown at shallow depth or lightly scratched into the soil in either the spring or fall. Fall-sown seed will generally flower the next spring. Once established, bluets self-seed with ease and also spread by rhizome extension.

COMPANIONS

Eastern trout lily, wood lily, eastern columbine, pasture rose.

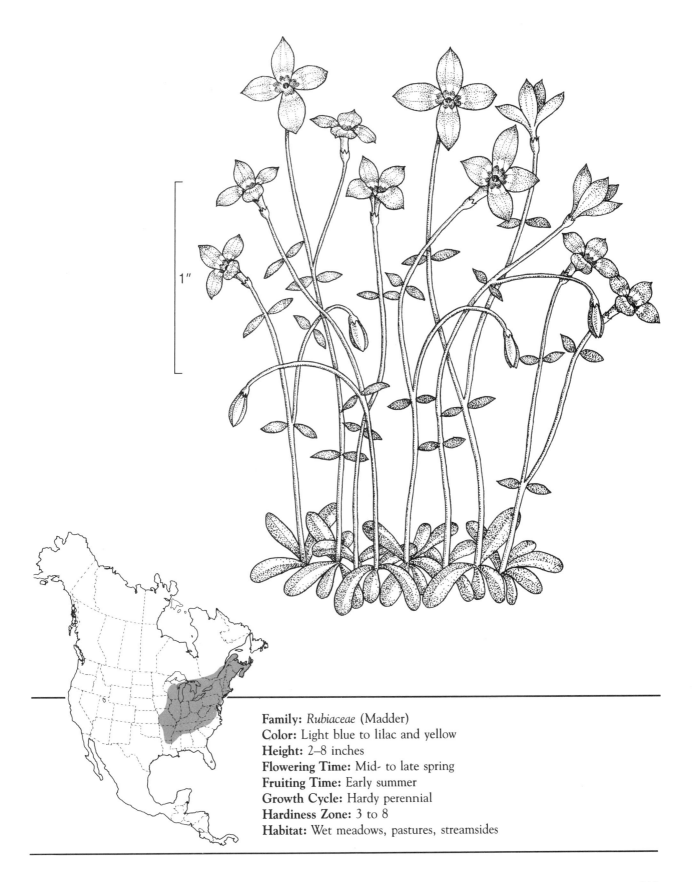

1″

Family: *Rubiaceae* (Madder)
Color: Light blue to lilac and yellow
Height: 2–8 inches
Flowering Time: Mid- to late spring
Fruiting Time: Early summer
Growth Cycle: Hardy perennial
Hardiness Zone: 3 to 8
Habitat: Wet meadows, pastures, streamsides

BLUETS (*Houstonia caerulea*)

PASTURE ROSE

Rosa carolina

Prairie rose, Carolina rose, *rosier de Caroline*

There is a simple elegance to this relative of fancy garden roses. A low (1–3-foot-high) shrub with single, upright stems arising from spreading underground stolons, pasture rose is a fine addition to the borders of the garden. The straight thorns of this rose are scattered sparsely along its stem. Fragrant 2-inch flowers are borne singly or in small groups, and have five pale pink petals encircling a ring of numerous, bright yellow stamens. The fruit, a ⅓-inch hip, turns from dark green to bright red as it matures. The hip contains several bony, tan, ⅛-inch seeds, and remains on the plant during the winter or until eaten by birds. The seeds that survive the passage through a bird's digestive system have an excellent germination rate. The hips, long used for making tea and jam, are a rich source of vitamin C.

CULTURE While pasture roses are one of the most shade-tolerant of roses, they grow best in open, sunny locations. They prefer moderately acid soils (pH 4.5–6), which are moist but well drained. Once established, pasture rose can tolerate fairly dry soils. This perennial requires relatively little care and is hardy to zone 4.

PROPAGATION Pasture rose can be propagated by seed, cuttings, and stolon division. The stems arising from the underground stolons can be separated and transplanted in the late fall or early spring. Divide the stolons with a sharp spade, being sure that each division has vigorous roots. Replant the divisions with the root crown just at the soil surface. Greenwood or softwood cuttings can be made in the early spring after vigorous shoot growth has just started. Cut 6–7-inch pieces and plant 3 inches deep in sand, keeping moist but not too wet, and provide shade. Replant in a permanent location after the stem loses its leaves in the fall. Collect seeds as soon as the hips have turned red in the late summer or early fall. The seeds should not be allowed to dry out or germination may be difficult. Remove the seeds from the pulpy hip and plant them thickly ¼ inch deep in a flat containing a mixture of sand and peat moss. Seeds require stratification (3 months at 40°F) and may benefit from scarification. Even under the best of conditions, seed germination may be slow, so leave the flat out the next winter as well before you become discouraged and throw out the soil. Transplant the seedlings when they become several inches high and have well-developed root systems. Some plants from seed may bloom the second year, but usually it takes 3 to 4 years to reach the flowering stage. Once established, pasture rose will spread by extension of its stolons.

COMPANIONS Black-eyed Susan, New England aster, wood lily, bluets, wild bergamot.

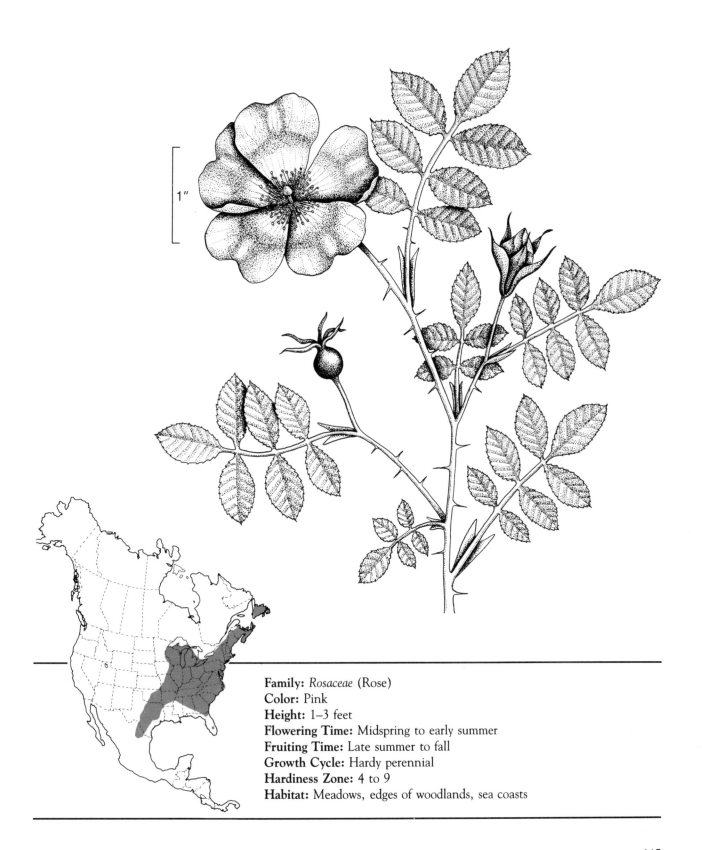

1"

Family: *Rosaceae* (Rose)
Color: Pink
Height: 1–3 feet
Flowering Time: Midspring to early summer
Fruiting Time: Late summer to fall
Growth Cycle: Hardy perennial
Hardiness Zone: 4 to 9
Habitat: Meadows, edges of woodlands, sea coasts

PASTURE ROSE *(Rosa carolina)*

BLACK-EYED SUSAN

Rudbeckia hirta
(R. serotina)

Brown-eyed Susan, *rudbeckie hérissée, rudbeckie tardive*

Black-eyed Susan is a hardy perennial that can be grown as an annual in most locations. Its first flowering signifies that summer has arrived, and its last flowering, that summer has gone. Originally a native of the Midwest and Lake States, black-eyed Susan reportedly expanded its range after its seeds were accidentally shipped to the East with clover seeds and planted in farm fields. The 1–3-foot-high stems and scattered 4-inch-long leaves are covered with short, bristly hairs. The 2–3-inch flower heads are borne on a relatively long stalk, making the black-eyed Susan an attractive cut flower. The individual flowers are of two kinds and cluster together in the flower head in a manner characteristic of members of the aster family. In the center is a hemispherical disc of tiny chocolate-brown flowers, surrounded by 10 to 20 petal-like, inch-long, rich yellow ray flowers. Sometimes the ray petals are darker at their bases. The root system tends to be fibrous and may be extensive in old, established plants.

CULTURE   Black-eyed Susan is a plant of sunny habitats, but can tolerate light shading. It is quite indifferent to soil conditions and will do well in dry, infertile soils if there is sufficient moisture for it to become established. It grows exceptionally well under cultivation and may even become somewhat aggressive if given abundant sun, moisture and nutrients. If started early, black-eyed Susan can be grown as an annual.

PROPAGATION   Propagate black-eyed Susan from seed since it is very difficult to divide the root system successfully. Propagation from seed is easy. Black-eyed Susan seeds require stratification for germination (3 months at 40°F); without it most of the seeds remain dormant. Sow the ⅕-inch-long black seeds about ⅓ inch deep in loamy soil as soon as they are ripe in the summer or early fall. Germination takes place in the spring after about 2 weeks of daytime temperatures between 65 and 75°F. Many of the plants will flower the first year, and nearly all will flower the second year. First-year plants tend to continue flowering later into the fall, so you can extend the flowering season by starting some new seed each spring. Since black-eyed Susan sometimes grows as a biennial, you may want to plant seeds two years in a row anyway. Seeds can also be sown in flats, left out over winter, and transplanted the following spring after the seedlings have become sturdy. Once established, they self-seed well.

COMPANIONS   New England aster, wild bergamot, pasture rose, wood lily.

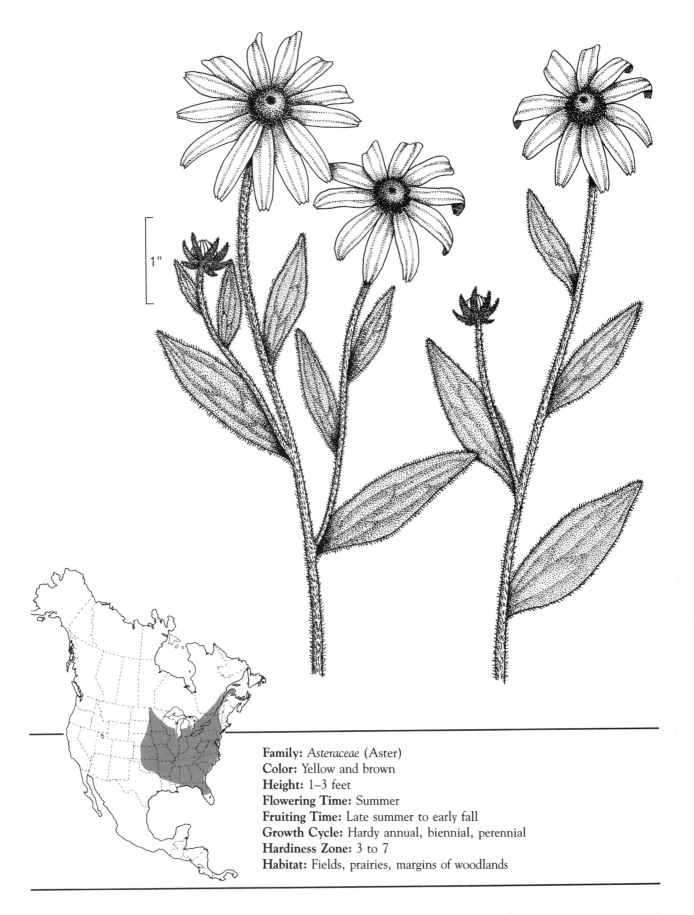

Family: *Asteraceae* (Aster)
Color: Yellow and brown
Height: 1–3 feet
Flowering Time: Summer
Fruiting Time: Late summer to early fall
Growth Cycle: Hardy annual, biennial, perennial
Hardiness Zone: 3 to 7
Habitat: Fields, prairies, margins of woodlands

BLACK-EYED SUSAN (*Rudbeckia hirta*)

WILD BERGAMOT

Monarda fistulosa

Monarde fistuleuse

Wild bergamot's membership in the mint family is indicated by its familiar square stems and irregular flowers. The name wild bergamot refers to the similarity between the aromas of this plant's foliage and the fruit of the bergamot orange tree of Europe. Indeed, the leaves have long been used for making herbal tea and a treatment for the common cold. The genus Monarda is named in honor of Nicolas Monardes, a European herbalist who wrote about North American native plants in the 1500s. The 2–4-foot-high fuzzy stems bear pairs of firm, 3-inch-long, hairy, gray-green leaves and a 2-inch whorl of lilac to pink flowers in clusters at the top of the plant. The 2-lobed upper lip of the tubular, 1-inch flowers bears a tuft of hairs and arches over the 3-lobed lower lip. The long stamens protrude from the throat of the flower and arch slightly upward. Many species of butterflies are attracted to the flowers. The seeds are 1/16-inch elliptical nutlets.

CULTURE

Wild bergamot is a widely distributed hardy perennial which grows well in full sun to light shade. While typically found growing in dry, open meadows, grasslands and woods, it responds well to moisture if the soil is well drained. Wild bergamot may develop mildew on its leaves if grown in too humid a location. Soil acidity conditions (pH 5–7.5) are not as important as situating the plants where they are exposed to the full sun at least part of each day.

PROPAGATION

The easiest way to propagate wild bergamot is from seeds. In the fall, plant the seeds ¼ inch deep in flats or in the desired location. They can also be planted indoors in the early spring. The seeds do not require stratification, although germination may be faster if they are given a chilling treatment. The seeds germinate quickly in the spring (1 to 2 weeks) and grow rapidly, sometimes producing flowers the first year. Most of the plants from seed will flower the second year. By the end of the first season wild bergamot will start to produce multiple shoots, and over time the plants may become bunchy, even crowding out other plants in their immediate vicinity. Clumps can be divided in the spring and the pieces of rhizome with buds set 1 inch deep and 1 to 2 feet apart. Avoid fall divisions since wild bergamot is susceptible to winter kill and frost heaving.

COMPANIONS

Black-eyed Susan, New England aster, pasture rose.

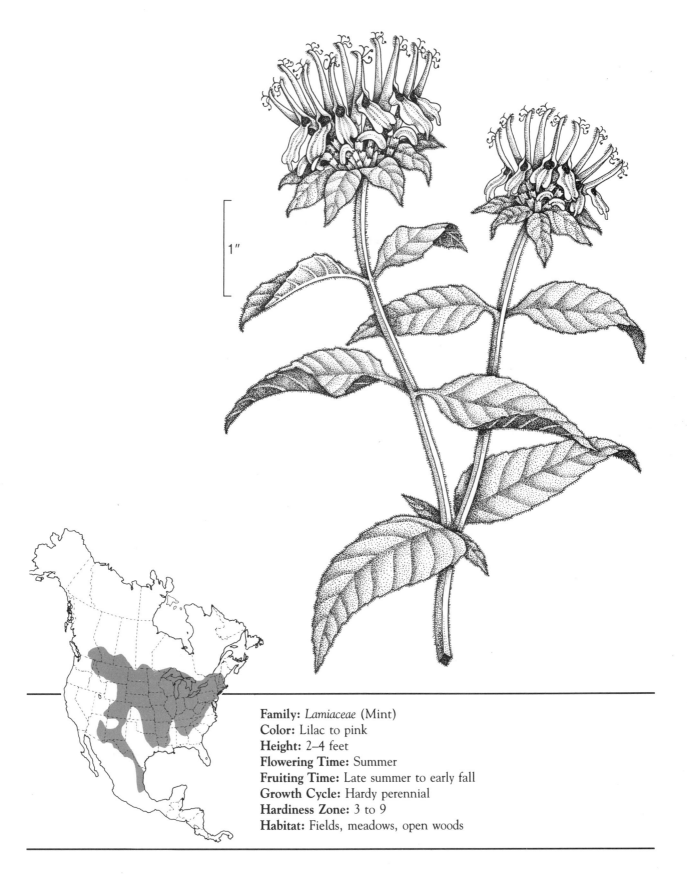

Family: *Lamiaceae* (Mint)
Color: Lilac to pink
Height: 2–4 feet
Flowering Time: Summer
Fruiting Time: Late summer to early fall
Growth Cycle: Hardy perennial
Hardiness Zone: 3 to 9
Habitat: Fields, meadows, open woods

WILD BERGAMOT *(Monarda fistulosa)*

NEW ENGLAND ASTER

Aster novae-angliae

Aster de la Nouvelle-Angleterre

Why bother planting a common garden variety of aster when there is this stunning native species? New England asters hardly confine themselves to New England, for they can be found growing in fields throughout the region and west to Colorado. This species can be cultivated as a perennial north to hardiness zone 3 and is the stock from which many of the horticultural varieties of hardy asters have been bred. Usually reaching a height of 2–4 feet, the New England aster has dense leaves covered with bristly hairs and bears clusters of flowers at the tips of leafy branches. The flower heads have violet-purple ray flowers surrounding the golden yellow disc flowers. New England asters attract many species of butterflies, and cross-pollination is necessary for this wildflower to produce seeds. It remains in flower until frost, although the ray flowers close over the flower head at night and on cloudy days. The disc flowers develop into ⅛-inch-long fuzzy seeds that are carried away by the wind. Native Americans smoked the dried roots and made an infusion from the plant to treat intestinal disorders.

CULTURE Grow New England asters in full sun to partial shade. They will not grow well if too densely shaded, but are easy to grow in fields and meadows. They grow nicely under a variety of soil acidity conditions from slightly acid to neutral (pH 5–7) and are best planted where soil moisture is ample throughout the summer. For a bushier form, prune New England asters in the late spring. They make attractive cut flowers in the fall but wilt quickly, so take your vase to the garden when you cut them.

PROPAGATION Although a perennial, New England asters can be grown as an annual. If the seeds are sown in the fall, plants usually flower the next fall. Seeds should be damp-stratified for 4 to 6 weeks prior to planting. Stratified seeds have three times the germination rate of non-stratified seeds and can be expected to germinate in 1 to 2 weeks. The seeds should be planted about ¼ inch deep in mineral soil with no mulch. The best time to propagate by root division is in the late fall. You should divide the roots every several years anyway, to keep the plants growing vigorously, so you might as well put the surplus material to good use. Space root divisions a couple of feet apart with the tops of the rhizomes just at the surface of the soil. Once established, New England asters will self-sow, if bare mineral soil and sufficient moisture are available.

COMPANIONS Black-eyed Susan, turtlehead, cardinal flower, closed gentian, pasture rose, wild bergamot.

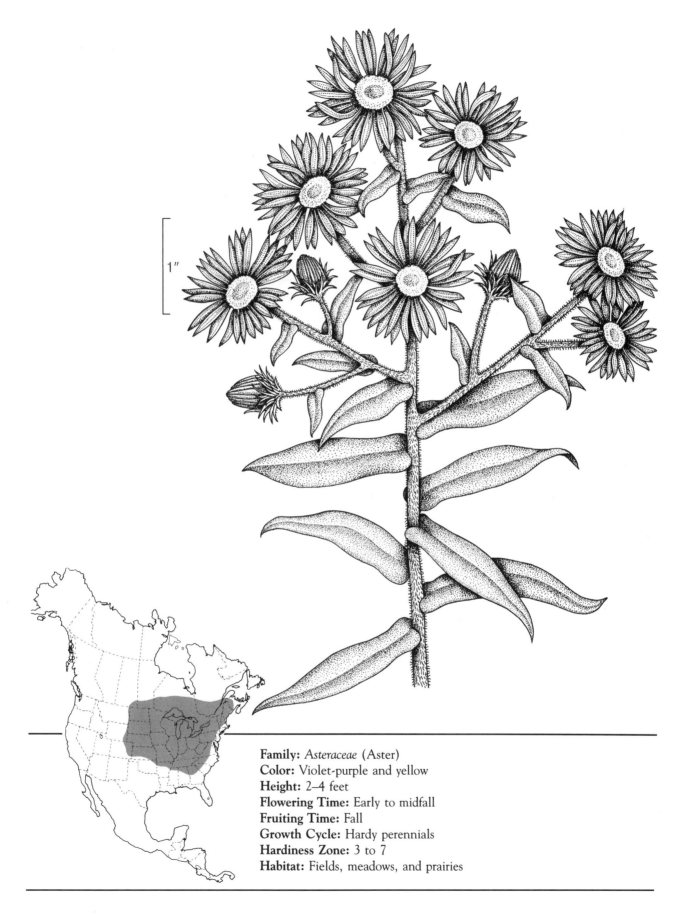

Family: *Asteraceae* (Aster)
Color: Violet-purple and yellow
Height: 2–4 feet
Flowering Time: Early to midfall
Fruiting Time: Fall
Growth Cycle: Hardy perennials
Hardiness Zone: 3 to 7
Habitat: Fields, meadows, and prairies

1″

NEW ENGLAND ASTER *(Aster novae-angliae)*

Appendixes

APPENDIX A
Suppliers

Send payment in the appropriate currency, i.e.: U.S. dollars to U.S. businesses and Canadian dollars to Canadian businesses.

Connecticut

Comstock, Ferre & Company
263 Main Street, P.O. Box 125
Wethersfield, CT 06109
Sells seeds and live plants, retail; seeds only, by mail order. Free catalog.

Illinois

Lafayette Home Nursery
R.R. Box 1A
Lafayette, IL 61449
309-995-3311
Sells seeds and live plants, retail and wholesale, by mail order (seeds only) and phone order. Send large SASE for catalog. Native prairie grass and wildflower mixes.

Midwest Wildflowers
P.O. Box 64
Rockton, IL 61072
Sells seeds retail by mail order. Catalog: $.50. Midwestern wildflowers.

The Natural Garden
38 W. 443 Highway 64
St. Charles, IL 60174
312-584-0150
Sells seeds and live plants, retail and wholesale, by mail order (seeds only) and phone order. Catalog: $2.00. Illinois native wildflowers and grasses.

R.H. Shumway
P.O. Box 777
Rockford, IL 61105

Sells seeds retail and wholesale, by mail order and phone order. Catalog: $1.00.

Sunshine Seed Company
R.R. #II, Box 176
Wyoming, IL 61491
309-286-7356
Sells seeds retail and wholesale, by mail order and phone order. Catalog: $1.00, refundable. Native seeds of Illinois, California and the Southwest.

Windrift Prairie Nursery
Dot & Doug Wade
Route 2
Oregon, IL 61061
815-732-6890
Sells seeds and live plants, retail, by mail order and phone order. Send 2 first-class stamps for catalog. Native Midwest prairie species.

Maine

Daystar
Route 2, Box 250
Litchfield, ME 04350
Sells live plants retail and wholesale, by mail order. Catalog: $1.00. New England rock garden plants.

Maryland

Native Seeds, Inc.
14590 Triadelphia Mill Road
Dayton, MD 21036
301-596-9818

Sells seeds and live plants, retail and wholesale, by mail order and phone order. Free catalog.

Massachusetts

Garden in the Woods
Hemenway Road
Framington, MA 01701
617-877-6574
Sells seeds and (at garden) live plants, retail, mail order. Free catalog. Sales are seasonal.

Lexington Gardens
93 Hancock
Lexington, MA 02173
617-862-7000
Sells seeds and live plants, retail. Free catalog.

Weston Nurseries, Inc.
P.O. Box 186, Route 135
Hopkinton, MA 01748
617-435-3414
Sells seeds and live plants, retail and wholesale, by phone order. Free catalog. Landscaping perennials including native plants.

Michigan

Dutch Mountain Nursery
7984 N. 48th Street, R-1
Augusta, MI 49012
616-731-5232

Sells seeds and live plants, retail, by mail order and phone order. Catalog: $.50. Mostly native shrubs, but some wildflowers as well.

Wavecrest Nurseries
2509 Lakeshore Drive
Fennville, MI 49408
616-543-4175

Sells live plants, retail, mail-order and phone order. Free catalog.

Minnesota

Prairie Moon Nursery
Route 3, Box 163
Winona, MN 55987
507-452-5231

Sells seeds and live plants, retail and wholesale, by mail order and phone order. Send 2 first-class stamps for catalog. Northern midwestern natives.

Prairie Restorations, Inc.
P.O. Box 327
Princeton, MN 55371
612-389-4342

Sells seed and live plants, retail and wholesale, by mail order. Free catalog. Sales limited to within 200 miles of Princeton, MN.

S & R Seed Company
Box 86
Cass Lake, MN 56633
218-335-2363

Sells seeds retail by mail order and phone order.

New Jersey

Thompson & Morgan
P.O. Box 1308
Jackson, NJ 08527
800-367-7333

Sells seeds and live plants, retail and wholesale, by mail order and phone order. Free catalog.

New York

Harris Moran Seed Company
3670 Buffalo Road
Rochester, NY 14624
716-594-9411

Sells seeds, retail and wholesale, by mail order and phone order. Free catalog.

Wildginger Woodlands
P.O. Box 1091
Webster, NY 14580
716-872-4033

Sells seeds and live plants retail by mail order. Catalog: $1.00, refundable.

Ontario

C.A. Cruickshank, Inc.
1015 Mt. Pleasant Road
Toronto, ONT M4P 2M1
416-488-8292

Sells seeds and live plants retail by mail order and phone order. Catalog: $2.00 for 2-year subscription. Woodland and bulb species.

Pennsylvania

Appalachian Wildflower Nursery
Route 1, Box 275A
Reedsville, PA 17084
717-667-6998

Sells seeds and live plants, retail and wholesale, by mail order and phone order. Send 1 first-class stamp for list.

Beachley-Hardy Seed Company
P.O. Box 336
Camp Hill, PA 17011
717-737-4529

Sells seeds wholesale by phone order.

W. Atlee Burpee Company
300 Park Avenue
Warminster, PA 18974
215-674-4900

Sells seeds retail and wholesale, by mail order and phone order. Free catalog.

Painted Meadow Seeds
P.O. Box 1865
Kingston, PA 18704
717-283-2911

Sells seeds retail and wholesale, by mail order. Free catalog.

Vick's Wildgardens
Box 115
Gladwyne, PA 19035
215-525-6773

Sells live plants, retail by mail order and phone order. Catalog: $.50.

Vermont

Putney Nursery, Inc.
Putney, VT 05346
802-387-5577

Sells seeds and live plants retail, by mail order and phone order. Free catalog.

Wisconsin

Boehlke's Woodland Gardens
County Aire Road W140 N10829
Germantown, WI 53022

Sells live plants retail by mail order. Catalog: $.50. Midwestern woodland and prairie species.

Cliffords Perennial & Vine
Route 2, Box 320
East Troy, WI 53120

Sells live plants retail and wholesale, by mail order. Free catalog.

Great Lakes Wild Flowers
Box 1923
Milwaukee, WI 53201

Sells live plants retail and wholesale, by mail order. Free list. Great Lakes natives.

Little Valley Farm
R.R. 1, Box 287
Richland Center, WI 53581
603-538-3180

Sells seeds and live plants, retail and wholesale, by mail order and phone order.

Catalog: $.25. Woodland, wetland, and prairie species.

Natural Habitat Nursery
4818 Terminal Road
McFarland, WI 53558

608-838-3376

Sells seeds retail and wholesale, by mail order and phone order. Free catalog. Prairie seed.

Prairie Nursery
Route 1, Box 365
Westfield, WI 53964

Sells seeds and live plants, retail and wholesale, by mail order. Free catalog. Prairie wildflowers and grasses.

Prairie Ridge Nursery
9738 Overland Road, R.R. 2
Mt. Horeb, WI 53572

608-437-5245

Sells seeds and live plants, retail and wholesale, by mail order and phone order. Catalog: $.50. Native prairie plants.

Prairie Seed Source
P.O. Box 83
North Lake, WI 53064

Sells seeds retail by mail order. Free catalog. Prairie species.

Sperka's Woodland Acres Nursery
Route 2
Crivitz, WI 54114

Sells live plants retail by mail order. Send 1 first-class stamp for list. Hardy native wildflowers and ferns.

Superior View Farm
Route 1, Box 199
Bayfield, WI 54814

715-779-5404

Sells live plants retail and wholesale, by mail order and phone order. Free catalog.

Wehr Nature Center
9701 W. College Avenue
Franklin, WI 53132

414-425-8550

Sells seeds retail by mail order and phone order. Free list. Native prairie wildflower mixes.

Wildlife Nurseries
P.O. Box 2724
Oshkosh, WI 54903

414-231-3780

Sells seeds retail by mail order and phone order. Catalog: $1.00. Wetland species for attracting wildlife.

APPENDIX B
Botanical Gardens

The following is a list of botanical gardens, arboreta, and nature centers that have gardens or natural areas dedicated to native plants. Many of these organizations provide additional services and have garden shops where books, seeds, and live plants can be purchased.

Connecticut

Audubon Center & Audubon
  Fairchild Garden
613 Riversville Road
Greenwich, CT 06830
203-869-5272
Entrance fee: $1.00 (adults), $.50 (children). Open all year, except holidays, 9 am–5 pm Tues.–Sun. Fairchild Wildflower Garden (½ mile from Center) open all year, daylight hours, $1.00 entrance fee.

Bartlett Arboretum of the University
  of Connecticut
151 Brookdale Road
Stamford, CT 06903
203-322-6971
Free. Open all year, 8:30–sunset.

The Connecticut Arboretum at
  Connecticut College
Williams Avenue
New London, CT 06320
203-447-1911
Free. Open all year, daylight hours. Emphasis on native woody perennials.

Connecticut Audubon Society's Larsen
  Sanctuary
2325 Burr Street
Fairfield, CT 06430
203-259-6305
Entrance fee: $1.00. Open all year, daylight hours. Sells seeds and live plants.

Elizabeth Park
915 Prospect Avenue
Hartford, CT 06119
203-722-6541
Free. Open all year, daylight hours. Rock gardens, rose gardens, and greenhouses.

White Memorial Foundation
Route 202, P.O. Box 368
Litchfield, CT 06759
203-567-0857; Museum 203-567-0015
Free. Open all year, daylight hours. Museum open 9 am–5 pm Tues.–Sat., 11 am–5 pm Sun.

Delaware

Winterthur Museum Gardens
Route 52
Winterthur, DE 19735
302-654-1548
Entrance fee varies. Sells seeds and live plants. Extensive gardens include native wildflowers. Call for information.

District of Columbia

Kenilworth Aquatic Gardens
Douglas Street NE
Washington, DC 20019

202-426-6905
Free. Open all year, 7 am–5 pm. Native aquatic and wetland gardens.

United States Botanic Garden
Maryland Avenue & 1st Street, S.W.
Washington, D.C. 20024
202-225-8333
Free. Open all year, 9 am–5 pm (winter), 9 am–9 pm (summer).

U.S. National Arboretum
3501 New York Avenue, N.E.
Washington, DC 20002
202-475-4815
Free. Open all year, 8 am–5 pm weekdays, 10 am–5 pm weekends. Workshops and symposia on native plants.

Illinois

Chicago Botanic Garden
Lake-Cook Road, P.O. Box 400
Glencoe, IL 60022
312-835-5440
Entrance fee: $1.00 parking. Open all year, except Christmas, 8 am–sunset. Sells seeds.

Chicago Wildflower Works
Daley Bicentennial Plaza
Grant Park between Monroe &
  Randolph Streets
Chicago, IL
Free. Open all year, all day. This extensive native and exotic wildflower garden, covering the roof of the Monroe Street

Parking Garage in downtown Chicago, was designed by artist Chapman Kelley and is maintained by the Chicago Park District.

Lincoln Memorial Garden
2301 East Lake Drive
Springfield, IL 62707
217-529-1111

Free. Open all year, daylight hours. Sells seeds and live plants.

Morton Arboretum
Lisle, IL 60532
312-968-0074

Entrance fee: $3.00 per car. Open all year, 9 am–7 pm (summer), 9 am–5 pm (winter). Prairie restorations.

Edward L. Ryerson Conservation Area
21950 N. Riverwoods Road
Deerfield, IL 60015
312-948-7750

Free. Open all year, 8:30 am–5 pm. Wide range of programs and native plant displays.

Severson Dells Environmental
  Education Center
8786 Montague Road
Rockford, IL 61102
815-335-2915

Free. Open all year, 8 am–4 pm Tues.–Sat., 1–5 pm Sun. Sells seeds.

James Woodworth Prairie Preserve
9831 Milwaukee Avenue (½ mile north
  of Golf Rd.)
Niles–Glenview, IL
312-965-3488

Free. Open June through September, except major holidays, 10 a.m.–3 p.m. A 5-acre virgin tallgrass prairie with interpretative center and demonstration gardens surrounded by suburbia. The University of Illinois acts as custodian for the site. Prairie Director, Department of Biological Sciences, University of Illinois

at Chicago, Box 4348, Chicago, IL 60680. 312- 996-8673.

Indiana

Christy Woods of Ball State University
2000 W. University Avenue
Muncie, IN 47306
317-285-8838

Free. Open all year, 7:30 am–4:30 pm Mon.—Sat.

Jerry E. Clegg Botanic Garden
1782 N. County Road 400, E.
Lafayette, IN 47906
317-742-0325

Free. Open all year, 10:00 am–sunset. Specializes in wildflower gardens.

Hayes Regional Arboretum
801 Elks Road
Richmond, IN 47374
317-962-3745

Free. Open all year, 8 am–5 pm Tues.–Sat., 1–5 pm Sun. Sells Seeds.

Iowa

Bickelhaupt Arboretum
340 S. 14th Street
Clinton, IA 52732
319-242-4771

Free. Open all year, daylight hours.

Kentucky

Bernheim Forest Arboretum &
  Nature Center
Route 245
Clermont, KY 40110

Free. Open Mar. 15–Nov. 15, 9 am–1 hour before sunset. Sells seeds and live plants.

Land Between the Lakes
Tennessee Valley Authority
Golden Pond, KY 42231
502-924-5602, Administration;
  502-924-5509, Nature Center

Free. Open all year, daylight hours. Woodlands Nature Center.

Maine

Perkins Arboretum & Bird Sanctuary
Colby College
Waterville, ME
207-872-3000

Free. Open all year, daylight hours. On the Colby College campus, administered by the Biology Department.

Wild Gardens of Acadia
Acadia National Park
Sieur de Monts Spring
Bar Harbor, ME 04609

Free. Open all year, daylight hours. Project of the Bar Harbor Garden Club.

Maryland

Cylburn Garden Center
4915 Greenspring Avenue
Baltimore, MD 21209
301-367-2217

Free. Open all year, 6 am–9 pm. Sells live plants.

London Town Publik House & Gardens
839 Londontown Road
Edgewater, MD 21037-2197
301-956-4900

Entrance fee: $2.00. Open all year, 10 am–4 pm Tues.–Sat., 12–4 pm Sun. Sells seeds and live plants.

Massachusetts

Alexandria Botanical Gardens &
  Hunnewell Arboretum
Wellesley College
Wellesley, MA 02181
617-235-0320

Free. Open all year, 8 am–4:30 pm (greenhouses); daylight hours (arboretum).

Arnold Arboretum
The Arborway
Jamaica Plain, MA 02130
617-524-1717

Free. Open all year, daylight hours. Part of Harvard University.

Berkshire Garden Center
State Routes 183 & 102
Stockbridge, MA 01262
413-298-3926

Entrance fee: $2.00 May–October. Open all year, 10 am–5 pm. Sells seeds and live plants. Wildflower displays.

Botanic Garden of Smith College
Lyman Plant House
College Lane
Northampton, MA 01060
413-584-2700, ext. 2742

Free. Open all year, daylight hours (grounds); 8 am–4:15 pm (Plant House). Wildflower garden, cultivated native plants. On the Smith College campus.

Garden in the Woods
Hemenway Road
Framingham, MA 01701
617-877-6574

Entrance fee: $3.50. Open April 16–Oct. 31, 9 am–4 pm. Sells seeds and live plants. Home of the New England Wild Flower Society.

Hopkins Memorial Forest
P.O. Box 632
Northwest Hill Road
Williamstown, MA 01267
413-597-2346

Free. Open all year, daylight hours. 2200-acre natural area. Buxton Garden, hiking trails.

Norcross Wildlife Sanctuary
Monson-Wales Road
Monson, MA 01057
413-267-9654

Free. Open all year, except holidays, 9 am–4 pm Mon.-Sat. Between Routes 19 & 32. Trails open Apr.–Nov.

Michigan

W. J. Beal Botanical Garden
Michigan State University
East Lansing, MI 48824
517-355-9582

Free. Open all year, daylight hours.

Fernwood Botanic Garden &
  Nature Center
1720 Range Line Road
Niles, MI 49120
616-695-6491

Entrance fee: $2.00 (adults). Open March–mid-Dec., 9 am–5 pm Mon.-Fri., 10 am–5 pm Sat., 12 pm–5 pm Sun. Sells seeds and live plants. 5-acre tallgrass prairie.

Hidden Lake Gardens
Route 50
Tipton, MI 49287
517-431-2060

Entrance fee: $1.00. Open all year, 8 am–sunset (summer), 8 am–4:30 pm (winter). Part of Michigan State University.

Matthaei Botanical Gardens
The University of Michigan
1800 North Dixboro Road
Ann Arbor, MI 48105
313-763-7060

Free. Open all year, 8 am–sunset (grounds), 10 am–4:30 pm (conservatory). Sells live plants. A variety of different native gardens, prairie restoration.

Whitehouse Nature Center
Albion College
Albion, MI 49224
517-629-2030

Free. Grounds open all year, daylight hours. Building open 9 am–5 pm Mon.-Fri., Interpretive Center open 1–5 pm weekends. Wildflower garden, woodland garden, restored prairie, and arboretum of native Michigan woody plants.

Minnesota

Eloise Butler Wildflower and Bird
  Sanctuary
Theodore Wirth Park
½ mile north of Highway 12
Minneapolis, MN 55409

612-348-5702

Free. Open April 1–Oct. 31, 7:30 am–sunset. Operated by Minneapolis Park and Recreation Board.

Como Park Conservatory
Midway Parkway & Kaufman Drive
Saint Paul, MN 55103
612-489-0868

Free. Open all year, daylight hours.

Minnesota Landscape Arboretum
3675 Arboretum Drive, P.O. Box 39
Chaska, MN 55317
612-443-2460

Entrance fee: $2.00. Open all year, 8 am–9 pm (summer), 8 am–6 pm (winter).

New Jersey

Leonard J. Buck Gardens
R.D. 2, Layton Road
Far Hills, NJ 07931
201-234-2677

Entrance fee: $.50 donation. Open all year, 10 am–4 pm Mon.-Sat., 1–6 pm Sun. (summer), 1–5 pm (winter).

Frelinghuysen Arboretum
53 E. Hanover Avenue
Morristown, NJ 07960
201-829-0474

Free. Open all year, except weekends Dec.–Feb. 9 am–sunset.

Emilie K. Hammond Wildflower Trail
The Taurne
Powerville Road
Boonton Township, NJ 07005

Free. Open Mar.–Nov., 8 am–sunset. Labeled wildflower trail.

Cora Hartshorn Arboretum
324 Forest Drive South
Short Hills, NJ 07078
201-376-3587

Free. Open all year, 2:30–4:30 pm Tues.–Thurs., 9:30–11:30 am Sat.; 3–5 pm Sun. in May & Oct.

Willowwood Arboretum
Longview Road
Chester Township, NJ 07903
201-829-0474

*Free. Open Mar.–Nov., 9:30 am–4 pm
Mon.–Fri., 10 am–4 pm Sat. & Sun.*

New York

Brooklyn Botanic Garden
1000 Washington Avenue
Brooklyn, NY 11225
718-622-4433

*Parking fee. Open April–Oct., 10:30
am–3:30 pm Tues.–Fri.*

Brooklyn Botanic Garden Research
  Center
712 Kitchawan Road
Ossining, NY 10562
914-941-8886

*Free. Open all year, daylight hours.
Workshops.*

Clark Garden
I.U. Willets Road
Albertson, NY 11507
516-621-7568

*Entrance fee: $1.50. Open all year, 9
am–4:30 pm. Sells seeds and live plants.
Affiliated with the Brooklyn Botanic Garden.*

Cornell Plantations
One Plantations Road
Ithaca, NY 14850
607-256-3020

Free. Open all year, daylight hours.

Bayard Cutting Arboretum
Montauk Highway
Oakdale, NY 11769
516-581-1002

*Entrance fee: $1.50, April–Nov. Open
all year, 10 am–4 pm Wed.–Sun.*

Institute of Ecosystem Studies
Mary Flagler Carey Arboretum
Route 44A
Millbrook, NY 12545

914-677-5343

*Free. Open all year, 9 am–4 pm Mon.–
Sat., 1–4 pm Sun. Sells seeds and live
plants.*

Knox Headquarters & Jane Colden
  Native Plant Sanctuary
Box 207, Forge Hill Road
Vails Gate, NY 12584
914-561-5498

*Free. Open all year, 10 am–5 pm Wed.–
Sun., 1–5 pm Sun.*

George Landis Arboretum
Route 20
Esperance, NY 12066
518-875-6935

Free. Open all year, daylight hours.

Mohonk Mountain House & Gardens
Mohonk Lake
New Paltz, NY 12561
914-255-1000

*Entrance fee: $4.00. Open all year, vary-
ing hours. A resort with gardens and trails.
Write or call for information.*

Museum of the Hudson Highlands
Box 181, The Boulevard
Cornwall-on-Hudson, NY 12520
914-534-7781

*Entrance fee: $1 donation. Open all year
except major holidays, 11 am–5 pm
Mon.–Thurs. and Sat., 1:30–5 pm Sun.
(summer), 2–5 pm Mon.–Thurs., 11
am–5 pm Sat., and 1:30–5 pm Sun.
(winter). Closed Fridays. A 3-acre
tallgrass prairie reconstruction, and 90
acres of woodlands.*

New York Botanical Garden
Bronx Park (Southern Boulevard)
Bronx, NY 10458
212-220-8700

*Entrance fee: $3.00 parking. Open
April–Oct. 8:30–4:30 pm. Sells seeds
and live plants. Detailed educational programs.*

Old Westbury Gardens
P.O. Box 420
Old Westbury, NY 11568
516-333-0048

*Entrance fee: $3.00 (adults), $1.00
(child). Open May–Oct., 10 am–5 pm
Wed.–Sun. Sells seeds and live plants.
Newsletter, workshops, symposia.*

Queens Botanical Garden
43-50 Main Street
Flushing, NY 11355
718-886-3800

*Free. Open all year, 9 am–sunset. Sells
seeds and live plants.*

Root Glen
Hamilton College
107 College Hill Rd.
Clinton, NY 13323
315-853-4502/859-4194

Free. Open all year, daylight hours.

Trailside Nature Museum
Ward Pound Ridge Reservation
Cross River, NY 10518
914-763-3993

Free. Open all year, daylight hours.

Ohio

Aullwood Audubon Center and Farm
1000 Aullwood Road
Dayton, OH 45414
513-890-7360

*Entrance fee: $1.50; National Audubon
Society members free. Open all year 9
am–5 pm Mon.–Sat., 1–5 pm Sun.
Closed major holidays. Marshes, woodlands, fen, wildflower trail, and native
Ohio restored tallgrass prairie. Seed collection program.*

Aullwood Garden
900 Aullwood Road
Dayton, OH 45414
513-278-8231

*Free. Open all year, Tues.–Sun., daylight
hours. Operated by Park District of Dayton–Montgomery County.*

Cedar Bog State Memorial
980 Woodburn Road
Urbana, OH 43078

513-484-3744

Entrance fee: $1.50. Open all year, by appointment only. 428 acres, operated by the Ohio Historical Society.

Cincinnati Nature Center
4949 Tealtown Road
Milford, OH 45150

513-831-1711

Entrance fee: $1.00 parking. Open all year, 7:30 am–8:30 pm Mon.–Fri. (summer); 8:30 am–7:30 pm Mon.–Fri. (winter).

Civic Garden Center of Greater
  Cincinnati
2715 Reading Road
Cincinnati, OH 45206

513-221-0981

Free. Open Jan. 16–Dec. 21, 9 am–4 pm Tues.–Fri, 9 am–3 pm Sat. Sells seeds and live plants. Periodic classes on native plant gardening.

Cleveland Museum of Natural History
Wade Oval, University Circle
Cleveland, OH 44106

216-231-4600

Entrance fee: $2.75. Open all year, 10 am–5 pm Mon.–Sat., 1 pm–5:30 pm Sun. Sells seeds and live plants.

Crosby Gardens
5403 Elmer Drive
Toledo, OH 43615

419-536-8365

Free. Open all year, daylight hours.

Dawes Arboretum
7770 Jacksontown Road, SE
Newark, OH 43055

Free. Open all year, daylight hours, except Thanksgiving, Christmas, and New Year's Day. Sells seeds. Wildflower walks, library.

The Garden Center of Greater Cleveland
11030 East Boulevard
Cleveland, OH 44106

216-721-1600

Free. Open all year, daylight hours.

Glen Helen
Antioch University
405 Corry Street
Yellow Springs, OH 45387

513-767-7375

Free. Open all year, daylight hours. Trailside museum open 10–12 am and 1–5:30 pm Tues.–Fri., noon–5:30 pm weekends. 1000-acre nature preserve, restored prairie.

Holden Arboretum
9500 Sperry Road
Mentor, OH 44060

216-946-4400

Entrance fee: $2.50. Open all year, 10 am–5 pm Tues.–Sun. Sells live plants.

Inniswood Botanical Garden & Nature
  Preserve
940 Hempstead Road
Westerville, OH 43081

614-895-6216

Free. Open all year, 8 am–4:30 pm Tues.–Sat., 12–5 pm Sun. Operated by the Metropolitan Park District of Columbus & Franklin Counties.

Kingwood Center
900 Park Avenue West
Mansfield, OH 43358

419-522-0211

Free. Open all year, 8 am–sunset. Sells live plants. Library.

Mount Airy Forest & Arboretum
5083 Colerain Avenue
Cincinnati, OH 45223

Free. Open all year, daylight hours. Wildflower programs.

Wildwood Preserve Metropark
5100 West Central Avenue
Toledo, OH 43615

419-535-3050

Free. Open all year, 7 am–sunset. Sells seeds and live plants. Programs, "Annual Prairie Celebration" in August.

Ontario

The Civic Garden Center/
  Edwards Gardens
777 Lawrence Avenue East
Don Mills, ONT M32 1P2

416-445-1552

Free. Open all year, daylight hours. Sells seeds and live plants. Courses on native plants, newsletter, plant sales.

Humber Arboretum
205 Humber College Boulevard
Toronto, ONT M9W 5L7

416-675-3111, ext. 445

Free. Open all year, daylight hours.

The Niagara Park Commission
School of Horticulture
Niagara Falls, ONT L2E 6T2

Free. Open all year, daylight hours. Interpretative services at the Niagara Glen.

Pennsylvania

Appleford
770 Mt. Moro Road
Villanova, PA 19085

215-527-4280

Free. Open all year, 9 am–sunset.

Barnes Foundation Arboretum
57 Lapsley Lane
Merion, PA 19066

215-664-8880

Free. Open all year, 9:30 am–4 pm Mon.–Sat., 1:30–4:30 pm Sun.

Bowman's Hill Wildflower Preserve
Washington Crossing Historic Park
Route 22
Washington Crossing, PA 18977

215-862-2924

Free. Open all year, 9 am–5 pm. Sells seeds and live plants. Monthly programs on native plants.

Delaware Valley College Arboretum
Delaware Valley College
Doylestown, PA 18901

215-345-1500

Free. Open all year, daylight hours.

Henry Foundation for Botanical Research
801 Stony Lane
Gladwyne, PA 19035

215-525-2037

Free. Open April–Oct., 10 am–4 pm Tues. & Thurs.

Longwood Gardens
U.S. Route 1
Kennett Square, PA 19348

215-388-6741

Entrance fee: $5.00. Open all year, 9 am–6 pm (summer), 9 am–5 pm (winter). Sells seeds and live plants.

Morris Arboretum
University of Pennsylvania
Hillcrest Avenue
Chestnut Hill, PA 19118

215-242-3399

Entrance fee: $2.00. Open all year, except Christmas & New Year's Day, 10 am–5 pm (spring–fall), 10 am–4 pm (winter). Sells live plants. Periodic courses.

Tyler Arboretum
515 Painter Road, Box 216
Lima, PA 19037

215-566-5431

Entrance fee: $3.00. Open all year, 8 am–5 pm, with extended hours in the summer. Sells seeds and live plants. Lectures, walks, native plant trail.

Wildflower Reserve of Raccoon Creek State Park
RD #1

Hookstown, PA 15050

412-899-3611/412-899-2200

Free. Open all year, 8 am–sunset. One of the most impressive stands of wildflowers in western Pennsylvania.

Québec

Ville de Montréal Jardin et de l'Institut Botaniques
4101 rue Sherbrooke est
Montréal, P.Q. H1X 2B2

514-872-1454

Free. Open all year, 8 am–10 pm. The Botanical Garden has several wildflower and native plant gardens.

Rhode Island

Blithewood Gardens & Arboretum
Ferry Road
Bristol, RI 02809

401-253-2707

Entrance fee: $2.00 (gardens). Open May–Oct., 10 am–4 pm. Programs and lectures.

Vermont

Park-McCullough House
West & Park Streets
North Bennington, VT 05257

802-442-5441

Entrance fee: $4.00. Open May–Oct., 10 am–4 pm.

Vermont Wildflower Farm
Route 7
Charlotte, VT 05445

802-452-3500

Entrance fee: $2.00. Open May–Oct., 10 am–5 pm. Sells seeds.

Virginia

Blandy Experimental Farm
Orland E. White Arboretum
University of Virginia
Boyce, VA 22620

703-837-1758

Free. Open all year, daylight hours.

Maymont Park
1700 Hampton Street
Richmond, VA 23220

804-358-7166

Free. Open all year, daylight hours. Sells seeds and live plants.

Norfolk Botanical Gardens
Airport Road
Norfolk, VA 23518

804-853-6972

Entrance fee: $2.00. Open all year, 8:30 am–sunset. Monthly newsletter.

River Farm
American Horticultural Society
7931 E. Boulevard Drive
Alexandria, VA 22308

703-768-5700

Free. Open all year, except holidays, 8:30 am–5 pm Mon.–Fri. Wildflower plantings and 5–acre wildflower meadow.

Wildflower Garden on Mill Mountain
Roanoke, VA 24014

703-343-6757

Free. Open March–Nov., 9 am–sunset. Part of the Garden Club of America.

Wintergreen Resort
Wintergreen, VA 22958

804-325-2200

Open all year, daylight hours. Annual "Wildflower Weekend" symposium in May.

West Virginia

Cathedral State Park
Route 50
Aurora, WV 26705

304-735-3771

Free. Open all year, 6 am–10 pm. Virgin eastern hemlock tract.

Core Arboretum
Department of Biology, P.O. Box 6057
West Virginia University
Morgantown, WV 26506-6507

304-293-5201

Free. Open all year, daylight hours.

Watoga State Park
Star Route 1, Box 252
Marlington, WV 24954

Free. Open all year, daylight hours. Trails through the arboretum.

Wisconsin

Alfred Boerner Botanical Gardens
Witnall Park, 5879 S. 92nd Street
Milwaukee (Hales Corners), WI 53130

414-425-1131

Free. Open April–Oct., 8 am–sunset. Native plant rock gardens.

Schlitz-Audubon Nature Center
1111 E. Brown Deer Road
Milwaukee, WI 53217

414-352-2880

Entrance fee: $1.00. Open all year, except holidays, 9 am–5 pm Tues.–Sun. Programs on native plant gardens.

University of Wisconsin Arboretum
1207 Seminole Highway
Madison, WI 53711

608-263-7888

Free. Open all year, 7 am–10 pm. Visitor center open 9 am–4 pm, weekdays; 12:30-4 pm, weekends. Extensive areas of restored plant communities.

Wehr Nature Center
9701 West College Avenue
Franklin, WI 53132

414-425-8550

Free (guided tours $1.25). Open all year, except Thanksgiving and Christmas, 8 am–4:30 pm. Sells seeds and live plants. Lectures, workshops.

Native Plant and Horticultural Societies

This is a listing of native plant societies, botanical organizations, and horticultural societies that are interested in native plants.

Connecticut

Connecticut Audubon Society
2325 Burr Street
Fairfield, CT 06430
203-259-6305
Publishes Connecticut Audubon Bulletin.

Connecticut Botanical Society
% Donald Swan
1 Livermore Trail
Killingsworth, CT 06417
Publishes a newsletter.

Connecticut Horticultural Society
150 Main Street
Wethersfield, CT 06109
203-529-8713
Publishes a newsletter.

The Nature Conservancy
Connecticut Chapter
55 High Street
Middletown, CT 06457
203-344-0716

Connecticut Natural Diversity
  Database
Natural Resource Center
State Office Building, Room 553
165 Capitol Avenue
Hartford, CT 06106

203-566-3540

Delaware

Delaware Natural Heritage Inventory
Division of Parks & Recreation
89 Kings Highway
Dover, DE 19903
302-736-5285

District of Columbia

Botanical Society of Washington
Department of Botany — NHB/166
Smithsonian Institution
Washington, DC 20560

Illinois

Chicago Horticultural Society
P.O. Box 400
Glencoe, IL 60022
Publishes Garden. *Parent organization of Chicago Botanic Garden.*

Illinois Audubon Society
P.O. Box 608
Wayne, IL 60184
312-584-6290
Publishes Illinois Audubon.

Illinois Native Plant Society
Department of Botany
Southern Illinois University
Carbondale, IL 62901
618-536-2331
Publishes The Harbinger *and* Erigenia.
Sells books on native plants.

Illinois Natural Heritage Inventory

Department of Conservation
Division of Natural Heritage
524 S. 2nd Street
Springfield, IL 62706
217-785-8774

The Nature Conservancy
Illinois Field Office
Suite 708
79 West Monroe Street
Chicago, IL 60603
312-346-8166

Indiana

Indiana Audubon Society, Inc.
Mary Gray Bird Sanctuary
RR 6
Connersville, IN 47331
317-825-9788
Publishes The Indiana Audubon.

Indiana Heritage Program
Division of Nature Preserves, IN DNR
605b State Office Building
Indianapolis, IN 46204
317-232-4052

The Nature Conservancy
Indiana Field Office
4200 N. Michigan Road
Indianapolis, IN 46208
317-923-7547

Iowa

Iowa Natural Areas Inventory
Bureau of Preserves & Ecological
  Services

Department of Natural Resources
Wallace State Office Building
Des Moines, IA 50319
515-281-8654

Iowa State Horticultural Society
State House
Des Moines, IA 50319
515-281-5402
Publishes Iowa Horticulturist.

The Nature Conservancy
Iowa Field Office
Suite 311
424 10th Street
Des Moines, IA 50309
515-244-5044

Kentucky

Kentucky Heritage Program
Kentucky Preserves Commission
407 Broadway
Frankfort, KY 40601
502-564-2886

The Nature Conservancy
Kentucky Chapter
P.O. 2125
Covington, KY 41012

Maine

Josselyn Botanical Society
% Dr. Charles D. Richards
Deering Hall, University of Maine
Orono, ME 04469

Maine Audubon Society
Gilsland Farm
118 Route 1
Falmouth, ME 04105
207-781-2330
Publishes Habitat *and* Journal of the
Maine Audubon Society.

The Nature Conservancy
Maine Chapter
122 Maine Street
Topsham, ME 04086
207-729-5181

*Administers the Maine Natural Heritage
Program.*

Maryland

Audubon Naturalist Society of the
    Central Atlantic States
8940 Jones Mill Road
Chevy Chase, MD 20815
301-652-9188
Publishes Audubon Naturalist News
and Atlantic Naturalist.

Maryland Natural Heritage Program
Department of Natural Resources
C-3, Tawes State Office Building
Annapolis, MD 21401

The Nature Conservancy
Maryland/Delaware Office
Suite 304 Chevy Chase Center
    Office Building
35 Wisconsin Circle
Chevy Chase, MD 20815
301-656-8673

Massachusetts

Massachusetts Audubon Society, Inc.
South Great Road
Lincoln, MA 01773
617-259-9500
Publishes Sanctuary.

Massachusetts Heritage Program
Division of Fisheries and Wildlife
100 Cambridge Street
Boston, MA 02202

Massachusetts Horticultural Society
300 Massachusetts Avenue
Boston, MA 02115
617-536-9280
Publishes Horticulture *and* The Leaflet.
*Offers courses and lectures on native plant
gardening.*

The Nature Conservancy
Massachusetts/Rhode Island
Room 740
294 Washington Street
Boston, MA 02108

617-423-2545

New England Botanical Club
Botanical Museum
Oxford Street
Cambridge, MA 02138
Publishes Rhodora.

New England Wild Flower Society, Inc.
Garden in the Woods
Hemenway Road
Framingham, MA 01701
617-877-7630
Publishes a newsletter.

Michigan

Michigan Audubon Society
409 West East Avenue
Kalamazoo, MI 49007
616-344-8648
Publishes The Jack Pine Warbler *and*
Michigan Audubon Newsletter.

Michigan Botanical Club
Matthaei Botanical Gardens
1800 Dixboro Road
Ann Arbor, MI 48105

Michigan Natural Features Inventory
Mason Building, 5th Floor
Box 30028
Lansing, MI 48909
517-373-1552

Michigan Nature Association
P.O. Box 102
Avoca, MI 48006
313-324-2626
Publishes Members' Newsletter. *Operates 99 sanctuaries, open to the public
without charge. Write for information.*

The Nature Conservancy
Michigan Field Office
Suite E
531 N. Clippert Street
Lansing, MI 48912
517-332-1741

Minnesota

Minnesota Native Plant Society
220 BioSci Center — University of
    Minnesota
1445 Gortner Avenue
St. Paul, MN 55108

Minnesota Natural Heritage Program
Department of Natural Resources
500 Lafayette Road
St. Paul, MN 55146
612-296-4284

Minnesota State Horticultural Society
University of Minnesota
St. Paul, MN 55108
Publishes Minnesota Horticulturist.

The Nature Conservancy
Minnesota Field Office
1313 Fifth Street, S.E.
Minneapolis, MN 55414
612-379-2134

Missouri

Missouri Native Plant Society
Box 6612
Jefferson City, MO 65102-6612
Publishes Missouriensis. *Meetings open
to the public.*

Nevada

Northern Nevada Native Plant Society
Box 8965
Reno, NV 89507
Publishes Mentzelia *and a newsletter.*

New Jersey

New Jersey Audubon Society
P.O. Box 125
790 Ewing Avenue
Franklin Lakes, NJ 07417
201-891-1211

New Jersey Native Plant Society
% Frelinghuysen Arboretum
Box 1295R
Morristown, NJ 07960

New Jersey Natural Heritage Program
Office of Natural Lands Management
109 W. State Street
Trenton, NJ 08608
609-984-1339

New Mexico

Native Plant Society of New Mexico
P.O. Box 5917
Santa Fe, NM 87502

New York

Horticultural Society of New York
128 W. 58th Street
New York, NY 10019
Publishes Garden *and a newsletter.*

The Nature Conservancy
New York Field Office
1736 Western Avenue
Albany, NY 12203
518-869-6959

New York Natural Heritage Program
Wildlife Resources Center
Delmar, NY 12054-9767
518-439-7488

Torrey Botanical Club
New York Botanical Garden
Bronx Park
Bronx, NY 10458
Publishes Bulletin.

Ohio

Cincinnati Wildflower Preservation
    Society
% Dr. Victor G. Soukup
Department of Biology
University of Cincinnati
Cincinnati, OH 45221

Inniswood Society
Inniswood Botanical Garden
940 Hempstead Road
Westerville, OH 43081
614-895-6216
Publishes Garden.

Native Plant Society of Northeastern
    Ohio
6 Louise Drive
Chagrin Falls, OH 44022
Publishes On the Fringe. *Monthly lectures and field trips.*

The Nature Conservancy
Ohio Field Office
1504 West 1st Avenue
Columbus, OH 43212
614-486-6789

Ohio Biological Survey
980 Biological Sciences Building
Ohio State University
484 West 12th Avenue
Columbus, OH 43210
614-422-9645

Ohio Natural Heritage Program
Division of Natural Areas &
    Preservation
Ohio Department of Natural Resources
Fountain Square, Building F
Columbus, OH 43224
614-265-6453

Pennsylvania

The Nature Conservancy
Pennsylvania/New Jersey Field Office
Suite 1002
1228 Chestnut Street
Philadelphia, PA 19107
215-925-1065

Pennsylvania Botanical Club
Academy of Science
19th and Parkway
Philadelphia, PA 19103

Pennsylvania Horticultural Society,
    Inc.
Independence National Historical Park
325 Walnut Street
Philadelphia, PA 19106
Publishes News *and* Green Scene. *Field
trips.*

Pennsylvania Native Plant Society
1806 Commonwealth Building
316 Fourth Avenue
Pittsburgh, PA 15222

Pennsylvania Natural Diversity
    Inventory
Bureau of Forestry
Department of Environmental
    Resources
34 Airport Road
Middletown, PA 17057
717-783-1712

Philadelphia Botanical Club
Academy of Science
19th and Parkway
Philadelphia, PA 19103

Québec

La Société D'Animation du Jardin et
    de l'Institut Botaniques
(SAJIB)
4101 rue Sherbrooke est
Montréal, P.Q. H1X 2B2
Publishes Liaison SAJIB *and* Bulletin
de la SAJIB.

Rhode Island

Audubon Society of Rhode Island
40 Bowen Street
Providence, RI 02903
401-521-1670
Publishes The Audubon Society of
Rhode Island Report.

Rhode Island Heritage Program
Department of Environmental
    Management
Division of Planning & Development
22 Hayes Street
Providence, RI 02903
401-277-2776

Vermont

The Nature Conservancy
Vermont Field Office
138 Main Street
Montpelier, VT 05602

802-229-4425
Administers the Vermont Natural Heritage
Program.

Vermont Institute of Natural Science
Church Hill Road
Woodstock, VT 05091
802-457-2779

Virginia

The Nature Conservancy
Virginia Field Office
619-B East High Street
Charlottesville, VA 22901
804-295-6106
Coordinates the Virginia Natural Heritage
Program.

Virginia Wildflower Preservation
    Society
Box 844
Annandale, VA 22003
Publishes Bulletin *and newsletters.
Several chapters, Wildflower Week events,
and other activities.*

West Virginia

The Nature Conservancy
West Virginia Field Office
Room 215
1100 Quarrier Street
Charleston, WV 25301
304-345-4350

West Virginia Native Plant Society
Herbarium, Brooks Hall
West Virginia University
Morgantown, WV 26506

West Virginia Wildlife/Heritage
    Database
Wildlife Resources Division
Department of Natural Resources
    Operations Center
P.O. Box 67
Elkins, WV 26241
304-636-1767

Wisconsin

The Nature Conservancy
Wisconsin Field Office
Room 209
1045 East Dayton Street
Madison, WI 53703
608-251-8140

Wisconsin Natural Heritage Program
Endangered Resources
Department of Natural Resources
101 South Webster Street
Box 7921
Madison, WI 53707
608-266-0924

National Organizations
UNITED STATES OF AMERICA

American Horticultural Society
P.O. Box 0105
Mt. Vernon, VA 22121
703-768-5700
Publishes American Horticulturist.
*Wildflower Rediscovery Project, Gar-
dener's Information Service, and other
programs.*

American Rock Garden Society
℅ Buffy Parker, Secretary
15 Fairmead Road
Darien, CT 06820
Publishes Quarterly Bulletin. *Twenty
regional chapters.*

Center for Plant Conservation
℅ Arnold Arboretum
The Arborway
Jamaica Plain, MA 02130
617-524-1717

Environmental Defense Fund
444 Park Avenue South
New York, NY 10016
212-686-4191

Environmental Protection Agency
    — Region I
John F. Kennedy Federal Building
Boston, MA 02203

617-223-7210

Includes CT, MA, ME, NH, RI, and VT.

Environmental Protection Agency
— Region II
26 Federal Plaza
New York, NY 10007

212-264-2525

Includes NJ and NY.

Environmental Protection Agency
— Region III
Curtis Building
6th and Walnut Streets
Philadelphia, PA 19106

215-597-9814

Includes DE, MD, PA, VA, and WV.

Environmental Protection Agency
— Region IV
345 Courtland Street, NE
Atlanta, GA 30308

404-881-4727

Includes AL, FL, GA, KY, MS, NC, SC, and TN.

Environmental Protection Agency
— Region V
230 South Dearborn
Chicago, IL 60604

312-353-2000

Includes IL, IN, MI, MN, OH, and WI.

Garden Club of America
598 Madison Avenue
New York, NY 10022

212-753-8287

Publishes Garden Club of America Bulletin.

National Council of State Garden
Clubs
4401 Magnolia Avenue
St. Louis, MO 63110

314-776-7574

Publishes The National Gardener *and the* Directory to Resources on Wildflower Propagation *($3.00).*

National Wildflower Research Center
2600 FM 973 North
Austin, TX 78725

Publishes Wildflower.

Operation Wildflower
National Council of State Garden
Clubs
Mrs. C. Norman Collard, Chairman
Box 860
Pocasset, MA 02559

Soil Conservation Society of America
7515 Northeast Ankeny Road
Ankeny, IA 50021

515-289-2331

Publishes Sources of Native Seeds and Plants *($3.00).*

U.S. Fish & Wildlife Service
Office of Endangered Species
Washington, DC 20240

703-235-2771

U.S. Fish & Wildlife Service
— Region 3
Federal Building
Fort Snelling
Twin Cities, MN 55111

612-725-3500

Includes IL, IN, IA, MI, MN, MO, OH, and WI.

U.S. Fish & Wildlife Service
— Region 4
Richard B. Russell Federal Building
75 Spring Street, SW
Atlanta, GA 30303

404-331-3580

Includes AL, AR, FL, GA, KY, LA, MS, NC, SC, TN, PR, and VI.

U.S. Fish & Wildlife Service
— Region 5
Suite 700
One Gateway Center
Newton Corner, MA 02158

617-965-5100

Includes CT, DE, ME, MD, MA, NH, NJ, NY, PA, RI, VT, VA, and WV.

World Wildlife Fund — U.S.
1255 23rd Street, N.W.
Washington, DC 20037

202-293-4800

CANADA

Canadian Botanical Association
Institut Botanique, Université de
Montréal
4101 rue Sherbrooke est
Montréal, P.Q. H1X 2B2

514-256-7511

Publishes CBA Bulletin. *Active Conservation Committee.*

The Canadian Wildflower Society
35 Bauer Crescent
Unionville, ONT L3R 4H3

416-477-3992

Publishes Wildflower.

References

Aiken, G.D., 1968. *Pioneering with Wildflowers*. Prentice-Hall, Englewood Cliffs, NJ.

A book on northeastern woodland natives written by the late senator from Vermont, a professional horticulturist.

Art, H.W., 1986. *A Garden of Wildflowers*. Garden Way Publishing – Storey Communications, Pownal, VT., 290 pp.

An illustrated guide to 101 native North American species and how to grow them.

Bailey, L.H., 1935. *The Standard Cyclopedia of Horticulture*. Macmillan, New York, NY. 3639 pp.

A classic gardening encyclopedia containing information on numerous native wildflowers as well as domesticated species.

Birdseye, C. & E. Birdseye, 1951. *Growing Woodland Plants*. Dover, New York, NY. 223 pp.

A guide to gardening with 200 northeastern native species of woodland habitats.

Bruce, H., 1976. *How to Grow Wildflowers and Wild Shrubs and Trees in Your Own Garden*. Van Nostrand/Reinhold, New York, NY. 294 pp.

East Coast woody and herbaceous perennials, presented in an anecdotal style.

Brumbrack, W.E. & D.R. Longland, 1986. *Garden in the Woods Cultivation Guide*. New England Wild Flower Society, Framingham, MA, 62 pp.

A handy guide to cultivating wildflowers by the propagator and garden director of The Garden in the Woods.

Cox, D.D., 1985. *Common Flowering Plants of the Northeast*. State University of New York Press, Albany. 418 pp.

A black-and-white field guide to the wildflowers of the region organized by habitat and plant family.

Crockett, J.U. & O.E. Allen, 1977. *Wildflower Gardening*. Time-Life Books, Alexandria, VA. 160 pp.

Coast-to-coast examples of natives for the garden, with color illustrations.

Durand, H., 1923. *Wildflowers and Ferns: In Their Homes and In Our Gardens*. Putnams, New York, NY. 394 pp.

An early classic on northeastern wildflowers.

Foster, H.L., 1968. *Rock Gardening: A Guide to Growing Alpines and Other Wildflowers in the American Garden*. Bonanza Books, New York, NY. 466 pp.

A classic with a good deal of information on native plants in rock gardens.

Hartmann, H.T. & D.E. Kester, 1975. *Plant Propagation*. 3rd ed. Prentice-Hall, Englewood Cliffs, NJ. 662 pp.

A standard text about plant propagation.

Hersey, J., 1964. *Wild Flowers to Know and Grow*. Van Nostrand, Princeton, NJ. 235 pp.

Concentrates on northeastern perennials and wildflowers.

Hill, L., 1985. *Secrets of Plant Propagation*. Garden Way Publishing, Pownal, VT. 168 pp.

How to propagate woody and herbaceous plants.

Hull, H.S., ed. 1982. *Handbook on Gardening with Wildflowers*. Brooklyn Botanic Garden, Brooklyn, NY. [*B.B.G. Plants & Gardens* 18 (1).] 85 pp.

A variety of articles about native plant gardening.

Jacob, W. & I. Jacob, 1985. *Gardens of North America and Hawaii*. Timber Press, Portland, OR. 368 pp.

A useful cross continent guide to gardens and arboreta with short descriptions and helpful state maps.

Kenfield, W.G., 1970. *The Wild Gardener in the Wild Landscape*. Hafner, New York, NY. 232 pp.

An interesting book on naturalistic landscaping in the Northeast.

Martin, A.C., H.S. Zim, & A.L.

Nelson, 1951. *American Wildlife and Plants*. Dover, New York, NY. 500 pp.

While not a book about wildflower gardening, this book is quite helpful in planning gardens to attract various wildlife species.

Martin, L.C., 1986. *The Wildflower Meadow Book*. East Woods Press, Charlotte, N.C. 303 pp.

A coast-to-coast treatment of native and exotic wildflowers that grow in fields and meadows.

McGourty, F., 1978. *Ground Covers and Vines*. Brooklyn Botanic Garden, Brooklyn, NY. (*Plants and Gardens*, Vol. 32, No. 3).

A useful booklet with articles on the use of both native and exotic plants as ground covers.

Montgomery, F.H., 1977. *Seeds and Fruits of Plants of Eastern Canada and Northeastern United States*. U. Toronto Press, Toronto, ONT. 232 pp.

A useful guide to seeds and fruits of native plants.

Newcomb, L., *Newcomb's Wildflower Guide*. Little, Brown & Co., Boston. 490 pp.

A useful field guide to wildflowers of the Northeast organized by the number of plant parts.

Newcomb, L. (translated by G. Morrison) *Guide des Fleurs Sauvages de l'est de l'Amérique du Nord*. Marcel Broquet, La Prairie, P.Q. 495 pp.

A French translation of *Newcomb's Wildflower Guide*.

North Carolina Wild Flower Preservation Society, 1977. *North Carolina Native Plant Propagation Handbook*. North Carolina Wild Flower Preservation Society, Inc., Chapel Hill, NC. 80 pp.

A handy guide to the propagation requirements of 98 species native to eastern North America.

Peterson, R.T. & M. McKenny, 1968. *A Field Guide to Wildflowers of Northeastern and Northcentral North America*. Houghton Mifflin, Boston. 420 pp.

One of the Peterson Field Guide Series, it is organized by flower color.

Phillips, H.R., 1985. *Growing and Propagating Wild Flowers*. U. North Carolina Press, Chapel Hill, NC. 331 pp.

Excellent book on eastern native plants, concentrating on seed collection and propagation methods.

Phillips, Norma, 1984. *The Root Book*. Published by the author, 6700 Splithand Rd., Grand Rapids, MN 55744. 107 pp.

A photographic guide to root systems and soil requirements of eastern North American wildflowers.

Roberts, E.A. & E. Rehmann, 1929. *American Plants for American Gardens*. Macmillan, New York. 131 pp.

Out of print, but worth a trip to the library for this classic work organized by habitats and ecological communities.

Sperka, M., 1973. *Growing Wildflowers*. Scribner's, New York, NY. 277 pp.

An excellent treatment of northeastern wildflowers.

Steffek, E.F., 1983. *The New Wild Flowers and How to Grow Them*. Timber Press, Portland, OR. 186 pp.

A sampling of wildflowers from North America, with useful tables of species from various regions and habitats.

Stokes, D.W. & L.Q. Stokes, 1985. *A Guide to Enjoying Wildflowers*. Little, Brown and Co., Boston. 371 pp.

An illustrated guide to 98 common exotic and native wildflowers found in the Northeast.

Sullivan, G.A. & R.H. Dailey, 1981. *Resources on Wildflower Propagation*. National Council of State Garden Clubs, Inc., St. Louis, MO. 331 pp.

A bargain at $3.00. Contains a wealth of technical information about plants native to various sections of the U.S.

Tanenbaum, F., 1973. *Gardening with Wildflowers*. Ballantine Books, New York. 165 pp.

A chatty book presenting northeastern native plants by habitat.

Taylor, K.S. & S.F. Hamblin, 1976. *Handbook of Wildflower Cultivation*. Collier Books, New York, NY.

Covers a variety of eastern wildflowers.

U.S. Environmental Protection Agency, Region I. 1981. *New England Wetlands, Plant Identification and Protective Laws*. U.S. EPA., Washington, DC. 172 pp.

A superb color photographic guide to Northeastern wetland species.

Wilson, W.H.W., 1984. *Landscaping with Wildflowers and Native Plants*. Ortho Books, San Francisco, CA. 96 pp.

Listings of native plants for various regions and habitats.

Woodward, C.H. & H.W. Rickett, 1979. *Common Wild Flowers of the Northeastern United States*. Barron's, Woodbury, NY. 318 pp.

An abridged version of the massive *Wild Flowers of the United States, Volume 1*.

Glossary

Annual. A plant whose life cycle from seed to mature plant, producing flowers, fruits, and seeds, is completed in a single growing season. After seeds are produced, the plant usually dies.

Anther. A pollen-producing sac attached to the filament in the male portion of a flower.

Axil. The point of attachment between stem and leaf.

Basal rosette. An arrangement of leaves radiating from a short stem at the ground surface. Most biennials have a rosette form during their first growing season.

Biennial. A plant whose life cycle extends over two growing seasons. The first year the seed germinates, producing a seedling that usually remains short over the winter. The second growing season the seedling rapidly elongates, flowers, produces seeds, and then dies.

Bolting. The rapid elongation and flowering of biennials during their second growing season.

Boreal. Pertaining to regions of the northern hemisphere that have cold winters and forests dominated by coniferous species.

Bract. A modified leaflike structure, often resembling a petal, surrounding a flower or flower cluster.

Bulb. A fleshy rootstock composed of leaf bases or scaly leaves.

Bunch grasses. Species of grass that form distinct clumps or bunches as they grow, in contrast to the sod-forming grasses usually grown for lawns.

Calyx. The collective term for the sepals of a flower.

Capsule. A dry fruit that splits open to release its seeds.

Complete flowers. Flowers with sepals, petals, stamens, and a pistil all present.

Composite flower. A flower made up of many individual florets clustered into a common head, as is typical in members of the aster family.

Compound leaf. A leaf that is divided into two or more separate leaflets.

Corm. A fleshy rootstock formed by a short, thick, underground stem.

Corolla. The collective term for the petals of a flower.

Crest. A ridge of tissue.

Deciduous. Pertaining to plant parts, usually leaves, that are shed annually.

Disc flower (disc floret). One of the small, tubular flowers that form the central disc of flower heads in many members of the aster family.

Dissected. Deeply divided or split into lobes.

Dormancy. The resting or inactive phase of plants or seeds. Dormancy of shoots is usually in response to unfavorable environmental conditions. The breaking of seed dormancy requires moisture and sometimes cold temperatures and abrasion of the seed coat.

Elaiosome. An oily, starchy appendage on some seeds that attracts ants and other insects, which act as dispersal agents.

Entire. A leaf margin that is smooth and lacking teeth.

Fibrous roots. A root system with many thin or branched root elements.

Filament. The anther-bearing stalk of a stamen.

Floret. One of the small flowers that is clustered together forming the composite flower head in members of the aster family. Florets may be either tubular disc florets or straplike ray florets.

Flowering shoot. A stem that produces flowers.

Flower head. A cluster of florets or small flowers gathered together on a common receptacle, typically found in members of the aster family.

Forcing. Inducing a perennial to flower out of season. Forcing often involves artificial chilling followed by warming the plant.

Germination. The breaking of dormancy in seeds or the sprouting of pollen grains deposited on a stigma.

Habitat. The kind of environment inhabited by a particular species.

Half-hardy. An annual plant that is sown in early spring and flowers in summer.

Hardiness zone. An index relating geographic regions to a plant's ability to withstand minimum winter temperatures. Hardiness zones developed by the U.S. Department of Agriculture range from zone 1, with a minimum temperature of $-50°F$, to zone 10, with minimum temperatures of 30 to 40°F.

Hardy annual. An annual plant whose seeds can withstand subfreezing winter temperatures and whose seedlings can withstand spring frosts.

Hardy perennial. A perennial plant that is not permanently injured or killed by subfreezing temperatures.

Herbaceous. Plants that lack woody tissues and therefore "die back" to the soil surface at the end of the growing season.

Humus. Soft brown or black amorphous substance formed through the decomposition of leaves, wood, and other organic materials.

Inoculant. A commercially formulated strain of rhizobium added to the soil to aid in the establishment of various members of the bean family.

Inoculation. The addition of rhizobia to the soil.

Keel. The lower, pouchlike lip of flowers of certain members of the bean family. The keel is formed by the fusion of two petals.

Leaflets. The individual segments of a compound leaf.

Legume. A dry, flattened pod fruit that splits open at both edges when mature, as is found in members of the bean family. The term is also applied to the species of the bean family.

Long-day plant. A plant that flowers in response to the short nights of late spring and early summer.

Moist chilling treatment. A means of enhancing the germination of some seeds by storing them under moist conditions at low temperatures prior to planting them.

Nodules. Outgrowths on the roots of plants in the bean family that are inhabited by nitrogen-fixing microorganisms known as rhizobia.

Non-flowering shoot. A stem that does not produce flowers; a vegetative shoot.

Ovary. The swollen base of a pistil, containing ovules. The ripening ovary, which is sometimes fused to the receptacle, becomes the fruit.

Ovules. The female sex cells that become seeds following fertilization.

Palmate. A pattern of compound leaflets or leaf venation, with elements radiating from a central point.

Peduncle. The main flowering stalk of a plant.

Perennial. A plant whose life cycle extends for an indefinite period beyond two growing seasons. These plants generally do not die following flowering.

Perfect flowers. Flowers with both stamens and a pistil, but lacking either sepals and/or petals.

Petal. A modified leaf attached to the receptacle outside the stamens and inside the calyx. Petals are usually showy and serve to attract pollinators to the flower.

Petiole. The stalk that attaches a leaf to a stem.

pH. A measure of the acidity/alkalinity of a substance ranging from 0 (strongly acidic) to 14 (strongly alkaline), with 7 being neutral.

Pistil. The female sexual part of a flower, consisting of the stigma, style, and ovary.

Plugs. A method of propagation by planting individual seeds in specially designed trays with small indentations. The root system of the seedlings fills the hole, forming a plug that can be easily removed and planted where desired.

Pollen. The powdery material produced in anthers, containing the male sex cells of flowering plants.

Pollination. The transfer of pollen from an anther to a stigma.

Propagation. Increasing the numbers of plants through seeds, cuttings, or divisions.

Ray flower (ray floret). One of the small flowers with a straplike petal, usually arranged in rings around the margin of flower heads in members of the aster family.

Receptacle. The fleshy tissue at the tip of a flower stalk to which flower parts are attached. Different species may have receptacles that are positioned below the ovary, form a cup around the ovary, or completely enclose the ovary.

Rhizobia. Microorganisms that inhabit nodules on the roots of members of the bean family. These organisms have the ability to take nitrogen from the air and create nitrogen compounds usable by their host plants.

Rhizome. A horizontal, usually branched, underground stem with buds and roots.

Root division. Propagating plants by cutting vertically between root segments.

Root rot. Plant diseases, usually caused by fungi, that lead to the degeneration of roots.

Rootstock. An underground stem of a perennial plant with its associated buds and roots.

Runner. A thin, creeping, horizontal stem that trails along the surface of the ground and gives rise to small plants.

Scape. A leafless stem bearing a cluster of flowers.

Scarification. Abrasion of the seed coat allowing the passage of water and oxygen into the seed, thereby enhancing germination in some species.

Seed coat. The outer protective covering of a seed.

Sepal. A modified leaf that forms the covering of a flower bud. Sepals are attached to the outer margin of the receptacle and are usually green. However, in some species the sepals are brightly colored and resemble petals.

Shoot. The aboveground or stem portion of a plant that bears leaves, buds, and flowers.

Shoot bud. A bud that develops into stem and leaf tissue.

Short-day plant. A plant that flowers in response to the long nights of fall or early spring.

Simple flower. A solitary flower borne on a single stem.

Slip. An old-fashioned name for a cutting used for propagation.

Sods. A method of propagation by densely planting seeds in flats or trays. The root systems of the seedlings intertwine, allowing the sod to be removed in a single piece and planted where desired.

Softwood cutting. A propagation technique of cutting green, rapidly growing portions of stems while they are pliable.

Spadix. A fleshy, spindle-shaped column bearing flowers in members of the arum family.

Spathe. A large, leafy bract that frequently envelops the spadix in members of the arum and other plant families.

Stamen. The male sexual part of a flower consisting of an anther and a filament.

Stigma. The top surface of a pistil upon which pollen grains are deposited.

Stolon. A thin, underground runner.

Stratification. Chilling seeds to enhance their germination.

Style. The portion of the pistil connecting the stigma and the ovary.

Taproot. A thick, strongly vertical root, usually extending to considerable depth, for example, the carrot.

Tender annual. An annual plant whose seedlings are killed by spring frosts.

Tender perennial. Perennial plants that are permanently damaged or killed by subfreezing temperatures.

True root. The descending, underground portion of a plant that is specialized to provide support and absorb water and nutrients. True roots usually lack buds.

Tuber. A rootstock formed by a fleshy, swollen tip of a stolon.

Vernalization. The cold treatment needed by some fall-germinating plants to promote flowering the following spring.

Weed. Any plant that grows where it is not wanted.

Wetlands. An area of low-lying land with soils that are submerged or wet for a significant portion of each year.

Wildflower. An herbaceous plant capable of growing, reproducing, and becoming established without cultivation.

Winter annual. An annual plant that usually germinates in the fall, overwinters as a seedling, and flowers the following spring.

Woody. Having hard, tough tissues that persist from year to year and are capable of producing shoot or flower buds. Woody plants also have the capacity to increase in diameter from year to year.

Index

Boldface numbers, such as **117**, indicate that illustrations, maps, or tables appear on that page.

A

Acid rain, 43
Acorus calamus, 124
Actaea pachypoda, 102
Adiantum pedatum, 81
Agricultural Experiment Stations, 46
Ail des bois. See Wild leek
Ail doux. See Eastern trout lily
Allium cernuum, 138
Allium tricoccum, 116 – 117, **117**.
　　See also Wild leek
American bellflower, 102
Anémone du Canada. See Canada
　　anemone
Anemone canadensis, 140 – 141, **141**.
　　See also Canada anemone
Annual precipitation of northeastern
　　North America, **58**
Anther, **25**
Apios americana, 132 – 133, **133**.
　　See also Groundnut
Aquilegia caerulea, 102
Aquilegia canadensis, 96 – 97, **97**.
　　See also Eastern columbine
Arboreta, 11
Arisaema triphyllum, 126 – 127, **127**.
　　See also Jack-in-the-pulpit
Asaret du Canada. See Wild ginger
Asarum canadensis, 94 – 95, **95**.
　　See also Wild ginger
Asclepias incarnata, 124
Asclepias tuberosa, 138
Aster de la Nouvelle-Angleterre.
　　See New England aster

Aster novae-angliae, 150 – 151, **151**.
　　See also New England aster
Athyrium filix-femina, 103
Audubon Society, 11

B

Balmony. *See* Turtlehead
Baneberry. *See* White baneberry
Beadruby. *See* Wild lily-of-the-valley
Beans, 53
Beds, 13
Bergamot, wild. *See* Wild bergamot
Black-eyed Susan, **77**, 146 – 147, **147**
Blanketflower, 138
Blind gentian. *See* Closed gentian
Bloodroot, 15, **63**, 84 – 85, **85**
Blue flag. *See* Larger blue flag
Blue violet. *See* Common blue violet
Blue bead lily. *See* Yellow clintonia
Bluegrass, 20
Bluets, **76**, 124, 142 – 143, **143**
Borders, 13
Boreal forest, 3
Botanical gardens, 11, 156
Botanical organizations, 12, 163
Bottle gentian. *See* Closed gentian
Bracts, 25, **25**
Brown-eyed Susan. *See*
　　Black-eyed Susan
Bulbs, 30, **30**
　division, **54**, 55
Bunchberry, **70**, 112 – 113, **113**, 124
Butterfly gardens, 13 – 14, **14**
Butterfly weed, 138

C

Caltha palustris, 125
Calyx, 24
Campanula americana, 102
Canada anemone, **76**, 140 – 141, **141**
Canada mayflower. *See* Wild
　　lily-of-the-valley
Cardinal flower, **74**, 130 – 131, **131**
Carolina rose. *See* Pasture rose
Cats, 48
Checkerberry. *See* Wintergreen
Chelone glabra, 134 – 135, **135**.
　　See also Turtlehead
Christmas fern, 81
Chrysanthemeum leucanthemum, 139
Cinnamon fern, 125
Clajeux. See Larger blue flag
Claytonia virginica, 80
Clean Water Act, 19
Climate, 31 – 32
Clintonia borealis, 110 – 111, **111**.
　　See also Yellow clintonia
Clintonie boreale. See Yellow clintonia
Closed gentian, 5, **75**, 136 – 137, **137**
Color, 26, **27**
Colorado columbine, 102
Columbine, **66**
Common blue violet, 4 – 5, **64**,
　　90 – 91, **91**, 124
Common polypod, 81
Companions
　meadow species, 138 – 139
　wetland species, 124 – 125
　woodland species

Companions (continued)
    early spring, 80 – 81
    late spring to summer, 102 – 103
Composite flowers, 25 – 26, **25**
Coneflower, 138
Confederate violet. See Common
    blue violet
Conservation, 7
    guidelines, 8
Container gardening, 15 – 17, **16**
Coreopsis lanceolata, 138
Corms, 30, **30**
    division, **54**, 55
Corn lily. See Yellow clintonia
Cornus canadensis, 112 – 113, **113**.
    See also Bunchberry
Corolla, 24
Cowslip, 125
Crackerberry. See Bunchberry
Cutflower garden, 14
Cuttings, 55 – 56, **56**

D

Dark treatments, 51
Day length, 33
Deciduous forest, 3
Deer, 48
Degree days, 31 – 32
Deptford pink, 139
Dianthus armeria, 139
Dicentra cucullaria, 88 – 89, **89**.
    See also Dutchman's breeches
Dicentre à capuchon. See
    Dutchman's breeches
Disc flowers, 25 – 26, **25**
Dish gardens, 17
Division, 53 – 55, **54**
Dogs, 48
Dogtooth violet. See Eastern trout lily
Dormancy, 40
Dryopteris noveboracensis, 103
Dryopteris spinulosa, 103
Dryopteris thelypteris, 125
Dutchman's breeches, **64**, 88 – 89, **89**
Dwarf cornell. See Bunchberry

E

Early yellow violet, 81
Eastern columbine, **66**, 96 – 97, **97**
Eastern trout lily, **64**, 86 – 87, **87**
Echinacea purpurea, 138
Ecotypes, 33
Elevation, influence on flowering, 32
Environmental Defense Fund, 7
Erythronium americanum, 86 – 87, **87**.
    See also Eastern trout lily
Erythronium grandiflorum, 80

F

False dragonhead, 138
False lily-of-the-valley. See Wild
    lily-of-the-valley
False miterwort. See Foamflower
False Solomon's seal, **69**, 108 – 109,
    109
Fawn lily. See Eastern trout lily
Federal Endangered Species Act, 7, 12
Ferns
    Christmas, 81
    cinnamon, 125
    interrupted, 125
    lady, 103
    maidenhair, 81
    marsh, 125
    New York, 103
    ostrich, 125
    royal, 125
    spinulous woodfern, 103
Fibrous root, 30, **30**
Filament, 24, **25**
Flame lily. See Wood lily
Flats, 51
Florets, 25
Flower beds, 13
Flowering season, 31 – 35
    extending, 33 – 35
Flowers, 24 – 26
    color, 26, **27**
    composite, 25 – 26, **25**
    disc, 25 – 26, **25**
    ray, 25, **25**

Flowers (continued)
    simple, 24 – 25, **25**
    timing, 34
Foamflower, **66**, 98 – 99, **99**, 124
Forcing, 16 – 17
Forest
    boreal, 3
    deciduous, 3
Frost-free period of northeastern
    North America, **59**
Fruit, 25, 26

G

Gaillardia aristata, 138
Gants de Notre Dame. See
    Eastern columbine
Gardens
    botanical, 11
    butterfly, 13 – 14, **14**
    container, 15 – 17, **16**
    cutflower, **14**
    dish, 17
    hummingbird, 13 – 14, **14**
    meadow, summer, **139**
    rock, 15, **19**
    theme, 13 – 23
    wetland, 18 – 19, **74**
        early summer, **125**
    woodland, 17 – 18
        early spring, **81**
        late spring, **103**
Gaulthérie couchée. See Wintergreen
Gaultheria procumbens, 122 – 123, **123**.
    See also Wintergreen
Gentiana andrewsii, 136 – 137, **137**.
    See also Closed gentian
Gentiane d' Andrews. See
    Closed gentian
Geranium maculatum, 102 – 103
Geranium, wild. See Wild geranium
Gingembre sauvage. See Wild ginger
Ginger, wild. See Wild ginger
Grasses, 19 – 20
Ground covers, 14 – 15, **20**
Groundnut, 18, **74**, 132 – 133, **133**
Growing degree days, 31 – 32

H

Habitats, 2 – 4
Hardiness zones, 38, **39**
  of northeastern North America, **60**
Height, 26, **28**
Heiracium aurantiacum, 139
Hepatica. *See* Round-lobed hepatica;
  Sharp-lobed hepatica
Hepatica acutiloba, 82 – 83, **83**.
  See also Sharp-lobed hepatica
Hepatica americana, 81
Herbicides, 21, 47
Hibiscus palustris, 124 – 125
Hot water treatments, 51
Houstonia caerulea, 142 – 143, **143**.
  See also Bluets
Houstonie bleue. See Bluets
Hummingbird gardens, 13 – 14, **14**

I

Indian potato. *See* Groundnut
Indian turnip. *See* Jack-in-the-pulpit
Innocence. *See* Bluets
Inoculants, 53
Insects, 48
Interrupted fern, 125
Iris versicolor, 128 – 129, **129**.
  See also Larger blue flag
Iris, wild. *See* Larger blue flag

J

Jack-in-the-pulpit, 5, 18, **73**,
  126 – 127, **127**

L

Lady fern, 103
Lady's slipper, 6
Lance-leaved coreopsis, 138
Landscaping ordinances, 22 – 23
Larger blue flag, 5, **73**, **74**, 128 – 129,
  129
Leek, wild. *See* Wild leek
Legumes, 53
Light
  conditions, 36, **37**
  hours of, 33
  treatments, 51

Lilium philadelphicum, 120 – 121, **121**.
  See also Wood lily
Lilium umbellatum. See Wood lily
Lily. *See* Eastern trout lily; Wild
  lily-of-the-valley; Wood lily;
  Yellow fawn lily
Lily-of-the-valley, wild. *See* Wild
  lily-of-the-valley
Lis de Philadelphie. See Wood lily
Lobélie cardinale. See Cardinal flower
Lobelia cardinalis, 130 – 131, **131**.
  See also Cardinal flower
Local conditions, influence on
  flowering, 32 – 33
Loosestrife. *See* Purple loosestrife;
  Spiked loosestrife
Lychnis flos-cuculi, 139
Lythrum salicaria, 124

M

Maianthemum canadense, 104 – 105,
  105. *See also* Wild
  lily-of-the-valley
Maïanthème du Canada. See Wild
  lily-of-the-valley
Maidenhair fern, 81
Mandrake. *See* Mayapple
Marsh fern, 125
Marsh marigold, 125
Matteuccia struthiopteris, 125
Mayapple, **67**, 100 – 101, **101**
Meadow beauty, 138
Meadows, 3 – 4, 19 – 23
  burning, 22
  garden, summer, **139**
  maintenance, 22 – 23, 22
  species, 138 – 151
    companions, 138 – 139
Meetinghouses. *See* Eastern columbine
Mertensia virginica, 80 – 81, 125
Mitchella repens, 114 – 115, **115**.
  See also Partridgeberry
Moisture conditions, 40 – 42, **41**
Monarda fistulosa, 146 – 147, **147**.
  See also Wild bergamot
Monarde fistuleuse. See Wild bergamot
Muguet. See Wild lily-of-the-valley

N

National Council of State Garden
  Clubs, Inc., 12
National forests, 11
National Wildflower Research
  Center, 12
National wildlife refuges, 11
Native plant societies, 12, 163
Natural Heritage Programs, 12
Nature centers, 11
Nature Conservancy, 11, 12
New England aster, **78**, 150 – 151, **151**
New England Wildflower Society, 6, 10
New York fern, 103
Nitrogen, 43
Nodding wild onion, 138
Nursery beds, 51
Nutrients, 43

O

Oignon sauvage. See
  Jack-in-the-pulpit
Orange hawkweed, 139
Osmunda cinnamomea, 125
Osmunda claytoniana, 125
Osmunda regalis, 125
Ostrich fern, 125
Ovary, 24 – 25, **25**
Ovules, 25
Ox-eye daisy, 139

P

Pain de pedrix. See Partridgeberry
Partridgeberry, **70**, 114 – 115, **115**
Pasture rose, **77**, 144 – 145, **145**
Patates en chapelet. See Groundnut
Patio containers, **16**
Pénacs. See Groundnut
Peat pots, 51
Peduncle, 24
Pests, 48
Petals, 24, **25**
Petit prêcheur. See Jack-in-the-pulpit
Petit thé des bois. See Wintergreen
Pets, 48
pH, 43 – 45, **44**
  changing, 46 – 47
  measuring, 45 – 46

Phragmities communis, 124
Physostegia virginiana, 138
Pink lady's slipper, 6
Pistil, 24 – 25, **25**
Plant descriptions, 24 – 30
Plant height, 26, **28**
Planting stock, 7 – 9, 10 – 11
  suppliers, 10 – 11
Planting techniques, seeds, 51 – 53
Plugs, 52
Podophyllum peltatum, 100 – 101, **101**.
  See also Mayapple
Polygonatum biflorum, 106 – 107, **107**.
  See also Solomon's seal
Polypodum vulgare, 81
Polystichum acrostichoides, 81
Pomme de Mai. *See* Mayapple
Potato bean. *See* Groundnut
Potting, 52
Prairie rose. *See* Pasture rose
Precipitation, annual, of northeastern
  North America, **58**
Propagation, 49 – 56
Puddingberry. *See* Bunchberry
Purple loosestrife, 124
Purple trillium, 5, **65**, 92 – 93, **93**
Purple-flowering raspberry. *See*
  Thimbleberry
Pyrola elliptica, 118 – 119, **119**.
  See also Shinleaf
Pyrole elliptique. *See* Shinleaf

Q

Quaker ladies. *See* Bluets
Quatre-temps. *See* Bunchberry

R

Ragged robin, 139
Ramp. *See* Wild leek
Ray flowers, 25, **25**
Receptacle, 24, **25**
Red lily, wild. *See* Wood lily
Red trillium. *See* Purple trillium
Reeds, 124
Rhexia virginica, 138
Rhizobia, 53
Rhizomes, 30, **30**
  division, 54 – 55, **54**

Rock gardens, 15, **19**
Root systems, 29 – 30, **29**, **30**
Rootstock division, 53 – 55, **54**
Rosa carolina, 144 – 145, **145**.
  See also Pasture rose
Rose mallow, 124 – 125
Rosier de Caroline. *See* Pasture rose
Rougets. *See* Bunchberry
Round-lobed hepatica, 81
Royal fern, 125
Rubus odoratus, 103
Rudbeckia hirta, 146 – 147, **147**.
  See also Black-eyed Susan
Rudbeckia serotina. *See*
  Black-eyed Susan
Rudbeckie hérissée. *See*
  Black-eyed Susan
Rudbeckie tardive. *See*
  Black-eyed Susan
Runners, 29, **29**
  division, 54, **54**
Running box. *See* Partridgeberry
Ryegrass, 20

S

Sang-dragon. *See* Bloodroot
Sanguinaire. *See* Bloodroot
Sanguinaria canadensis, 84 – 85, **85**.
  See also Bloodroot
Scarification, 50 – 51
Sceau-de-Salomon à deux fleurs.
  See Solomon's seal
Seeds, 7 – 11, 25, 26
  collecting, 9, 49
  dark treatments, 51
  dissemination, 26 – 29
  dormant, 50
  hot water treatments, 51
  light treatments, 51
  mixtures, 9 – 10
  planting techniques, 51 – 53
  propagating with, 49 – 53
  scarification, 50 – 51
  stratification, 50
  suppliers, 10 – 11
  wildflower-grass mixtures, 19 – 20
Sepals, 24, **25**
Sexual parts of flowers, 24 – 25

Sharp-lobed hepatica, **63**, 82 – 83, **83**
Sharp-lobed liverleaf. *See*
  Sharp-lobed hepatica
Sharp-lobed liverwort. *See*
  Sharp-lobed hepatica
Shinleaf, **71**, 118 – 119, **119**
Simple flowers, 24 – 25, **25**
Slope, influence on flowering, 32
Slugs, 48
Smilacina racemosa, 108 – 109, **109**.
  See also False Solomon's seal
Smilacine à grappes. *See* False
  Solomon's seal
Snakehead. *See* Turtlehead
Sods, 52 – 53
Soil
  conditions, influence on
    flowering, 33
  mixes, 52
  moisture conditions, 40 – 42, **41**
  nutrients, 43
  pH, 43 – 45, **44**
    changing, 46 – 47
    measuring, 45 – 46
Solomon's plume. *See*
  False Solomon's seal
Solomon's seal, **68**, 106 – 107, **107**
Solomon's zigzag. *See* False
  Solomon's seal
Spiked loosestrife, 124
Spinulous woodfern, 103
Spring beauty, 80
Squawvine. *See* Partridgeberry
Stamens, 24, **25**
Stem cuttings, 55 – 56, **56**
Stigma, 24 – 25, **25**
Stinking Benjamin. *See* Purple trillium
Stolons, 29, **29**
  division, 54, **54**
Stratification, 50
Style, **25**
Swamp milkweed, 124
Sweet flag, 124
Sweet white violet, 125

T

Taproot, 30, **30**
Teaberry. *See* Wintergreen

Temperature, 38 – 40
Terrariums, **16**, 17
Tête de tortue. See Turtlehead
Thelypteris noveboracensis. See
    Dryopteris noveboracensis
Thelypteris palustris, 125
Theme gardens, 13 – 23
Thimbleberry, 103
Tiarella cordifolia, 98 – 99, **99**.
    See also Foamflower
Tiarelle cordifoliée. See Foamflower
Trille dressé, 92
Trillium. *See* Purple trillium; White
    trillium
Trillium erectum, 92 – 93, **93**.
    See also Purple trillium
Trillium grandiflorum, 81
Trinitaire. See Sharp-lobed hepatica
Trout lily. *See* Eastern trout lily
True roots, 30, **30**
Tubers, 29, **30**
   division, 54, **54**
Turtlehead, **75**, 134 – 135, **135**
Twinberry. *See* Partridgeberry
Two-eyed berry. *See* Partridgeberry
Two-leaved Solomon's seal. *See*
    Wild lily-of-the-valley

V

Vegetation of northeastern North
   America, **57**

Viola pallens, 125
Viola papilonaceae, 90 – 91, **91**.
    See also Common blue violet
Viola rotundifolia, 81
Violet. *See* Common blue violet;
    Early yellow violet; Sweet
    white violet
Violette papilionacée. See Common
    blue violet
Virginia bluebells, 80 – 81, 125
Virginia Wildflower Preservation
    Society, 6

W

Wakerobin. *See* Purple trillium
Weeds, 47 – 48
Wetlands, 3 – 4
   garden, 18 – 19, **74**
     early summer, **125**
   protection laws, 19
   species, 124 – 137
     companions, 124 – 125
White baneberry, 102
White trillium, 81
Wild bean. *See* Groundnut
Wild bergamot, **78**, 146 – 147, **147**
Wild columbine. *See* Eastern
    columbine
Wild geranium, 102 – 103
Wild ginger, **65**, 94 – 95, **95**
Wild iris. *See* Larger blue flag
Wild leek, 71, 116 – 117, **117**

Wild lily-of-the-valley, **68**, 104 – 105,
   105
Wild red lily. *See* Wood lily
Wildflowers
   conservation, 7
    guidelines, 8
   culture, 36 – 48
    grass seed mixtures, 19 – 20
   joys of, 4 – 5
   plugs, 52
   seed mixtures, 9 – 10
   sods, 52 – 53
Wintergreen, **72**, 122 – 123, **123**
Wood lily, **72**, 120 – 121, **121**
Woodland gardens, 17 – 18
   early spring, **81**
   late spring, **103**
Woodland species
   early spring, 80 – 101
    companions, 80 – 81
   late spring to summer, 102 – 123
    companions, 102 – 103
World Wildlife Fund, 7

Y

Yellow adder's tongue. *See*
    Eastern trout lily
Yellow clintonia, **69**, 110 – 111,
   111
Yellow fawn lily, 80
Yellow violet, early. *See* Early yellow
    violet